Lush!

Joanna Page

Lush!

From Swansea to Stacey and Everything in Between

SPHERE

SPHERE

First published in Great Britain in 2025 by Sphere

3 5 7 9 10 8 6 4 2

A CIP catalogue record for this book
is available from the British Library.

ISBN 978-1-4087-2427-9

Typeset in Bembo by M Rules
Printed and bound in Great Britain by
Clays Ltd, Elcograf S.p.A

Papers used by Sphere are from well-managed forests
and other responsible sources.

Sphere
An imprint of
Little, Brown Book Group
Carmelite House
50 Victoria Embankment
London EC4Y 0DZ

The authorised representative
in the EEA is
Hachette Ireland
8 Castlecourt Centre
Dublin 15, D15 XTP3, Ireland
(email: info@hbgi.ie)

An Hachette UK Company
www.hachette.co.uk

www.littlebrown.co.uk

For Eva, Kit, Noah and Boe, the best gang in the world.
For James, my big Northern bull. For Mum and Dad, thank you
for everything. And for Daisy, it all began with you.

Contents

Introduction

'You have to have made it by the time you're thirty'

April 2006

I was working in a shoe shop in East Dulwich when I got the call. I was inside a massive cardboard box full of loose Crocs and I heard the faint buzz of my mobile phone coming from the other side of the stockroom.

I almost didn't answer it. I was too busy rummaging around trying to find a men's size twelve in brown to make up a pair for a customer waiting out front. And it would only be my mum or my husband, James, ringing for a chat, I thought. I could phone them back later.

But then I remembered that James was spending the day locked in a studio, recording voiceovers, so it wouldn't be him. And Mum, who only ever used her mobile phone in dire emergencies, was off visiting my Auntie Kirsteen, so it wouldn't be her, either. My friends all knew I was working

at the shop, or they were working themselves, so that left . . .
who? Who would be ringing me on a Tuesday afternoon?

Oh my God! I thought, with a sudden rush of excitement.
My. Agent.

I shot out of the cardboard box and across the stockroom
floor faster than you could say Kenneth Branagh. As I reached
my phone the screen went dark, but not before I'd caught a
glimpse of that longed-for number – the main switchboard
of the talent agency, Peters Fraser + Dunlop. I quickly called
back, pushing aside the doubts I'd lately been having about
ever getting another acting job again. I hadn't worked all
year, but maybe my luck was changing. I was desperate to
act again.

My agent was a legend in show business – some of the
actors he represented were my absolute idols. He had put
me up for some fantastic parts in the time I'd been with him
and, although I was still a jobbing actress (currently working
part-time in retail), I couldn't help my imagination running
away with the possibilities as to why he might be calling.
An audition for a costume drama at the National, perhaps?
A screen test for a big-budget TV drama series? Maybe even
a movie?

'Darling, how are you?' he asked, in his deep, smoulder-
ing purr.

'What's the news?' I asked him breathlessly, once we'd said
our hellos and how-are-yous.

But it wasn't what I was hoping for.

'They're turning *Dirty Dancing* into a musical and putting
it on in the West End,' he said. 'Will you go and audition for
the part of Baby's older sister, Lisa?'

I hesitated. I loved the *Dirty Dancing* film – I knew it inside
out – and a role in a West End production was a big deal. But
this wasn't the sort of thing I normally went up for; I saw

myself as a serious dramatic actress, and I thought my agent did, too. I wanted to be the next Kate Winslet. I didn't do musical theatre – I'd hardly done any singing in the eight years since I'd left drama school – and I was usually cast as the sweet, innocent type, the 'ingénue', so I couldn't see myself playing a character like Lisa – vain, sexy and sure of herself. That wasn't me.

But there's a first time for everything, isn't there? And who was I to turn down the chance to be in a massive new musical with guaranteed regular earnings? I'd be part of a company again, in a tight-knit group of actors and the backstage crew. After months without acting work, I suddenly wanted the part of Lisa more than anything.

'What shall I do for the audition?' I asked my agent, in a panic. 'I'm fine with the acting side of it, but what shall I sing?'

He had some sheet music ready. 'Lisa's song is called "Hula Hana" and I'm going to email it to you. Can you work on it before you go?'

'I'll try,' I promised.

'And it's a General American accent. Just do your best.'

I swallowed. 'Okay.'

I was used to having to perform in an accent that wasn't my own. Welsh parts were practically non-existent, so if you were Swansea born and bred like I was, accents came with the job. I'd worked in a northern accent, Scottish, cockney, New York, American southern and many times in standard southern British – or RP, as it is usually known. It wasn't easy, because there is only so much you can give to a role when you're not speaking with your natural accent, but I could more or less do them all. And a few years earlier, I'd played a New Yorker in a production at the Almeida Theatre in London. Even though I wished that for once he'd say a job had come in for a Welsh actress, at least I knew I could do the American accent.

'Any luck with those size twelves?' came a call from out front in the shop.

'Give me a second!' I yelled back, my hand cupped over the phone.

I quickly said goodbye to my agent and jumped back into the enormous box of Crocs.

Later, at home, I sank into gloom as I looked over the sheet music for Lisa's song. *What's the point?* I thought. I wasn't a singer. I didn't even know where to start, and there wasn't time to book a session with a singing teacher before the audition. So I did what I always do in an impossible situation: buried my head in the sand, right up until about two hours before I was due to meet the director and his team at Pineapple Dance Studios in Covent Garden. Then I frantically started preparing – too late. I'm glad there isn't any record of my attempt to sing 'Hula Hana' at the audition. It was so much more difficult than anything I'd attempted in drama school. *Flipping heck, that was terrible!* I thought when I'd finished. I left Pineapple Studios expecting never to hear from the *Dirty Dancing* team again.

On to the next thing, I mused dejectedly, hoping there would be a next thing.

But to my surprise the casting director got in touch the next day. 'We really like you,' she said. 'We'd like to meet you for the part of Baby.'

My hopes soared again. Lisa's innocent younger sister, Baby, was much more my kind of role. Innocent and idealistic, she's on the cusp of womanhood when she falls in love with a dance instructor while on holiday with her family at a smart vacation resort. Their romance is at the centre of the drama.

I'd practically been brought up on *Dirty Dancing*! What young girl hasn't imagined writhing around on Patrick Swayze while carrying a watermelon? We'd all practised the bit with our friends when he's being all sexy stroking down her arm, and she gets a fit of the giggles! And now, this was my chance to play the Jennifer Grey role, my dream – could this really be happening?!

'And she's the only main character in the production who doesn't have her own song,' the casting director added.

Even better! If I didn't have to sing a solo, it was the perfect part for me. Like Baby, I was naive, shy and unsure of myself. *Yes, I am Baby*, I thought. *I can play this part.*

Back at Pineapple Studios a couple of days later, I did a reading from the script and someone from the creative team joined me. 'I thought you were Baby from the first minute I saw you,' she gushed. 'You *are* her. You *are* Baby.' She gave me a lot of encouragement.

Maybe I'll get the part! I thought, although I'd had enough near misses to know I couldn't take anything for granted.

I flashed back to a memory of a film director who'd kept saying, 'I think you're wonderful. You are perfect. Your face is wonderful,' and then given the part to another actress. I pushed the thought away. *Be positive*, I told myself.

Over the next few months I went back to read for the *Dirty Dancing* team over and over again. I started to pin my hopes on getting the part, especially as nothing else was coming in from my agent. I tried to imagine every aspect of Baby's character, and practised my American accent to myself all day long in the shoe shop.

It was a gorgeous summer and James and I were living a happy, carefree life in East Dulwich, a pretty area of South London with lots of green spaces and little restaurants. We'd come home from work each day and spend our evenings making dinner and watching *Survivor*; our favourite John Mayer CD was constantly on loop; it was a wonderful time. And it was fine working at the shoe shop. It was a simple enough job, pressure-free. I didn't really like being out front and having to deal with customers – I preferred being in the stockroom – but it was a lot better than sitting at home fretting about when my next acting job would come in. That's why I had applied to work there in the first place – to have something to do. The teachers at my drama school had often talked about how long you could last as an actor. You needed nerves of steel to get through the times when you weren't working, and I had this constant, gnawing sense of time slipping away. I'd read somewhere that Hugh Grant had said you had to make your name in the industry by the age of thirty, or it wouldn't happen, and this thought kept whirring around my mind. I was twenty-nine.

At last my agent rang and said, 'You're getting really close now. You're down to the final three.'

I bit my lip. I'd been in this situation so many times before.

My heart was in my mouth when I went to the next audition. As I waited to be called, the same enthusiastic creative started chatting away like mad to me again.

'You're perfect for Baby, even your outfit is perfect,' she raved, admiring the spotlessly white vest and tracksuit bottoms I was wearing. 'Great choice! You are Baby down to a tee.'

She's behaving as if I've already got the part, I thought with rising excitement. By now I could absolutely see myself playing the role of Baby. *This has to happen*, I kept thinking. *It will happen. I will succeed.*

We spent the morning learning a dance routine. I was partnered with a West End star who was up for the part of

Johnny, Baby's love interest. He was six foot four, massively built and very extrovert. I felt tiny next to him, in every way. And maybe it was because I came across as small and shy, or it was just his way of dispelling his own jitters, but as we went through the moves he was talking to me as if I were a nervous wreck. 'You're going to be fine,' he kept saying. 'Just relax. You're all right.'

'I'm fine. I feel confident!' I wanted to tell him. 'You don't need to keep going on and on.'

We spent hours rehearsing, which was exhausting, and during one of the breaks I quickly wolfed down a family-sized chocolate bar to keep me going. It worked and I bounced back into the studio, raring to go again. But then – oh the horror! – when I looked at my reflection in the mirror on the wall, I saw a great big smear of brown chocolate across my white vest top. I was furious with myself. Why hadn't I brought a change of clothes?

The next stage of the audition was doing a scene with Josef Brown, the actor who eventually got the part of Johnny (played by Patrick Swayze in the film). Josef was a trained dancer with model good looks – he was absolutely gorgeous. He was wearing a black singlet and tight black trousers, just like Patrick Swayze had in the film.

'This is the scene where Baby goes up to Johnny's hut before she sleeps with him for the first time,' the director said.

I drew an anxious breath. It was that pivotal moment where Johnny opens up and shows his vulnerability, and Baby passionately declares her feelings for him. They have an intense exchange, charged with awkwardness and sexual tension, and Baby asks Johnny to dance with her. Things develop from there.

All the key members of the production team were lined up to watch. A stagehand dragged a mattress into the room and dropped it on the floor. The director said, 'Just keep going until we shout stop.'

Josef, who no longer had his top on, started acting out the scene, and I joined in. We ran it through to the end, until there weren't any lines left to say.

By now the atmosphere was quite charged, but no one shouted, 'Stop!' So we had to keep going.

Oh Jesus, what does she do in the film? I thought.

Then I remembered: as they are dancing, Baby begins to stroke Johnny's arms and shoulders. Breaking away, she walks around him and brushes her lips against the dip in his muscular back. And then she trails her fingers down his spine and touches his bum.

Oh my God! I could feel myself blushing at the thought of it. I've always felt uncomfortable playing this sort of scene. I think it's because it's inbuilt in me to be the 'good girl' and 'Head Girl', after going to an all–girls comprehensive school. Still, Josef was incredibly chiselled and had a lot of charisma, and I told myself that we were only acting, after all.

I tried to take it slow and sensual as I caressed him and touched his back, but I was trembling slightly. And then I reached down and felt his bum.

In one very swift move, Josef lifted my leg up onto his thigh and spun me around. It was so sudden that it shocked me, but he was so strong and in control that I couldn't help enjoying the sheer thrill of it. Before I knew it, he'd pushed up my arms and was lifting up my top.

I had completely forgotten that Johnny starts undressing Baby as they dance. *I hope he's not going to try and take my top off!* I thought in alarm. Although I have to say, I was thoroughly enjoying it, and one hundred per cent had now experienced real life *Dirty Dancing*!

He went on lifting it until it was all the way up to my

bra – and I just let him do it! Then, *oh my God*, he went even further and started taking it up over my bra ...

'Stop!' the director shouted.

I quickly pulled my top back down and walked out of the studio, feeling completely flustered and, I imagine, exactly how Baby would've felt! I paced up and down the corridor, fanning myself with my hand, and tried to collect my thoughts. Had it gone well? Actually, yes! It had been good. I was excited to hear what the casting director would say.

A couple of minutes later, she came out to find me. 'Thank you very much, Jo,' she said briskly. 'We don't need you any more. You can now leave.'

I stared at her blankly as the meaning of her words caught up with me.

'Oh! Oh my! Okay,' I stuttered.

I've been cut! I thought, reeling in shock as she walked away. *After all these months. After doing that!*

In the blink of an eye, my dream of playing Baby was over.

I was too stunned to think; all I knew was I had to get out of there fast. *Don't cry, don't cry*, I urged myself, as I hurried to find my coat.

The other two actresses trying for the part were in the dressing room waiting to be called. It was between them now: one of them would get to be Baby. I was out.

'Bye, everybody!' I said, brightly. 'Good luck. Hope it all goes well.'

I rushed out of the building onto the street, turned and stumbled blindly down to the Strand, barely able to see where I was going through the tears welling up in my eyes. Just then, a taxi sped past, flanked with a poster blazing the words, 'Dirty Dancing The Musical – coming soon!'

It was cruel timing and, despite myself, I couldn't stop the tears. After months of suspense, after a summer of hoping and fretting, I'd been left with nothing. The words of the creative echoed in my mind: 'You're perfect for Baby. You *are* Baby.'

I can't believe it, I thought. *I hate this industry! This has happened too many times. I just can't take it any more.* I didn't know what to do with myself, but I knew I didn't want to stand around in the street crying and attracting attention. I needed somewhere to hide away and lick my wounds – and it had to be somewhere close by, because I really didn't want to go home and face reality yet. Reality was a huge gaping hole of nothingness. It was the constant worry of waiting and hoping for another acting job to come in.

I looked around and saw the Savoy Hotel on the other side of the road – the flamboyant, opulent Savoy Hotel, a favourite haunt of theatre lovers and performers for more than a century. Suddenly the Savoy was the place I wanted to be. I crossed the road and walked through its grand entrance into the art deco foyer, where hundreds of actors and actresses had walked before me in years gone by.

I was in my trackie bottoms and this white vest. I'd literally just started my period, and there was chocolate smeared down my top.

Sobbing, I went up to the desk and asked, 'Do you have a room?'

'Yes, miss,' said the concierge. I stopped crying and gave her my credit card. She looked at me suspiciously; I must've looked a right state. I'd just dropped three hundred quid on a room, was covered in chocolate, sweaty and sobbing, but I was past caring. 'Do you have any bags that you need taking up?'

'I haven't got any luggage. I haven't got anything,' I said miserably.

'I'll show you upstairs,' one of the porters offered.

As I got in the lift with him, I burst out sobbing again. His rugged face broke into a sympathetic smile.

'I'm really sorry,' I said. 'I'm an actress and I've just lost out on a part, and I don't want to go home, and . . .'

'Don't worry, miss, you're here now,' he said.

I don't know what it is about hotel porters, but they always seem to say the right thing at the right time. And all dignity had certainly left me at that point.

After he'd shown me my room and the door had shut behind him, I threw myself on the bed and sobbed and howled into a pillow, pummelling the mattress with my fists. It was a relief to let out all my frustration and fury with nobody around to see the mess I was in. I had never felt so low in my life.

Five minutes later, I heard a knock at the door. Worried that I'd been making too much noise, I quickly sat up and tried to compose myself. I grabbed a wad of tissues, dried my eyes and opened the door. A young waiter stood in the doorway, holding out a plate of handmade chocolates. 'We thought these might help cheer you up,' he said with an embarrassed smile. 'Compliments of the Savoy.'

It was such a nice thing to do. 'Thank you,' I said, trying to smile back at him. Then my face crumpled and I quickly shut the door again.

I felt utterly hopeless. I didn't know what to do. I popped a chocolate into my mouth. It collapsed and melted on my tongue. I took off all my clothes, because I'd bled through my pants and I was covered in chocolate. I washed my pants and stood under the shower, feeling like I was drowning in sorrow.

After my shower, I wrapped myself in a towel, sat on the toilet and stared at the tiled wall for a very long time. Eventually, I went to find my phone, called James and left him a message saying that I wasn't coming home. 'Going to switch off my phone now,' I added. 'Just can't face speaking to anybody.' I think it was the lowest I'd felt in my life.

Next, I opened the mini bar and inspected the drinks inside. I went for the bottle of champagne first. I popped it open, filled a tall flute glass and drank it down in one. Then I poured another and put on the telly. The Labour MP John Prescott's face filled the screen. He was giving a speech, looking a bit downcast, I thought. I sat on the bed and ate a whole packet of Pringles as I watched him.

Then I slowly worked my way through the mini bar, naked, while my pants dried on the radiator in the bathroom. I went on pouring myself drinks until I'd drunk the mini bar dry – wines, spirits, cocktails, the lot. And then I collapsed in a heap on my big, luxurious Savoy bed and slept like a baby.

The next morning, James kept trying to ring me, but couldn't get through to my mobile or the phone in my room, so he rang the Savoy reception and asked them to go up and check on me. 'Can you just make sure she's okay?' he said, in case I'd done something stupid.

I called him blearily a few minutes later. 'I'm fine, except my head hurts,' I said.

'Come home,' he said. 'I've been worried about you.'

'Not yet. I can't face it, sorry.'

It was check-out time, so I hurriedly put on my damp rag of a vest and grubby trackie bottoms and went downstairs to settle my bill. Then I headed to Topshop on the Strand and bought myself some new pants, a pair of tracksuit bottoms and a top. I strode to Charing Cross train station with my carrier bag, went into the women's toilet, had a wash in the sink and put on my new outfit.

God knows why I didn't just stay in the Savoy, nip out and get some clothes and come back! I can only think that after my failed foray into musicals, I was so engrossed in the drama of it all, I was now finally living it. There was no bringing me back from this one.

I spent the next few hours walking dolefully around town, a symphony of depressing thoughts playing in my head. Then, at last, I got on the train and made my way back to our house in East Dulwich.

I burst out crying when I saw James. 'I just feel such a failure,' I said.

He wrapped his arms around me and pulled me close. 'Don't worry, something else will come along.'

'No, it won't! That's it – my acting days are over,' I wailed. 'I'm no good – I'm rubbish, and I hate it! I hate this feeling so much. I can't do this any more!'

In the days that followed, I completely bombed. It felt as if my whole life to this point had been focused on acting and now my dreams and everything I had worked for had been smashed to bits.

'I've tried as hard as I can, but I've reached a limit where it's just not working any more,' I told my mum and James. 'I'm never going to work as an actress again. I'm going to have to find something else to do. That's it.'

They kept trying to reassure me, but soon I was running through new career possibilities in my head. *Interior designer, yoga teacher . . . I could retrain as a nurse . . .* I kicked myself for not facing reality sooner and starting earlier. *If I'd started a year ago, instead of waiting for a job to come in and panicking all day long, I could be a trained yoga teacher now,* I kept thinking.

Of course that's the life you choose if you decide to be an actor – only, I'd been lucky and had constant work until the last year. But I couldn't stand it any longer. In my mind I was a rubbish actor. I was worthless. My anxiety about not working had led me into an unbearably negative space and

I was terrified of how much further down I would spiral if I didn't walk away.

Two weeks later, while I was still licking my wounds, my agent phoned. 'A TV script has just landed on my desk and I think you'll like it,' he said. 'It's a sitcom about a Welsh girl and an Essex boy who fall in love, and it's very funny.'

I hesitated. A sitcom? But I was a serious dramatic actress . . . wasn't I?

'Wait a minute. Did you say a *Welsh* girl?' I asked.

1

A Swansea life

There was a big wooden cupboard on the landing at my Auntie Iris's house and when you opened it all her costumes and clothes tumbled out. Amid the satin, lace and sparkly trim, the gauzy petticoats and military jackets, I remember a turquoise feather boa so soft and iridescent, so floaty and sinuous, that it almost came alive when you wore it. I was obsessed with that turquoise feather boa. It was a little piece of magic, from a completely different world to mine.

Auntie Iris did am dram and threw fancy-dress parties. She had a piano, and I had never seen a piano in anyone's house before. I know I'm Welsh, and everyone is singing and there's music all the time, but that was at school or in chapel or in church. To actually go to someone's house and see that they owned a piano was amazing and exciting in my eyes.

Auntie Iris lived in Mumbles, a pretty seaside village on the western tip of Swansea Bay. Her house was full of exotic things. She had an antique Singer sewing machine. She had a little blue budgie in the living room. And at Christmas she had

Thornton's Viennese truffles – just one layer in a really nice little box. I had to really hold myself back from those truffles. I'd head straight for the box, let myself have one, then find myself stealing another one, and then another. But obviously you couldn't eat them all, because it was just one layer.

Everybody on my mum's side of the family – the Fosters – lived down in Mumbles. Mum's family prided themselves on having good manners and being polite, hard-working, well-respected people. 'You must say *lady*, not woman,' my gramps once told me, after I'd got it wrong in a sweet shop in Mumbles. But I was the first grandchild on that side, and hugely adored.

My dad's family – the Pages – were in the more built-up areas of Swansea, in Blaen-y-Maes and Mayhill. Although, when they were small, they lived in the beautiful countryside of Parkmill. I think that's where my Dad's fear of snakes came from. Many a time his older brother, Bobby, would chase him through the fields holding a grass snake in his hands, trying to get him with it. My dad was one of eight, so I had loads of cousins, which was really exciting, and when I went to see Auntie Wendy – my dad's sister – everything was loud, vibrant and busy. It was noisy, full-on fun. You were out playing. It felt free. Mum would pick me up from there, and Auntie Wendy would let her know what I'd had for tea. 'Mandarins! She doesn't eat mandarins! She won't even try them!' Mum would exclaim. 'She does in my house,' Wendy would say with a laugh.

My mum, dad and I lived in Treboeth, in Swansea, and we were a tight, happy unit of three. My father, Nigel, was a mechanic who specialised in MOTs; my mother, Susan, had worked in a bank until she got pregnant with me. I was their only child. They wanted more, but my mum had two ectopic pregnancies and other complications after she had me. She

lost babies and must have gone through a lot of disappoint-
ment and sadness. Eventually, she and Dad decided to stop
trying. They accepted they weren't having any more kids and
poured everything into me. I was showered with love. I had
a very happy childhood.

We lived in a little semi-detached house on a sloping street
called Llangyfelach Road. There was a living room and a
kitchen downstairs; upstairs there were three small bedrooms
and a tiny bathroom. When we moved in, my parents put an
extension on the back of the house, a little porch, where our
two cats, Smarty and Sooty, used to live on either side of the
window in their little baskets.

I also had a cat called Tiddles. When I was about seven, I
was told she had run away because she'd found another family
who really, really loved her. For years, I couldn't understand
how I'd loved this kitten so much and she'd just abandoned
me. It really affected me to think that I'd given so much love
to this little cat, and she just left.

It was only when I got to thirty-five that Mum told me
that Tiddles had, in fact, been found run over on Rogers
Street. They'd decided not to tell me that my cat was dead,
but instead to tell me that she had basically abandoned me
and found somebody else who loved her more.

I absolutely loved our house. Even though it was small, it
felt big enough for us. Mum and Dad would move the light-
pink leather sofa round to watch telly in the evenings, and I'd
be under the stairs on the other side of the living room, either
pretending to be someone else in a makeshift den, or with
my little ghetto blaster, making up dance routines, singing
and acting. Or I'd be playing out the back in the big piles of
sand Dad left after he cemented over the garden, and later
with my netball, hitting the wall constantly.

Aside from me prancing around in my own magical world,

there was no one else. It was very quiet: I did a lot of reading, and I loved being on my own. My room was neat and
tidy, and I was proud of my things. I looked after everything
incredibly well. So it felt very strange when my cousins,
Claire, Ian and Paul came to stay and were suddenly in my
space. They wanted to play with all of my toys and basically
trashed everything. This was my space. 'Only child' vibes
were starting to seep out.

At one point, they told me it was a good idea to get into
a sleeping bag, and Ian tied the top and started swinging it
around his head with me inside. I was enjoying it – it was
good fun – and I don't think any of us realised how dangerous it could have been. They were the brothers and sister
I never had, and I loved them with all my heart and sank
myself into the energy and vibrancy and love they brought
with them.

Mum went back to work when I was three, but she didn't
return to the bank, even though she'd been to grammar
school and was brilliant with numbers, systems and counting
money. I'm told that Mum had been the best worker in her
section at the bank, so good that they put her in charge of for-
eign money. She was also declared the Best Legs in Swansea
Lloyd's Bank by all the boys. So she was pretty popular.

But when Mum returned to work, she took a part-time job
at Mothercare in Swansea, so we could still spend as much
time together as possible. She says she enjoyed chatting to
people, helping them to find what they needed and organising
the stock. And she took great pride in being able to wear sky-
high heels all day long on the shop floor. Mum was gorgeous:
five-foot-four tall, slim and fashionable, with beautiful long
dark hair, which she later cut into a Mia Farrow crop. She
always says that she wonders if I was swapped at birth, because
I'm nothing like her, and I look nothing like her either. She's

always been taller and slimmer, and I've always been shorter and rounder. But the undeniable proof that she is my mother is that we have exactly the same voice!

I was always aware that something was going on with Mum's pregnancies, even though it was never spoken about. I remember sitting on the top bunk bed, saying goodbye to her. She said she was going to visit someone, but I knew she was going into hospital, and I knew it was serious. I wasn't told the truth, but I sensed it.

I remember me and Dad wheeling her on a stretcher down to the operating theatre at Morriston Hospital. We wheeled her all the way to the theatre doors and said goodbye. There was always a lot of medical stuff going on; there was also a lot of death. Nan's mum Nanny Jones died first. Grandpa Jones died. Then Gramps. Then Grandpa Page. A lot of people died when I was still quite young, but it never felt frightening. It was just something that happened. Nan was a nurse, Auntie Iris worked on the reception desk at the hospital. And Kirsteen and Uncle Leslie worked for the NHS. There was always something medical going on.

I think I dealt with a lot of grown-up things when I was little. They probably thought I could handle it – and I just got on with it. I was an only child. I spent a lot of time with adults. I listened, I picked up on things that they didn't realise I was noticing.

My mum is very methodical, organised, loves counting money and making lists, is very precise about everything, and that's where I get that side of me from. Dad is creative and brilliant at drawing, and would have made an amazing archaeologist. But he never had the chance to do anything like that, because they had a very big family, not much money and there were a lot of them to support. He left school when he was fifteen and had to go out and get a job.

Some Christmases, when he was little, he had no presents. He was completely selfless and always made sure the younger kids, his brothers and sisters, were looked after and had gifts. That's Dad, through and through. He will sacrifice anything for us. He is a giver and a feeder. He wants to look after you all the time. His mother was the same. Nana Page died when I was two years old. But for those two years she had me, she used to wrap me in a shawl 'Welsh fashion' and hold me to her bosom. She was a true Welsh matriarch. She'd sit by the table, next to the window downstairs, wanting to know all the news and everything that was happening with her children. She had a frying pan that was never washed, and loved it when Mum took me to visit her.

Originally, Dad applied to work at the Post Office, but eventually ended up at WG Davies, a car-servicing garage, doing MOTs, which was much more his cup of tea. Everybody knew Nigel Page in Swansea, from the council to the fire service, and everybody loved him. Dad gets on with everybody, no matter what class they're from, who they are or what they do. He's a big, solid Welshman, very gentle and unassuming, and people are drawn to confide in him. He only has to go for a walk down the beach and he'll meet someone who will tell him their life story.

Dad's customers were always giving him bits and bobs as thank-yous. He'd come home with anything from a big crate of pop to a new settee. And if you wanted something, you just had to ask 'Pagey' and he would get it for you. No questions asked.

I get my impulsivity from Dad. He was wild when he was young, full of energy and freedom. He had long, flowing blond hair and he'd put flowers in it. Dad was a catch. Women loved him. He had trials for Swansea City Football Club, but didn't turn up for them because he was too busy going out on the town. There's a Peter Pan quality to him, as well. Even now, in his seventies, he looks incredibly young. I take after him much more than I take after my mum, and physically, as I get older, I seem to be turning into him.

I was a very confident little girl around my family. Nan used to take us to the Kardomah, a coffee shop in the centre of Swansea where they served the most wonderful pancakes with ice cream. Mum and Nan would sit and gossip about everything, and I would lean over and put my hands over their mouths when I wanted a turn to speak.

Growing up in Treboeth, life was simple. Everywhere was within easy walking distance. My little school, Gwyrosydd Primary, was just down the road. Mum would take me in the mornings and I would happily run through the gates to meet my friends. I was so excited about going to school, about learning.

On my first day in Reception, I marched into the class-room and straight up to the teacher and said, 'Miss, here is a picture I've drawn for you.' I gave it to her proudly.

Shortly after that, a boy came up to me and whispered, 'Come under the table with me.'

I straight away dipped underneath the table with him, and I don't think I surfaced for the rest of the day. His name was Michael and somewhere along the line, he asked me to be his girlfriend – and I stayed his girlfriend for the rest of our time at Gwyrosydd. Michael would give me a single rose on Valentine's Day; he came to my birthday parties bringing cards, boxes of chocolates and teddy bears. Throughout junior school, my parties were all little girls and Michael, the only boy.

I was more reserved at school than at home. My reception teacher told my mum, 'Joanna's very quiet. She doesn't really talk to anybody when she comes in.'

'What does she do, then?' Mum asked.

'She goes straight to the dressing-up box and becomes somebody else for the day,' they said. 'And every day it's a different person.'

After school, I'd go up to my bedroom and start being someone else – a princess or a queen. I'd dress up, come downstairs and prance around, pretending to have an argument with a prince or fight a baddie. I was already quite dramatic, even then. When that scene was over, I'd go back upstairs, change and start acting something new: a doctor, a fashion designer or a rock star.

I had a Wonder Woman costume and a nurse's outfit. Everything else was conjured out of my dressing-up box with beads, scarves, a pair of shorts, a dressing gown, my mum's blouse, different belts and other accessories that would help me become different people. One day we went to London and Mum took me to Hamleys, where on the second floor I bought a long blonde wig. That wig was incredible.

There's a photo from my childhood that makes me laugh. I must be about seven and I'm in the living room. I'm wearing a pullover, a tartan skirt and long socks, and my hair is in the Lady Diana style, which I'd requested from Mum's hairdresser. I'm leaning against the wall with one hand on the radiator behind me. In the other hand I'm holding up a glass of sherry.

The sherry was my nan's suggestion. She thought it would cure my fussy eating, which had developed after a bout of chicken pox several years earlier. 'It'll be good for her appetite,' Nan told Mum.

So Mum would occasionally give me a small glass of sherry before a meal. Or I'd have melon with sherry poured all over it. I don't know if it worked as it was supposed to, but it explains why I'm so fond of sherry now and find it so comforting – I was practically weaned on it!

Nan had some strange suggestions. If you didn't like veg, she would say, 'Just put sugar on it.'

My uncle Anthony, her son, had hated vegetables, so she'd give him lettuce and cover it in sugar; she'd give him broccoli and cover it in sugar. She'd cut up an apple and put a little sugar on the side to dip the apple into.

If in doubt, Mum would give me an omelette. I'd always eat those. She made a lot of omelettes during my childhood. And still makes the best to this day.

Mum worked at Mothercare on Saturdays and Dad did MOTs at the garage, so I would either go to Auntie Iris or Nan and Gramps for the day. As the first grandchild on Mum's side of the family, I was absolutely adored. Every work surface in Auntie Iris's kitchen would be covered in flour and pastry when you arrived, because when she wasn't giving parties or doing am dram, she was cooking. Pasties, pies, cakes and sponges: she baked them all. Dad loved going there. We all did.

Auntie Iris didn't have children, so she could still run around in her lovely high heels and spend money on nice clothes and shoes. I remember her bedroom so clearly. She had all her shoes lined up under the window. 'You can wear those ones, those ones and those ones,' she'd say. 'But not those – they're new and for best.'

Every other Saturday I would go to my nan and gramps, who lived in Newton, above Mumbles, in a flat attached to the Glynn Vivian Home for the Blind, where Nan was the matron. Nan had been headhunted from her role as matron on the ENT ward in Singleton Hospital, where she ran a really tight ship and was feared and respected by the nurses.

From an early age, I'd help Nan with the cleaning and dusting there on a Saturday. She had me cleaning the toilets and all the rooms, nothing was off limits. She would come in behind me, wipe the top of the door, find a bit of dust, and say, 'See, you haven't done it properly.' She always found something.

I liked the practical work, and I liked caring for people. The residents were a captive audience for me. All the old people wanted me to sit with them, have lunch with them, perform for them, dance and sing. I remember once, Auntie Ethel and Auntie Winnie had a full-on tug of war over me in the day room. Each one had an arm and was pulling me from side to side.

Every time I saw Nan she'd say, 'Have you opened your bowels today?' I'd laugh, while Mum would be mortified. I was fascinated by Nan's hospital stories. Tales of worms being found in bed pans, disgusting eye infections, Nan performing the Heimlich manoeuvre on Gramps, in the middle of the living room, when he was choking on a piece of steak! They would make Mum heave, but I loved it and took them all in.

The only reason I wouldn't want to go and visit sometimes was that Nan and Gramps would argue and bicker. Nan was a lovely, interesting and incredibly strong woman. She was amazing, but she'd been affected by the difficulties she'd had in life. Sadly, she had married an alcoholic, my grandpa – Gramps – who was charming and lovely when he wasn't having a drink. But most of the time, he was.

Alcoholism is an awful disease, because it's not just the person who is addicted who suffers, but also everybody around them.

It was a double-edged sword staying at Nan and Gramps's house. Nan could be irritable and would shout at Gramps. He would sneak off with his bottles of whisky. Mum and Dad didn't really argue, so hearing Nan and Gramps bicker felt uncomfortable. But they were both loving people, and they were my grandparents. Gramps used to put me to bed and I would always be homesick and have trouble sleeping, so he made me a cassette tape of Beatles and Mantovani songs to play to soothe me. I had no idea who I was listening to, no idea who The Beatles were, but I would lie in bed with the instrumental 'Eleanor Rigby' hypnotising me to sleep, all as chosen by Gramps.

There was a lot to admire about Nan. She worked hard all her life. She was very strong, physically and mentally, and she wouldn't let anything beat her down. I think of her often. Any time that I've been low in my life, I think of Nan telling me, 'Shoulders back, head held high, you're just as good as anyone else.'

Sometimes we'd visit my gramps's brother, Uncle Leslie, who was married to Auntie Kirsteen and also lived in Mumbles. Mum and I used to get nervous going down there, because Leslie and Kirsteen didn't have children and were always just a bit posh. I wanted to make a good impression, so I'd be on my best behaviour and try to be perfect.

My whole existence was about having to be perfect. When I was small, I was perfectly dressed and my hair was always perfect – I looked like a doll. But the pressure to be perfect growing up didn't come from my parents, it came from me. As an Aries I was a determined child. I felt this drive, this ambition, this need to be the golden girl.

I was a good girl at school and was only ever told off once. I can still remember how mortified I was. It happened because I was walking along a corridor and a group of boys started running alongside me, just as the headmaster was coming the other way. I wasn't running, but the head saw us together and said, 'You shouldn't be running in the corridor. Go and stand in the assembly hall, until I come and get you.'

I hated the idea of being naughty and this felt like serious trouble. What made it worse was that the head promptly forgot about us and so we stood in the assembly hall for the rest of the day. Some of the others left, but I wouldn't budge.

Finally, one of the mums came into the assembly hall. 'What are you doing?' she asked.

When we explained, she went and found a teacher and really shouted at them. 'This is absolutely ridiculous. They've been there all day.'

I was still very quiet when I wasn't with my family. When I was about nine, my mum was chatting to my Auntie Diane, who was just my mum's friend, not my real auntie. Auntie Diane was talking about her daughters, Karla and Sasha, going to elocution lessons and doing LAMDA exams with a teacher called Ros Taylor. We didn't have a clue what LAMDA exams were, but Mum liked the sound of me learning elocution. She wanted me to be able to speak confidently, so she enrolled me for lessons with Ros Taylor.

For the LAMDA exams, you recite a piece of prose and a poem. Ros Taylor said to Mum, 'She's good at this. Have you thought about signing her up for the drama classes?'

'She's so quiet that I can't imagine she'd want to, but go on then,' Mum said. So I started doing the drama classes too.

Every year at Swansea Grand Theatre, there was a show called *The Bumbles of Mumbles*, which was about a group of imaginary creatures that could be found on Mumbles Beach. All the local dance schools would take part and do a big dance routine and a song.

My first year I shared the main part of Dearlo with another girl. I danced and mimed on stage wearing a big gold puff-ball skirt, a gold hat on my head, pink ballet tights and ballet slippers. It went really well, and the next year I did it alone. I'll never forget standing in the wings, seeing all the lights, feeling the electricity of the audience – and then going out on stage. It was my first real experience of acting. It's where it all began.

I really enjoyed performing. Soon I was winning awards for performing songs, reciting poems and acting out scenes at the school Eisteddfods. The Eisteddfod is a massively important date in the Welsh calendar. It's a huge annual celebration of Welsh culture, with arts and music competitions, concerts, gigs and exhibitions. If you did well in a school Eisteddfod, you went on to compete against other schools. Then you might be selected to go the National Eisteddfod in August – and if you did well there and reached the final round, you had a chance of appearing on Welsh telly. That was my dream.

I went on to be head girl in my last year at junior school. When I was eleven I moved to Mynyddbach Comprehensive School for Girls, which was directly across the road from our house. Mynyddbach was a hard, rough school. You'd see girls pulling the taps off in the science block, so the water would shoot out like a fountain; you'd see them sitting on the bathroom floor with lighters and cans of hairspray, making flamethrowers so teachers couldn't come in, and supply teachers were always getting sanitary towels stuck on their backs. I remember seeing two girls fighting once. In the fray, their shirts came off and they carried on in their bras. One girl had three big scrams down her face.

There was a lot of bullying going on at Mynyddbach and I was spat on a couple of times. I was called a swot because I wanted to study and was constantly picked on. It was basically like St Trinian's and pretty difficult to get through, but I think it stood me in good stead for the rest of my life. It taught me how to put a wall up and be strong.

Luckily, I had a good friend in Charlotte Evans. She was in my class, and we used to go back to her house and put music on – New Kids On The Block. We would dance on her mum's rowing machine and imagine that New Kids On The Block were hiding in the wardrobes, looking at us through the slats. Then they'd open the doors, see us and say, 'Wow, you're really amazing dancers. Will you please come and join us on tour?' We used to spend night after night doing that, and we were obsessed with Gary Lineker, as well.

My other good friends were Sheree Williams – another girl who really wanted to study – Nicole James, Kerry Ace and Louise Verbeck. And then there were girls who one minute would be your enemy, and the next minute they would be your new best friend. It was very weird, being in an all-girls environment. It could be really quite bitchy, but then suddenly it would switch.

Luckily, at home, me, Mum and Dad were the happiest little family. We did everything together. And I had lots of hobbies. I was always busy. I went to St John Ambulance classes, ballet, jazz and modern dance classes, acting, swimming and horse-riding lessons.

I was still spending alternate Saturdays with Auntie Iris and Nan and Gramps. Keeping Gramps away from drink was always on our minds. When I was about eleven, my nan left me in the flat with Gramps to sort something out in the old people's home. I was in her bedroom, and the mirror on the wall was angled in a way that I was able to see Gramps going into the living room. When I heard the clink of the whisky decanter, I thought, *I must stop him from drinking!*

I went into the living room and found Gramps pouring a drink. I started chatting to him and managed to get him away from the whisky and out of the room, and we had a cup of tea together instead, although I expect he managed to sneak back for a tipple later on. Poor Gramps, he just couldn't help himself.

Even though he was an alcoholic, he was gentlemanly,

very funny, incredibly charming – and he looked like David Niven. But Nan was constantly tense about what might happen next. There was a time when we all went for a walk in the Mumbles, the bit where the beach is on one side and the golf course on the other. I didn't realise it, but Gramps was already half cut. Suddenly he lost his footing and fell down the bank onto the golf course, just as someone on the green was about to swing his club.

Gramps plunged headlong into the bushes and just hung there, upside down. 'Where's my glasses? Where's my glasses?' he was shouting. We had to drag him out while he kept shouting about his glasses, which were perched right on top of his head. Nan was mortified, but the rest of us thought it was hysterical. Stuff like that was always happening to Gramps.

It was around this time that we started openly talking about Gramps's drinking and trying to do something about it by going to AA meetings. It was a big thing for an eleven-year-old to be going to AA meetings and dealing with all of that, and I can't say that I really wanted to, either, but I went along with it.

Mum was very particular about the way we spent our Sundays, because she hadn't enjoyed Sundays when she was growing up. Nan had made her clean the house on a Sunday. She'd have to do her bedroom, dust the living room, put the washing out on the line. So she wanted Sundays to be fun days. We'd normally put our best clothes on, I'd be allowed a glass of sherry, and then we'd play games.

We also started going to St Alban's Church, in Treboeth, and that's where I went to Sunday School, which I loved. But we left St Alban's – because they wouldn't let me join the choir for ages. One week, Mum came looking for me after Sunday School, and there I was in the front pew watching them all sing. I'd been told I had to watch for three weeks before I was allowed to join in! Talk about the church and their rules! So with that in mind, we went instead to a beautiful Grade II listed Welsh Baptist Chapel on Llangyfelach Road, just opposite us. Maybe they would let me sing.

I always say that Mum forced me to go there every week, but to be honest we went because I wanted to perform. I was always up in the pulpit reading out passages from the Bible, singing songs, reading poems. As much as I enjoyed it, I didn't like being taken to chapel all the time, especially as there was quite a lot of pressure on me from the elders (all men) and the reverend to be baptised. *No, I don't want to stand in that big thing of water with some strange man, and be pushed under by him,* I thought, and so I refused.

Something funny would always happen in chapel – funny haha but also funny peculiar. There was a married couple who came every week. They'd get up to sing together and the woman's singing voice was a lot deeper than the man's. He'd start singing really high, she'd start singing really low, and sometimes it would set me and Mum off giggling. You had children being sick in the pews and, in the row in front of us, there was an old man who kept falling asleep. We'd watch intently as his head went further and further forward, until eventually it went all the way and he'd smack it on the pew in front of him and wake up with a yelp.

The highlight of my week was the Thursday evening youth club in the community hall round the corner. This was the best youth club ever. At the entrance, there was a shop selling penny sweets in little white paper bags, and you'd pick out a selection on your way in. Inside the hall, there was a table-tennis table, always some footballs and a disco on the go, but mostly you would just run around, play and talk.

In those days I shopped in Tammy Girl, where the clothes were 1980s business chic and made you look as if you were going to an office. I felt very sophisticated. I had the most fantastic tartan dress with a cowl neck, and slip-on shoes that I'd managed to convince Mum to buy for me after having a full-on meltdown in Clarks, refusing to wear T-bar shoes any more. I was becoming a woman. One Thursday I turned up to the youth club in a pleated navy skirt that came down to my calves, and a big, flamboyant 1980s-style blouse. I'd curled my Lady Di cut with Mum's hot brush and I was ready to go. That was the evening I decided to try out wearing Mum's bra. Being eleven, pushing twelve, I was completely flat-chested, which lasted until I was thirty-five, so before I left the house, I stuffed the bra with a load of kitchen roll and went off to the youth club feeling very grown-up.

On arrival, there was a buzz in the air. Some of my friends had decided to lock me in a downstairs room with Michael, who I'd now been going out with for seven years. Our friends had decided that the moment had come, and Michael and I weren't being let out until we'd kissed.

Inside the room, I stood against the wall, expectantly, hoping I could keep a hold of my kitchen roll. What I wasn't expecting was for Michael to start doing a sort of shimmying action as he brushed his hands up and down my body. It was too close for comfort. I wished I'd plumped for the cotton wool instead.

'Actually, I don't want to kiss you,' I said.

He wasn't too upset. 'Okay, let's just stay in here for a bit, so they think we've kissed, and then we'll leave,' he suggested. Shortly afterwards, he dumped me for football.

I still see Michael every now and then. He's a conductor on the trains and sometimes we'll both be on the Swansea to Paddington line, and he'll sit down next to me and we'll chat away about life and our memories of school.

I didn't mind being dumped. I was becoming much more

focused on my interests. At every chance, I'd put myself forward to recite or sing in Welsh at the school Eisteddfod, on my own or in a group. Mrs Jenkins, my lovely Welsh teacher at Mynyddbach, worked really hard with me on my Welsh recitals. There's something about being from South Wales. Lots of us can't speak or understand Welsh, so she would painstakingly take me through the meaning of the poem, line by line, and once I understood it I'd be able to act it out, learn it and perform it.

There were two groups in the twelve-to-fifteen age category – Welsh speakers and non-Welsh speakers. The first year I entered, I got through to the final few, but fell short because some of the other non-Welsh speakers in my group were better at speaking Welsh than they let on, and so they won. I vowed to enter again, and win.

When the new term started, the West Glamorgan Youth Theatre Company held auditions at our school. They were very well regarded, but I'd never ever heard of them. I didn't know that you could join a company like this and put on plays. Mrs Fullard and Ms Davies, my two drama teachers, introduced me to Derek Cobley, one of the directors, and I launched into my monologue, playing a mad woman who'd regressed to being a child again. Not one to go with the comedy, I always liked a bit of drama! It was an amazing opportunity and, because it was funded by Swansea council, you didn't have to pay for it. And so that's how, at the age of fourteen, I came to spend two weeks rehearsing and putting on a play in West Cross in Mumbles, sleeping in a dormitory just down the road from Auntie Iris's house.

It was very exciting, but also terrifying, because everything about the experience was new, although luckily Ros Taylor was one of the teachers. For the first time in my life I was part of an acting troupe, putting on a proper production. It was also my first time staying away from home.

Since Michael dumped me, I hadn't had much contact with the opposite sex. Now I was plunged into this whole world of boys, many of them far older than me, and the environment was very creative and loose. In the evening, we'd have dinner, and then there'd be discos and stuff. People played games then – you'd all go in a circle, and when the music stopped, you had to kiss the person opposite you. I just used to hide in the corner to avoid anything like that, like some weird nerd. I joined in with the dancing, but stayed with the girls and didn't really speak to the boys. And I made some good friends who really looked after me – Helene Morris and Tonya Smith, among them.

The first production I did at West Glam was *Fuente Ovejuna* by Lope de Vega, a seventeenth-century play about a Spanish farming community rising up against a cruel overlord. It's quite a full-on drama with lots of blood and gore. In one scene, Spanish soldiers are raping and pillaging the villagers, and I played a young child being dragged off to meet a violent end. I remember really loving it, because I got to shout and wail and let out a huge swell of emotion. I didn't have any lines, but I did sing something with another young girl. We were on the top of a cart, just before we were dragged off, and we got to sing a song of defiance and protest. I had no idea what I was doing or what was going on, but I was absolutely loving being carried away with all the drama of it.

It was my first experience of older girls being friendly, because my secondary school was so rough that you didn't go near the girls who were in the years above. Suddenly I was in a dorm with these strong young women and it felt exciting and new. They'd write things on my script, like 'Men use affection to get sex. Women use sex to get affection.', which made me feel rather liberated and womanly, and like I was part of something – even though I hadn't even kissed anybody and didn't have any idea what sex was like.

I started my period surrounded by all these lovely girls. Luckily, I was prepared for it because Mum had given me the book *Are You There God? It's Me, Margaret*. She was always very good talking about these things. When I did the same with Eva as she turned twelve, it was a real full-circle moment.

Fuente Ovejuna was our winter show. We did the musical *Salad Days* for the summer show, which was much more light-hearted and just as much fun. I loved every moment.

I also remember we'd always do an improvised piece. This time it was a rap about Florence Nightingale. While one of the boys was rapping, me and Martha Jaquest had to do a contemporary dance with each other. We started giggling – it was all too much to handle – and while stroking Martha's face I completely lost control and wet myself. I had to carry on the production with soaking wet, smelly leggings. The show finished with fake snow falling from the roof, gathering in large white clumps on the inside of my thighs, and people saying, 'Jo Page smells of wee.' I loved it. I think there's something about being on stage for me – I get a thrill from it, but I'm always right on the edge. It's not the most professional thing, I know, but I just find it addictive – that buzz, that unpredictability.

West Glam wasn't just for aspiring actors; it was for anyone who wanted to be involved in theatre production. So there were students working in the wardrobe department, making costumes, and there were students learning stage management and doing all the lighting and sound. When we finished a show, we all had to help with the 'get out', the process of dismantling and packing away the entire production.

You'd each be assigned a job: taking down the lights, folding the costumes or boxing things up. I used to love that bit. It felt good to have the whole company working together.

Then came the end-of-show party and a total clothes crisis for me. I really panicked. They'd told me it was black tie and I thought, *I don't know what the hell you're meant to wear.* I was used to my tartan cowl necks and denim skirts, I'd never worn a cocktail dress before.

We managed to find a black dress in Tammy Girl. Mum had to take the shoulders up, and she couldn't sew, so she just pulled the shoulders all the way up until the neckline came halfway up to my chin. And I wore it like that. I remember feeling completely terrified. It was a big party, everyone was kissing, and I just stood in the corner in my little cocktail dress, looking like I was about thirty-five. When I think back on it, I wonder what all the fuss was about. I was fourteen, for goodness' sake; I honestly could have worn anything.

My life had been quite closeted until then. I was brought up to be a good girl and stay close to my family. Mum knew I wouldn't rebel, so if I wanted a perm, she'd say, 'Go on then, have one.' Or if I wanted a piercing, she'd say, 'Yes.'

She actually didn't want me to have any of those things. She just knew I didn't have that rebellious streak, which only really appeared once I started having children. All the way through being young, I just wanted to be good.

I certainly wasn't the type to hang around the streets of Swansea with my school friends, but doing West Glam Theatre made me curious for new adventures. 'Everybody is going down to the park tonight and I want to go,' I said to Mum one day when I was back home.

She smiled. 'You're not going to like it.'

'I should be allowed to see if I want to hang around with my friends,' I said defiantly.

'Okay, you can go,' she said.

So my friends came to call for me and off we went. We walked down the hill and they bought two flagons of cider. Then it was off to the park, where there was a group of boys hanging out. My friends started smoking and drinking, but I didn't want to do either. I looked on in horror as they gulped down cider and then straight away threw it up again, in front of all the boys.

'This is awful! Why would you do that? Do you not even want to look attractive?' I asked them.

But they were already drunk by then. I mean, looking back now, who the hell was the most empowered out of us all? My friends expressing themselves and doing what they wanted? Or me, panicking about looking attractive to the boys?

When we came out of the park, don't ask me why, but we wandered over to a nearby Jehovah's Witness place of worship, went in and sat at the back. My friends started throwing things at people and laughing and shouting.

What on earth are they doing? I thought. *I have to get out of here, because any minute someone is going to have a row.*

I was terrified by the thought of getting in trouble. I still hadn't recovered from being told off by the headmaster at primary school. But this was something else.

I left the chapel and started walking up the hill to go home. Suddenly, I heard a police siren and a police car sped past me in the opposite direction. *They must be going to the chapel!* I thought. *Something's kicking off.*

I started running, worried that the police would soon come to arrest me for causing a disturbance in the back of a Jehovah's Witness place of worship. I sprinted all the way home and through the door before they could get me.

'How was it, love?' Mum asked, looking up from the telly.

'It was awful, Mum!' I burst out.

'See, I was right, I knew you wouldn't like it.'

I was so angry with Mum for being right! 'But I should be allowed to see if I want to do something or not,' I retorted. 'Yeah, I didn't like doing it and you were right that it's not the sort of thing that I'd want to do, but it still should be allowed.'

And that was as far as my rebellious side extended – for the time being. I went back to focusing on my interests and entered the Eisteddfod again in the twelve-to-fifteen age group. This was my second attempt and I was desperate to come first. I made it to the last round again, and was among the final few competitors, but halfway through my recitation, suddenly conscious that all eyes were on me, I panicked, dried and completely forgot my lines.

'Oh, miss!' I burst out, turning to look at Mrs Jenkins.

She smiled reassuringly, and I managed to pick up where I'd left off and carry on.

Afterwards, the judges said that if I hadn't turned and spoken to her, I would have gone on and won the National Eisteddfod. I was gutted.

I entered again the next year, and this time I went all the way through to the final round at the Nationals. My performance was broadcast live and my Auntie Iris saw it while she was working on the reception desk of Singleton Hospital.

So there I was on my third attempt, halfway through reciting this very long extract of a Welsh epic poem on live TV, when it happened again. *Oh, my gosh*, I thought, *I do not have a clue what the next verse is. I just can't remember what I've got to say.*

My mind raced to my Welsh class and what we'd been learning recently. Without stopping to think, instead of the verse I was meant to be reciting, I launched into a paragraph about being on a caravan holiday and going to the youth club with my friends last night. Maybe it sounded strange to have this interlude in the middle of a great epic about Welsh knights and dragons, but at least it meant there wasn't an embarrassing gap before I could gather myself and pick up where I'd left off.

And this time, finally, I came first! 'You got lost along the way, but it didn't matter at all,' the judges wrote in my report.

I've won! I've done it at last, I thought.

Mrs Jenkins tried to push me to enter again the following year, but I didn't want to go through it all again. I was already feeling quite panicky because I was starting to get ready for my GCSEs, and I decided it would be too much pressure to have to learn and perform a long Welsh poem on top of everything else.

My Auntie Iris died soon after this and we were all very sad, especially Mum. Auntie Iris had been like a mother to her. Auntie Iris left her house to Mum. It was really important to her that we live there. All of a sudden we were moving to Mumbles, half an hour's drive away.

I was really upset when Mum and Dad told me. I didn't want to up sticks and leave all my friends. Yes, Auntie Iris's house had been in the family for years. Gramps had been born there, Uncle Leslie had been born there. I'd spent so many happy times there. But it wasn't my home. 'I don't want to go,' I yelled.

Mum dithered for a while. She and I are very different: when she makes a decision, she will talk about it for ages before actually doing the thing, whereas I'll just make the decision and get on with it. If I've decided I'm going to buy something, I'll go and buy it there and then. Mum, though, before she buys a chair, say, will go to about fifty shops and sit in every single chair she sees, before she then goes back to the first chair she liked – and that'll be the one she buys. Mum doesn't like change, or having to make a decision. So this was hard for her.

Mum's indecision meant it was a while before she could bring herself to move to Auntie Iris's house. She panicked and worried about it so much and it was a month before we actually went. Once we were there, it wasn't as much of a wrench as we'd all thought it would be. I missed our little home, but I carried on going to the same school, and it didn't take too long to get used to the bus journey.

Mum had gone back into finance a few years earlier and had started working for a local loan company. My Auntie Wendy was the first to go into it, and had said, 'Why don't you come and work with us? You're brilliant with money.' So Mum went along, did an interview, and got the job straight away. Mum would have her little book of customers that she'd collect from on a Monday and Friday, then she'd come home, balance her books and organise the money.

She absolutely loved it and her customers adored her. She was firm, but fair and very nice with it. One of her skills was helping her clients see sense about the size of the loan she was prepared to give them and how much she calculated they would be able to pay back in weekly instalments. She gave out great advice and helped them understand money better and how to manage their finances. With some of them she was also a bit of a counsellor, talking through their problems and issues on her Monday and Friday rounds. I used to go with her sometimes and sit in the car while she did her visits.

Mum saw some difficult things during her time there. Once, she went round to collect on a Friday and the client had hung a noose from the kitchen light, they were about to hang themselves. 'My life's a mess,' they were saying. 'I've lost my kids. I don't want to live any more.'

Mum went in, sat down and talked them down from killing themselves. It was a pretty tough job. She saw all sorts.

Mum is a great organiser and enjoyed keeping her papers

and filing in order. She'd come home on a Friday and have to balance her books. So if she was supposed to have collected £150 that night, and only had £130 cash, she would have to work out what she had missed and find the difference. That was her favourite part. Sometimes she spent hours doing it, but she always found it and balanced the books perfectly. She's still very good at figures. I think she'd have been very successful in finance if she'd stayed at the bank and worked her way up.

We didn't have a lot of money, but Mum would save all year so we could have a holiday. We'd always go abroad some-where, but we could never afford anything fancy and we'd often book those holidays where you turn up at the airport not knowing where you're going. You'd suddenly find out you were off to Ibiza or somewhere, and it was always brilliant.

But there was one year when Dad came home from the garage and said he knew a fella who worked in a travel agents and could get us a free holiday. Mum said, 'Okay, that sounds great.'

We were told we had to drive to Cardiff, show our pass-ports, not ask any questions, and definitely not draw any attention to ourselves. We turned up to Cardiff Airport, all excited but a bit on edge. Then we went off to Spain and had the most amazing time.

Coming home, we were at the airport in Spain and got our return flight details. It said we were landing in Luton. Mum went mad. 'We parked in Cardiff. We can't land in Luton! How the hell are we going to get home?' She gave Dad the full silent treatment. He was panicking. So we landed in Luton, hired a car, drove all the way back to Cardiff to get our car, and then drove home. But it was an experience, and it was fun. That was the kind of holiday we had. And I loved it.

Aside from our yearly trip abroad, we used to go down to our caravan in Llandovery. I must have been about twelve when we bought that old caravan. It was very simple and basic, but some of my happiest childhood memories are of being there, eating ham, egg and chips with Mum and Dad, playing cards.

One day, Dad came home from work with a portable toilet. It looked like a plastic bin with a flip lid. You'd basically squat over it, do your business, then put the lid back down. It was like a throne to us. We were over the moon. No more walking to the cement block loos in the middle of a field. Dad would put up a curtain across the middle of the caravan, and whoever needed the loo would go behind it, squat, and then Dad would take it out and dispose of it. Honestly, it made the holiday. We thought it was the best thing in the world.

It's funny, because I always cry whenever I drive past our old house in Treboeth. I haven't lived there for thirty years, but as I'm coming up the hill towards it, I recognise everything, every detail, and the tears always start. Simply because it's the house that I grew up in, it still feels like my house. Sometimes I think I'd love to pull over and knock on the door and ask the owners if I can go in and have a look around my old bedroom. But I think I'd probably just walk through the house crying and it would freak them out.

I lived in that house when life was lovely and simple. It's the house where we got our first dog, who would only drink water from the tap in the bathroom. She would run upstairs when she heard the tap go and jump up on the sink, and that's how she'd drink her water. Mum definitely didn't want to have a dog. We already had cats. But Dad and I were desperate and so we went on and on and on. Mum eventually said she'd think about it and by that afternoon, Dad and I were out looking at English Springer Spaniels.

That's how we got our beautiful first dog, Lady, who was named after the heroine in *Lady and the Tramp*. She was the most devoted dog you could ever get and absolutely wonderful.

One of the most vivid memories of living at that house is when Mum organised a surprise party for Nan's sixtieth birthday. Mum had already made herself ill with the stress of it all. She couldn't eat and had to go the doctors. Mum and Dad went to pick Nan up, saying they were going to take her out for a meal. All her side of the family and her friends came to our house and hid in the living room.

'But first, you've got to come back to the house and come in to say goodnight to Joanna,' Mum told Nan in the car. She wants to wish you happy birthday.' So Nan came into the house and we all surprised her! Everyone was there, hiding! The party went fantastically, and was topped off when Auntie Thelma sat heavily on our glass coffee table, the table top smashed and she fell right through it.

At that same party, I remember everybody being shocked at Lady's behaviour. She had eaten a big bowl of salted pea-nuts – the whole lot – and was so thirsty that she sat outside the bathroom door throughout the party, trying to burst in for a drink of water every time anybody went to wash their hands.

There were always parties, and family Christmases and Mum's friends coming round for Avon or Tupperware at Treboeth. It was a lively, fun and busy house.

Our new home in Mumbles had the smell of Auntie Iris, which wasn't surprising, given she had lived there for many years. One night I came out of my bedroom onto the land-ing and caught the scent of lavender – Auntie Iris's signature smell. I remember a strong sensation of her presence, which went right through me. I don't believe in ghosts, or any of that sort of stuff. I think, when we die, that's it. We're probably like stardust – we return into some sort of universal matter and then re-form as something else. But in that moment, I really felt that Auntie Iris was there. Then the smell disappeared and she was gone. I'll never forget it.

I soon settled into our new home and grew to love it. But I missed Treboeth, I still do. It was our first proper family home and I'll never forget it. I felt safe. I felt loved. When we moved to Mumbles, it was the end of an era. I was starting to grow up, starting to change. I drew a line under my childhood.

2

'People like us don't become actors'

I had one question on my mind when I was fifteen and we started having career talks at school. 'How do you become an actor?'

No one seemed to take it seriously. 'What do actors do?' I asked a teacher at school.

'Well, they go to drama school,' she said. 'But people like us, we don't do that.'

I couldn't understand it. She'd praised my acting and given me support and encouragement all the way through my time at secondary school. I absolutely idolised her. She used to wear soft lambswool jumpers and short knee-length skirts, with thick black tights and flat shoes. I started dressing like her. I even bought Narcisse perfume, when I figured out it was the scent she wore. I was heartbroken that she didn't think I could be an actress.

I thought it was something I could do, I mused. *She obviously doesn't see that in me.*

I don't think she was being unkind – just real. I mean, I was from Swansea, who the hell did I know who'd become an actor?

I only knew of one young actress from Swansea who was making a living out of acting. Her name was Melanie Walters and Mum had taken me to see her in *Educating Rita* at Swansea Grand Theatre – she had flaming red hair and was really good.

I felt so confused, because I'd got into West Glam Youth Theatre, I'd won the Eisteddfod, I loved performing and everyone said I had something. But most of all, I could feel it, it was there, I needed to act. So what kind of people *did* become actors, then?

I hadn't doubted myself until this moment.

But now that I thought about it, although people were giving me praise when they saw me in something, they never followed it up by saying, 'You could do this professionally. Have you thought about becoming an actor?'

Why not? I was certain that if I wanted to I could make it happen. Why didn't other people believe in me?

When I passed the audition for the National Youth Theatre of Wales a few months later, it confirmed for me that acting was something I was good at. Out of the many kids that applied, only a few had been chosen to go on the sought-after summer residency, living in Aberystwyth. My parents were very proud of me.

The summer after I did my GCSEs, I set off to Aberystwyth for a month of acting workshops and performances with the National Youth Theatre of Wales. It's quite funny to think of my parents letting me loose after so many years of cushioning and protecting me. But in their eyes, I was still very much the good girl – and I was. I'd been to an all-girls school for the past five years; I was head girl at my primary and secondary schools; I didn't have a clue how to talk to boys, and I never went out unless it was to a dance or acting class.

I felt nervous on the car journey. I knew that some of the students I was about to meet would be older and more experienced than I was. What would they think of me? As we drove north, from the bottom of Wales to the top, I tried to comfort myself with the thought that there'd be quite a few familiar faces from West Glam there, including Tonya. Yet there was a rising sense of anxiety inside me when we arrived.

In my little room on campus, Mum and Dad put all my clothes in the wardrobe and helped get me sorted. 'Okay, then, we're off,' they said.

I felt bereft as I waved goodbye to them. But there was no point moping in my room, so I went to find Tonya downstairs.

And then something magical happened: the world suddenly burst into colour. Surrounded by people who loved performing arts as much as I did, I went on to have the most brilliant four weeks of my life.

When I look back on that time, it feels almost as if I went through an invisible revolving door that evening: I went in as a child and came out the other side as a young adult. I had never drunk alcohol before – apart from Mum's medicinal sherry and the occasional festive Babycham at our neighbours' house – but now I developed a taste for the deliciously light and fruity combination of Taboo and lemonade. Five, to be exact, in order to get the job done, and although I was only sixteen and looked about twelve, I got away with it by flashing a European ID card that I'd forged my date of birth on. I was never, ever tempted to try drugs, though. Lectures from

Mum had persuaded me that trying any drug at all would lead straight to heroin addiction and death.

Boys were suddenly of huge interest to me. I mean, massively so. I was thrilled when Tonya told me that a fella named Craig fancied me and wanted to take me out for a drink. Craig and I spent the evening together, and ended up back in his room, kissing – the first time I'd kissed a boy properly, aside from a fumbled snog I'd had in a pub by the sea. Unfortunately, as I was kissing him, I was thinking, *He's good-looking but I don't really fancy him.*

I had a Wonderbra on and Craig spent the whole evening trying to scoop my boobs out of it. As I was completely flat-chested, there was literally nothing to push out. But God love him, he never stopped trying.

After kissing him all night, I walked around campus for the whole of the next day holding his hand, still thinking, *I just don't fancy him.*

I didn't know how to tell him, so I told Tonya, and she dumped him for me. Luckily, he went on to become a friend, and much merriment was made of the boob scooping.

In actual fact, I'd had my eye on someone else that I'd spotted, when I'd first arrived. He was much older than me, eighteen, he had a lovely smile, and his name was Greg. The problem was, I had absolutely no idea how to talk to him, so Tonya's skills were employed again and off she went to go and do her business. Shortly after, when he asked me if I'd like to go for a Chinese takeaway, I jumped at the chance.

I'd never had Chinese food before and had no idea what to order when we got there. I chose a little carton of egg fried rice. That was it, just a tiny carton of rice, which I ate in the street as we walked back to my room. It was gone by the time we'd done about ten paces.

That night, Greg and I kissed. This time I actually fancied

the person I was kissing – and he must have felt the same, because we went out with each other for the rest of our time in Aberystwyth.

It was during those weeks that I also discovered Paul Weller (not personally, but on cassette tape), Levi's jeans, Wonderbras and dolphins. We were staying on the Aberystwyth seafront and there were many mornings when I'd wake up, look out of the window and see dolphins jumping in the bay.

We did loads of improvising on the course. We improvised a half-Welsh, half-English production called, *Why Don't You Talk to Me?* It was all about issues that affect young people, and it felt extremely liberating to be able to have a voice. I played the best friend of a teenage girl who fell pregnant; somebody else was in an abusive relationship; another was discovering their sexuality. We sang and acted during the day, improvising to our hearts' content, then at night we wandered the Aberystwyth seafront, heading to the Bear, a local pub, where I would have my five Taboo and lemonades lined up. It was bliss. We put the whole production together ourselves and I loved doing it.

I was learning loads from the teachers and the other students and was like a flower bursting into bloom. But although most of my experiences during those weeks were very positive, some weren't so good, and I had a couple of near disasters.

One evening, Greg and I had a massive argument and ended up falling out. I flounced off with another boy and shut myself in a room with him. After making sure that Greg knew we were in there together, I decided that I was going to purposely kiss him, just to spite my now ex-boyfriend.

It was teenage drama at its most combustible and ridiculous. Greg started banging on the door, shouting, 'Let me in, let me in!'

'No!' I yelled back. 'Leave us alone.'

If I was being deliberately dramatic to draw passionate dec-larations of love from my eighteen-year-old boyfriend, then it worked, because by the time I'd got home he'd written me a love letter. It was adorable, but now that he was declaring his love for me, I wasn't interested. 'For God's sake, he's written saying that he's in love with me,' I told Mum, letting his letter drop from my hand into the bin.

I soon realised that I had some sort of power over the op-posite sex. I wasn't sure what it was, or what to do with it, but I was enjoying the new-found confidence it gave me, and after spending the last five years purely with my girlfriends, I was ready to mingle.

I never wrote back.

That September of 1993, I started at Gorseinon College in Swansea, where I'd signed up to do A levels in dance and the-atre studies, English lit and psychology. Gorseinon College was massive and had at least a thousand students, maybe more, and I was so excited to be in this new world, specialising in what I really loved.

Yet I was soon wishing I had chosen to be in with the BTEC students, studying performing arts. Their world was seductive and exciting. There was an openness about them that wasn't there in the people in my academic classes: every-body was in dance gear, throwing themselves around; it was all about performing, being creative, and the boys were in touch with their feminine side. They were dancing, singing, completely free and expressive, I loved being around them, soaking up their energy, but I couldn't quite be like them, or dance or move the way they did. I was seduced by their energy, but I just wanted to be a serious actress. That's what I had in my head.

After five years in a single-sex school, it took me a while

to get used to sitting next to boys in class and seeing them in the common room and canteen. *This is insane!* I thought. *They're everywhere.* They were like aliens, and I had no idea how to talk to them.

But, at last, I had a social life and started going out in the evenings. A group of us would meet in Neptunes, overlooking Bracelet Bay, or Cinderella's, known as Cinders, near the pier – two of the legendary 1990s drinking spots of Mumbles. We'd end up going down to the beach and messing around until late. Then we'd head into Swansea and go to Ritzy's, where you'd be lucky to make it across the dance floor in one piece.

I had a scary encounter in a bar one night, when I bumped into a Welsh actor who had been teaching improvisation at a workshop I'd once attended. He must have been about forty-five and there was something very edgy about him: you could see in his face that he was a heavy drinker, and I don't know what he was doing hanging round a bar full of teenagers. But I'd had a few sherbets myself and didn't think too deeply about it when he came up to chat and suggested going into an empty side room where it was quieter. 'I want to talk to you about something,' he said.

'Okay,' I said, wondering what it could be.

As I walked into the room, he suddenly pushed me inside, circled round me and shut the door. 'I think you're gorgeous,' he said, blocking my exit. 'I'm in love with you and I'm going to kiss you. Kiss me!'

'No, I'm not going to kiss you,' I said.

I didn't feel scared at first, but then he tried to force himself on me. 'Get off me!' I yelled, shoving him away. 'Let me out of here.'

Thankfully, a few of the students I was out with had noticed him leading me away. One of them heard my muffled shouts and called the others over. They forced the door open and the Welsh actor sprang away from me. 'What's the fuss about?' he said, trying to laugh it off.

It was all over so quickly that I didn't really register that I might have been in danger – I just thought I was dealing with a lairy but harmless, boozed-up old lech. Being the innocent that I was, I think I felt more like a damsel in distress who had been rescued by a gang of knights in shining armor. I didn't stop to think how much worse it could have been if they hadn't come to save me.

Before long I realised I didn't want to go to places like Ritzy's and have the fellas just grab you and have a grope, it was much more fun at the gay clubs. I wanted to be surrounded by all of the gay boys and girls, and dance to the most amazing music with them in a lovely safe space.

I ended up having a very brief fling in my second year of A levels with this boy who was bisexual. He was making a half-hearted attempt at going out with me, and he really shouldn't have, because he quite clearly wasn't into girls. But I was going out with him because he was very charismatic, and I was so attracted to that whole world that I just wanted to be with him.

One night we were coming out of a gay club, and I suddenly felt a massive blow to the side of my head. It was my first experience of being mugged and of homophobia. A random fella had punched me, called me names and stolen my handbag.

I didn't care about being hit, what I was really concerned about was my A level copy of *Oedipus Rex* in my bag, with all my study notes in it. My ear throbbing, we phoned the police and they drove us around Swansea city centre looking for the fella that night. Then we went back to the police station and they got out a load of books with photos of different men, and flicked all the way through them in front of us. We looked through them all to see if we recognised anyone, but we didn't. That was the last I ever heard of it. I never got my book back.

I went on seeing this boy and going to gay clubs with him. One night we went to a drag show and he got really drunk. All of a sudden, I saw him in the middle of the drag queens and someone was taking off his clothes. When he was down to his pants, I saw him falling to the floor, and then some form of sexual act went on. I only half glimpsed it, but it looked like he was getting a blow job. I was in shock – and what made it worse was that everybody was turning around to look at me, knowing we were together. One of my friends tried to save face by shouting, 'Don't worry, she loves it!'

Do I?!! I thought.

After that, we amicably parted ways, and I thought, *No, don't go out with a gay fella, because it's just not going to work. He won't be devoted to you. Just be his friend, his best friend.*

I quickly dropped A-level psychology. There were too many boys to give my attention to, and so I concentrated on my English, dance and drama. I was slowly being pushed down the Oxbridge route, when they could drag me away from the drama studio. Being academic, it was deemed a waste to not have anything to fall back on, but life was too much fun. We were doing two shows: Lorca's *Yerma*, and I'd just got the part of Hermia in *A Midsummer Night's Dream*. When we did that, I came alive. I wasn't interested in putting pen to paper.

I remember sitting in my theatre studies class one day and deciding to make myself cry and look really upset. And the weird thing is, I actually started feeling it. I just felt like emoting for a bit. So I sat there looking really sad, as if I had the weight of the world on my shoulders.

My teacher, Simon Pirotte, looked at me and said, 'Jo, are you all right? Is something the matter?'

'No, no, it's fine, it's fine.'

It wasn't about showing off. I just wanted to do emotions. I wanted to sit in that feeling and play with it.

Even though I was busy emoting every which way I could, I still found it really difficult to cry on stage. One of my last productions at West Glam was *Nicholas Nickleby*, and I played Kate Nickleby. There was one big moment where Kate is being attacked by several men, and I was supposed to cry, but I just couldn't get the tears out. My teacher was starting to get impatient with me, so I began panicking, thinking, *What am I going to do?* Which only made the situation worse.

I decided to head to Boots, bought some Vicks VapoRub, and before I went on, I opened the little stick and rubbed it under my eyes, totally underestimating the effect it would have. The vapour shot up and hit me like a brick wall. I threw my hands up to my eyes to rub them, forgetting I had it all over my fingers, and blinded myself. I was in agony. I couldn't open my eyes. I stumbled on stage, rubbing my face, tears pouring. But it worked. My teacher was really impressed and thought I'd pulled it out of the bag, emotionally.

Fine, he doesn't need to know, I thought. Whatever works.

There was no telly on demand in the nineties – it was just what happened to be on. So I'd come home from school, sit down with my food on a tray on my lap, and watch *Blockbusters*, *Grange Hill* and *The A-Team*. I didn't really watch dramas in the evenings, because of bedtime, but every now and then I'd catch something by chance while flicking through the channels.

That's how I discovered the things I loved: *French and Saunders*, Ruby Wax, Maggie Smith, *Blackadder*. I remember stumbling across Miranda Richardson playing Queenie opposite Rowan Atkinson, and feeling terrified and totally fascinated by this woman, who was dramatic and hilarious at the same time. *How do you do something like that? How do you become someone like that?* I wondered.

Years later, when I ended up working with her on *Gideon's Daughter* – Stephen Poliakoff's film – I could barely speak. I just stood there staring, thinking, *Oh my God, it's Queenie.* She was beyond wonderful. She had this real menace about her, in the best possible way.

It was the same when I saw Miriam Margolyes in *The Life and Loves of a She-Devil*, and later in *Blackadder*, and was utterly mesmerised. These women were so comedic but also really dark. *I want to be part of this*, I thought. *How do you become someone like that? How do you do this?* Then my mate Helene Morris introduced me to Victoria Wood (not personally, just on tape!), and that was that.

I got into Shakespeare and that led me to Kenneth Branagh and his films. I became completely and utterly obsessed with him. I read his autobiography from cover to cover, and thought, *RADA, that's where you need to go. That's how you get into this world.*

I began finding my way – shopping in charity shops, picking out old men's velvet jackets and flares, going up to the RSC to watch Kenneth Branagh in *Hamlet*, and just thinking, *I want to be part of this. I want to be in this world. But how do I do it? I'm from Swansea. No one in my family is in theatre or TV. There's nothing like this here.*

But I knew, I just knew – that's what I wanted.

I was really not enjoying studying for my English lit A level. My tutor was a very skinny and sharp-featured woman. I found her lessons incredibly boring. There'd be the most amazing piece of text that I'd want to read and perform, and we'd analyse it and pull it apart so much, until all the heart and soul had been stripped of it.

Under her tutelage, I didn't bother to finish reading *Persuasion* by Jane Austen, I hated doing haiku, and *King Lear* left me cold. I didn't want to analyse things and take them apart, I wanted to jump in and become them.

Either way, I wasn't committed to making sure I had something to fall back on. There was only one thing I wanted to do, and so Mum, Dad and I started looking into how to apply to drama school and sending off for brochures and application forms.

The summer before my A levels, I was invited back to the National Youth Theatre of Wales for the summer residency. This time it was in Cardiff, which was nowhere near as romantic a setting as Aberystwyth. We were doing the Stephen Sondheim and John Weidman musical, *Assassins*, which focuses on nine people who have assassinated, or tried to assassinate, the presidents of the United States. I'd recently been introduced to Sondheim's work at West Glam. The last show we'd done was *Into the Woods*, a musical, intertwining the plots of several fairy tales, and I'd been cast as Cinderella, a dream role, and an introduction to Sondheim's genius for combining music, lyrics and character. It was a fantastic production to take part in. And now here I was, about to start on my second Sondheim.

The same group of actors from the previous year were on this course too, give or take a few new ones and, very quickly, after being forgiven for not responding to the love letter, Greg and I got back together again. So quickly, in fact, that it came as quite a shock to the fella next door, when he peeked in to chat to Greg that first evening. Greg's neighbour had corkscrew curls, was skinny and quite gangly looking – and it turned out to be Rob Wilfort, who, little did I know, was going to end up playing my brother Jason in *Gavin & Stacey*.

Greg and I were with each other all the way through the residency, but this time something felt different. Maybe it was something to do with being in a less romantic setting (it's amazing how much atmosphere a dolphin can bring!), but I found him a bit weird and controlling. Whatever it was, I reacted against this by purposely doing things I felt he didn't approve of.

One night, a group of us were in a bar, playing dares, and somebody dared me to wee on the sofa.

'If you do that, then I'm dumping you,' Greg said.

I can still see us now, in my mind's eye, staring each other down. *How dare you try and control me?* I thought.

Looking back, as a forty-eight-year-old woman, I can see he had a point. If any boyfriend of mine had turned around and announced he was going to wee in the corner of the room, I'd probably have had something to say about it too. But I was on my high horse, and I wasn't going to be told by any man what I could and couldn't do. Promptly I stood up, pulled my pants down and weed on the sofa. At that, Greg turned around, walked out, and dumped me on the spot.

There was a real theme of trying to control me in my earlier dalliances with men. I think they loved how small and sweet and innocent I was, like a little bird waiting to be captured. But then I'd surprise them with a feistiness that even I didn't know was in there. I remember one boy saying, 'We've sorted out your hair and make-up. Now we've just got to do your nails. Then you'll be perfect.' Like I was a little doll. He didn't last long. I sometimes wonder what happened to him; he's probably opened his own beauty parlour now!

Greg and I made up and stayed with each other throughout the rest of the course, but it wasn't the same. He was angry and controlling; I didn't know how to deal with it. But I also didn't want to lose him. Not an ideal first romance.

I continued to see him after he went off to drama school that September. I went to visit him about a month before I turned eighteen, in early 1995, and spent the day and night there.

A week later, I found out that he was seeing the girl he was sharing the flat with. One of our friends knew about it, but just didn't know how to tell me – so it was only now that I was finding it out. It was a real blow; I was really quite badly burnt by it all.

If only I'd just replied to that love letter. Karma's a bitch.

My first proper long-term relationship was with Marc, who I met at West Glam. He was tall, with dark hair, and very funny. We'd known each other for years, but a spark had ignited as I was starting to blossom, and I'd caught his eye. It was great at West Glam – the students had a really social time, but we also did Brecht and Ibsen. The plays were full-on. I remember doing *The Woman* by Edward Bond. I didn't have a clue what I was doing, but I got to wear a fantastic pink tweed power suit, which I loved. Sharing dormitories and doing shows together can be quite dangerous when first love blooms, but Marc and I were taking full advantage of it, and during the interval of a matinee had sneaked off into a room together. Thank God I'd already done my costume change, because as I was straddling him on a chair, kissing him, oblivious to everything else, I suddenly heard the voice of Siwan Morris, my friend, saying the opening line for Act Two over the tannoy.

And then she said the line that was before mine.

I have never jumped off anyone so fast in my life. It's really weird as an actor, because you can be doing anything at all, but when you hear your cue line it just brings you out of it. 'Oh my God!' I screeched.

I dived off him, sprinted down the corridor and didn't stop until I burst through the door, legged it through the wings and ran straight out on stage, said my line, and carried on with the play.

Siwan said to me later that she just knew I'd make it. She was pretending to be blind and had her eyes closed, but she committed to saying the line, confident that I would appear on stage in time.

I blame the power suit. Put me in a costume and I'll get straight into character.

At the start of my final year at college, I began going to auditions for drama school. Although I couldn't ignore the fact that most of the other applicants seemed a lot more so-phisticated than I was, I was quietly confident. *I can do this*, I thought. I might have been young, but I could act. I was also able to read a text and quickly make sense of it. My one weakness was that I often felt too shy to speak up and vocalise my thoughts.

It's funny, because when I'm not acting I don't like people watching me. At Christmas time, I never wanted to join in when the family were doing charades, or trying to get me to sing something. But if you put me in a costume on a stage and give me a script, I love it. Being somebody else gives me a feeling of freedom.

When I was acting, I never really thought about being funny or doing comedy – it just didn't occur to me. I loved drama and darkness. That was the world I wanted to be in. So much so that when I auditioned for RADA, where you're supposed to do two speeches, one serious and one comedic, I went my own way and chose two very serious pieces.

The first was Philomele from *The Love of the Nightingale*. In the speech, she's been raped by her brother-in-law and had her tongue cut out. It was pretty full-on.

My second piece was Queen Katherine from Shakespeare's *Henry VIII*, kneeling and begging the king to believe that she has been a true and faithful wife, or otherwise to 'give me up to the sharp'st kind of justice.' Again, heavy and full of pleading and drama. I was fully committed to the tragedy.

The RADA teachers didn't say anything about the fact I hadn't brought in a comedy monologue. But when I did Katherine's speech, they asked me, 'What do you think Katherine is saying?'

I thought about it. 'She's begging him not to leave her,' I said. 'She doesn't want to be divorced.'

'Yes, but what does she actually mean when she says, "the sharp'st kind of justice"?'

I paused. Then it hit me. 'Oh my God, she's challenging him to have her beheaded if he can prove she's been untrue!'

I remember that moment so clearly. It was the first time I fully understood the weight of what I was saying. I realised the speech was not just about heartbreak. It was about survival.

'Do it again, but with that thought in your mind,' they said. And I did, this time knowing what it really meant.

That's when everything shifted for me.

I found London quite terrifying. Mum and I went on the Tube and when I looked at the map of the Underground, I thought, *There's no way in hell I'm going to be able to work this out.*

I felt so overwhelmed down there that I went all dramatic and grabbed hold of Mum, saying, 'Oh! I'm going, I'm going . . .' Mum had to hold me up, because I nearly passed out.

Thank God for that, she thought. *She's not coming to London.*

Right from the get-go, I was very dramatic. That's what I could tap into. In my final recall for RADA, we had a two-day workshop. I was given a comedic speech where I was a northern girl on the back of a motorbike. I hated it. I didn't like it or think I was in the least bit funny. I did it through gritted teeth.

At the end, in front of everyone, when we had to perform a speech, they encouraged us to do the new one. But I decided to go back to my trusted favourites, because I just thought, *I'm not a comedy actress.*

They told us that if you had got in to RADA, Nicholas Barter, the principal, would phone you. I was on the toilet one morning and Mum called out, 'Jo, Jo, Nick Barter is on the phone!'

I had to get off the toilet and run into Mum and Dad's bedroom to pick the phone up. 'Oh, hello, Joanna, it's Nick Barter here. I'm phoning to tell you that we would really like to offer you a place at RADA.'

I remember keeping it together and being really quite calm. 'Oh, thank you very much,' I said, staying composed. But then I put the phone down and we went absolutely ballistic.

I would have been happy with the idea of staying closer to home, but when I got in to RADA to do a Diploma in Acting, I thought, *If you get in to RADA, you must go to RADA.* And I wanted to be the next Kate Winslet.

There was only one problem with going to RADA, though: I was an only child. I loved living at home and spending time with my parents. I didn't want to go and live in London, where just the sight of the Tube map made me feel faint.

Wait, there was another problem, a bigger one: it was astronomically expensive to go to RADA – from the fees to the living expenses – and there was no way my parents could afford to pay for it, we didn't have that kind of money.

Still, determination runs deep in our family. Mum started writing letters to everybody she could think of, trying to source funding. They were begging letters, really, addressed to individuals like the Welsh actor Sir Anthony Hopkins, and to a range of different trust funds and foundations.

Mum was amazing. There were no computers. We didn't have the internet. She would go to the library, get down all the big reference books and look through them for hours on end, patiently searching for any possible means of support for my drama-school training.

When I think about Mum devoting so much time and effort to doing this research for me, I realise how lucky I've been to have such devoted parents. I've never, ever doubted their love and they've always been so determined on my behalf.

Mum's research went deep. She was dead set on finding me a way to go to RADA. I'm amazed to think of all of the work she did and all the letters she wrote. Eventually, her enquiries led her to the Atlantic Foundation, a Cardiff-based charity that provides grants for a wide range of causes, from education, to famine and poverty relief overseas. She discovered that there was a certain fund set aside to give grants to relatives of people who had been in the Navy. As both my grandpas had been in the Navy, we were eligible to apply. That was a red letter day for our family. All because of Mum's incredible investigative powers.

After weeks of work and months of waiting, Mum managed to get enough pledges, grants and donations to fund my course at RADA. I was all set. I was going to London.

The night before I left was horrific. Mum locked herself in the bathroom crying all night. I was watching *The Lion King* downstairs with Marc and I could hear her sobbing. Later on, I began taking all my posters and cards down off the wall in my bedroom, dismantling my life. It was awful.

Mum loved me so much that she didn't want to hold me back. She was so selfless that she had actively found a way for me to leave home. But she was only in her early forties and it must have felt like her heart was being ripped out. Still, she managed to put on a brave face the next day as we drove to London.

There's a side of me that would have loved to have stayed in Swansea. I would have lived down the road from Mum and Dad, worked in the local shop, married a boy from Swansea, and had kids straight away.

But then there's a side of me that likes travelling and moving and living out of a suitcase. I don't like being in one spot for too long – I'm restless – I like going from job to job, the unpredictability of it all, being able to move at the drop of a hat.

But it would have been easier if I'd stayed closer. I already had friends here. I would have been with Mum and Dad. I would have had their safety and security. It was such a difficult decision to go to London, and it's not always been good. I've missed a lot from family life – weddings, funerals, parties and the day-to-day.

But that's what you do when you become an actor. You sacrifice a part of your life for your career. And then you get older, and you get to an age, and you think, 'Was it worth it?' And yes, it was worth it, because it was a life choice I made, even though I still wonder about what the other life might have been.

I made the choice. I was leaving my lovely family unit. Now it was time to start the rest of my life. I was about to grow up.

3

Breathe through your anus: the RADA years

Mum and Dad drove me to London. I was so upset and scared that they promised to stay up for my first week and help get me settled. They booked a bed and breakfast on Gower Street, right next to my halls of residence. It made a difference to have them close by. I was only eighteen and felt a long way from home. At the same time I had a head full of Kenneth Branagh-inspired hopes and dreams for the days ahead.

I was staying at Bonham Carter House, which was a halls of residence for student nurses, and this was the first year that they had allowed RADA students in. I had no idea how central it was. At the weekend I would cross the road and get on the Tube at Goodge Street to go down to Covent Garden, not realising that I could have just come out of my building, turned left, and walked there in less than five minutes.

My tiny room was on a corridor with shared bathrooms halfway along, and a kitchen at the end. Mum, Dad and I unpacked my stuff and put it away.

I went to the bathroom and, on my way back, a man came up to me. He was probably about thirty and had a friendly enough face. 'Would you like to come to my room and have a look at my holiday photos?' he asked.

I don't want to, I thought. *I don't know who you are, but I'm going to have to be polite and say yes.*

I was so naive. 'All right then,' I said reluctantly.

He led me into a room and said, 'Sit on the bed.'

I sat down, and he shut the door and locked it. Then he turned the radio up.

Oh God, I thought, instantly feeling uncomfortable. I took a closer look at him. He was thin and rangy, with slightly protruding eyes and straggly hair. Normal enough, but then again . . .

He asked me why I was in London and I said that I was starting at RADA. 'I work at RADA!' he exclaimed, his eyes lighting up. 'I'm the caretaker there.'

He sat down next to me, got out a load of photos and started showing them to me. 'This was when I was in Thailand,' he said, pausing when he came to one of the photos. He laughed and tapped it with his finger. 'I was buying drugs in this picture.'

I was horrified that he was talking to me about drugs, but I simply said, 'Oh, that's lovely,' and, 'That's really nice.'

I sat there for a bit longer, looking at his photos with him, and then I said, 'I need to go back now, because my parents are in my room. I need to go back to my room.'

His smile faded. 'All right, go on then. Go and open the door.'

I stood up and went to the door, but I couldn't open it. He

came and stood behind me. 'You can't get out, can you? And nobody can hear you.'

Loud pop music was playing on the radio, but I couldn't hear it any more, as everything had seemed to stop and be hanging heavily in the air.

'Can you let me out? Please?' I said, the panic rising in my voice. I was desperately wishing that I could press the rape alarm my Uncle Anthony had given me before we left, but it was back in my room. 'Can you just let me out?'

He left me waiting for about thirty seconds, the longest thirty seconds of my life. My heartbeat pulsed in my ears. At last, he moved forward and turned the lock.

I opened the door and shot straight out. My room was a few numbers down and I started banging on the door. Mum opened it.

'Mum! Oh my God, I've just been stuck in a strange man's room.'

'What?' Mum and Dad were appalled to hear what had happened. They sat me down and gave me a cup of tea. 'For God's sake, don't go into strange men's rooms!' they said.

Mum shook her head worriedly. 'I can't believe that we're leaving our daughter here, when this has happened, just as she's literally only gone to the toilet.'

I never saw the man again.

That evening, it had been arranged for some of the new students to meet each other over a drink. One of the fellas there started chatting to me. He lived in London, quite far out, and at about half past eleven, after I'd gone to bed, he knocked on my door. 'I can't get home,' he said. 'There are no buses running this late. I'm going to have to stay in your room tonight.'

'No, you're not,' I said.

I definitely wasn't getting trapped in a room with a man twice in one day.

'But I have no way of getting home,' he whined.

'Tough. It's not my problem. You're not staying in my room tonight.'

I found out the next day that he knocked on another girl's door and she let him into her room. When she turned the lights off to go to sleep, he jumped on top of her and started touching her up, and she chucked him out.

This all happened – and I hadn't even started the course yet!

The next morning, my heart was in my mouth as I walked into RADA's main building in Gower Street. Meanwhile, on the pavement outside, my parents were hiding behind a tree with their camcorder. They were in such a fluster that they missed me going in and only caught me when I crossed the road a bit later to go to another building.

'Look at you!' they said, when they showed me the video later.

'That's ridiculous,' I laughed. 'What did you do that for?'

Now that I've got children, I completely understand. It was my first day at RADA, the most famous drama school in the world. It was huge.

As I stepped inside the entrance, I was bubbling up with excitement. I loved acting and was confident of my ability. Kenneth Branagh had thrown himself into the diploma course and gone on to great things. Now it was my turn. I was on my way to becoming the next Kate Winslet.

For my first day, I wore surfer tie-dye trousers and a surfer-style jacket. I was literally head to toe in tie-dye. I didn't even own a winter coat. That was my first day at RADA.

It was September, and I was bloody freezing. It became quite obvious that I needed a coat and so Mum and Dad took me down to John Lewis and bought me a long, classic winter overcoat, which I still have upstairs. It had a proper collar, it was cinched in at the waist and it flowed all the way down to my ankles, so I looked like I'd come out of a Laura Ashley catalogue. I loved that coat, it was the first piece of grown-up clothing I'd ever had. The last coat Mum had bought me was my school one from C&A. We'd had a massive row in the street because I didn't want one with a hood, and now I was finally wearing one that made me feel like I was in a nineties romantic film starring Meg Ryan.

After an introductory talk in the theatre, we were sent to room nine, where our acting classes would be held, and told to form a big circle. Standing there in my surf trousers and T-shirt, I looked around at the people I was going to be spending the next three years with. To my dismay, they all looked a lot more grown-up than me. Most of them had been to university and were in their early twenties. They had names like Candida, Philippa and Sophie. One of them was thirty. Meanwhile, I was straight out of my A levels at Gorseinon College in Swansea and utterly clueless. There was a yawning gap of experience between us.

The only other person my age on the course was Rob Wilfort, who I knew from the National Youth Theatre of Wales in Aberystwyth. I was glad to see a familiar face. Even though we didn't massively bother with each other, at least I knew someone – and he went on to be a lifeline during my years at RADA.

We were told to go round the circle and take turns saying one thing about ourselves. This was our first 'exercise'. I re-member one boy saying his name was Johnny and he liked bananas. Halfway through, a student walked in, looking flustered. 'I'm so sorry I'm late!' she said. 'I'm Maxine Peake. I got lost.'

The teacher who took us for Alexander technique went

absolutely berserk with her. He really simpled her. 'How dare you! This is your first day. You've turned up late.'

It wasn't as if she'd come late for the whole day. We'd gone from one room to another after the introductory talk, and she'd genuinely got lost on the way to his class. I was speechless. It seemed like a huge overreaction. *Oh my gosh!* I thought. *There's no need to be like that.*

'If this is going to be your attitude,' he thundered on, 'if you think you can just treat us like this, without respect, then you're not going to last here.'

There was utter silence in room nine.

I don't like it here, I thought, with a shudder.

I soon discovered that the ethos at RADA was to treat the students like complete shit. We were supposed to be there to learn how to act, but firstly they wanted to break us down, strip us of all of our bad habits, get rid of everything that marked out our individual identity and render us completely neutral.

In their eyes, everything about me was wrong. I was too sweet. I was too lovely. I was too prissy. I was too clean. I was too closed off. I began to wonder what they'd seen in me in the first place.

I was told, 'You can't do it,' so many times in my first few days that my confidence dropped away. It was a self-fulfilling statement: I couldn't relax and do any of the classes freely, because every time I tried something I was told 'You're rubbish, you can't do it, that's wrong.' Very quickly, I seized up.

Every morning, I would wake up and go next door, through the famous stone pillars into the building, my stomach knotted with nerves but with an optimistic front. Val would be there behind the desk, to greet us. A cockney woman with a cheery voice, she was like our mother. She had experience of this business being the mother of the actress

Lisa Maxwell, so she had a warmth and homeliness to her that was much needed.

All the students were given the same treatment, so by the second year everybody had really good Alexander technique-trained posture and was talking like a BBC newsreader. 'You need to get rid of your accent,' I was told, time and time again.

I felt ignorant compared to everybody else. I was bewildered a lot of the time; I didn't know what to think when the teacher in our voice class said, 'We're going to do RP so I suggest you turn on Radio Four and listen to their voices.'

What is Radio Four? I thought. I'd grown up listening to the charts on Radio One. That was it. I didn't listen to anything else. *How do you find Radio Four?* I was too frightened to ask anybody.

The other students seemed to know all this stuff. They were English and already spoke RP; they were a completely different class to me. I was a graduate of youth theatre, and I was going off my natural instinct with acting. I didn't think about any other way of looking at anything or reading anything. It was just what you felt.

And I felt different being Welsh.

There just wasn't anybody else like me, except maybe Maxine Peake, who became a good friend. I didn't have the three years of going out and getting drunk, doing university degrees, being in lectures, talking and analysing stuff. I'd just been messing around with the B Techers and having fun.

I dreaded it when we were given a text to analyse. I just felt stupid. I didn't have the right words and I didn't feel safe enough to offer my opinion on anything. We'd all sit there and analyse the script like we were writing a bloody English essay on it when all I wanted to do was just get up and act it out.

All this talk, talk, talk. I'd sit there and feel frustrated. I didn't have anything intelligent to say about why someone decided to write something that way, or that it was set in the 1930s when such and such was happening. Yes, there are social differences – the way you dress, how women were seen, what was going on in the world – but when it comes down to it, humans are humans. It's just about feelings and thoughts and what you want.

It came as a shock, as well, to see how talented some of the others were. Growing up, I'd been led to believe that I was just amazing at everything I did. I was a hard worker, didn't ever want to step out of line or misbehave, and I was the head girl of both my junior school and my comprehensive. I was used to doing well. So I had a bump down to earth when I realised there were lots of people who were just as good as me, and some were better.

It knocked me for six. I went through a huge and very sudden drop in self-esteem.

I began to dread my classes. Each morning we'd be given an exercise to do, where we had to explore the characteristics of whichever character we were playing at that time, and mine always seemed to consist of someone old, or dominant or sexy or maternal.

I remember playing a lesbian child killer with my classmate Hannah. We had to start by being in bed and kissing, and I was so self-conscious and nervous I turned up wearing my thermal vest underneath my red pyjamas with cats on them.

Another time, I had to chase Rob Wilfort with a pair of scissors around a room, jump over the bed and kiss him. Then I was cast as Arcadina, from *The Seagull*, an older dominant actress in her fifties. For the exercise they wanted me to explore my sexiness and strength and power in my body. They insisted on me wearing an evening gown, putting my hair up and wearing a lot of make-up. 'This will make you feel strong, confident and sexy,' the teacher said. 'Well, it won't,' I replied. 'I feel like a little girl in my mother's clothes. If you want me to feel sexy then let me wear my hair loose and messy. I'll put on my jeans and a vest and no bra, that'll make me feel earthier.'

But no, I was forced to do it her way. I felt false, I didn't feel truthful. I felt uncomfortable. She told me this was because I couldn't act.

I'd find myself crippled by shyness because I was so worried about being criticised. It didn't feel like a safe environment where I could experiment. It was their way or the highway – and if they felt you'd got it wrong, they'd humiliate you. *I have absolutely no idea how to do this*, I'd be thinking. *I don't know how to get to any of these emotions the way they want me to.*

We were studying Stanislavsky's 'the method', which was the only technique we ever did. No other techniques were taught. It was this or nothing. If you couldn't get it right, or it didn't work for you, it meant you couldn't act. 'The method' encourages actors to draw on their own life experiences to create a character.

In real life, I'd never been in love, never had children, never been pushed to the brutal limit of something so awful happening in my life that I'm on my hands and knees and feel like I can't carry on. But this was 'the method', and you had to draw on your own life experiences. Aged eighteen, I didn't have any life experience, I'd just 'acted', and I'd had no problems reaching this depth of emotion before. I mean I was begging for my life in my audition speech, and they seemed to think I had something then, so I couldn't understand why it felt like they needed to destroy me. Couldn't we just 'act'?

I didn't like the emphasis on marking everything out

methodically in advance. You'd have your lines, and they would want you to write down how you were going to play each one. It might be 'to soothe' or 'to strike' or 'to hit' or 'to relax' – and that is how you would say each line. Every time. If you veered from it, you'd got it wrong. If you ignored it, and just did it how you felt in the moment, you'd got it wrong. It was so rigid. Taking away all instinct. I'd done it by feeling before, and been so free, and receptive and open. This was too fixed for me. I was happy to have a go at all the exercises, but if it didn't work for you they'd say, yet again, 'Well, you can't act.'

At my audition one of my teachers had expressed surprise at how relaxed and open I was. I just wanted to try something different every time and see where it took me. That was the way I liked to discover how I was going to do something – not by thinking and planning and marking it out. If I'm working opposite someone, I want to bounce off them. I want to have fun in the moment, have no idea what choices they're going to make, no idea what choices I'll make in return. Now I was being held captive in a box. How can you make something so creative and free and instinctive into something so rigid and set? And how can you be an acting school and see that someone is obviously talented, but because they get to where they need to be by using other means as opposed to yours, you say they're shit?

James says that when he was at LAMDA, it was all about having fun. Yes, you'd be acting out different things and trying different techniques to see what worked and what didn't, but it was enjoyable. Nobody ever said to him, 'You can't act. You're shit.' You just got up and tried out different bits and bobs, and if it worked it worked, and if it didn't, it didn't.

One day my acting teacher stood me up in front of

everyone and said, 'This is the perfect example of everything that is wrong with an actor.'

Everything that had been a positive before going, suddenly became a negative. It seemed the worst thing I could've done was turn up to RADA being an eighteen-year-old Welsh girl. My innocence seemed to be a problem that needed fixing. I was trying my best to fit everything in after being in an all-girls school for the last five years, but I was still only eighteen and had just left home for the first time. I was sorry if I couldn't portray someone really sexual convincingly, but I'd only kissed someone for the first time the year before. I started thinking there was something wrong with me. This thing I had done instinctively with relish and enjoyment, actually it turned out that I wasn't very good at it.

I remember being in a class with Maxine Peake. We had to squat on the floor and move around the room. It felt quite silly, but everybody was doing it. Then the teacher said in her booming voice, 'Breathe through your anus!'

Maxine was crying – I think she felt humiliated – but I was in hysterics because I thought it was so funny.

The exercises continued. One day, I was told, 'Don't wash for a week, because we want to dirty you up a bit. You're too Welsh and you're too sweet.'

Maxine was a bigger girl then, and one day one of the teachers said to her, 'If you keep eating all those chips, you'll never play Juliet.'

Quick as anything, Maxine said, 'I don't want to be Juliet. I want to play the nurse. It's a far better part.' She was brilliant.

At the end of each term, I insisted on packing up the whole of my room in my halls of residence. Dad would come early and wait for me at Sidoli's Café, just around the corner, which I'd read in Kenneth Branagh's book was where he and his friends used to go. Meanwhile, I would be throwing up over the side of the bath with a raging hangover because I'd been to the goodbye party at RADA the night before. Eventually, Dad would pick me up, and we would take everything out of my room – all my pots and pans, every single item of cutlery, every jumper and everything off the walls. I'd strip the room bare, take it all back home for the couple of weeks I had off, and then come back and set it all up again. I think I just needed to feel I was leaving for ever each time.

No one came close to being as awful as my acting teacher. She was vile. Lots of people liked her, she had her favourites – obviously I wasn't one of them – but she was always late for her own classes. Bear in mind, we're paying a fortune to go to RADA. The reason was always the same: she hadn't been able to park. She had a massive collection of twenty-pence coins and she'd send different students down to put money in the parking meter outside the front of the RADA building. For half of her lesson, you'd be sorting out her parking.

This teacher was really mean to me. 'These are your two children,' she said to me in class one day, pointing at two other students. 'Social services are coming tomorrow to take them away from you. This is your last evening together. Start acting.'

If I'd been at West Glam, I would have thrown myself into it. I would've enjoyed improvising and seeing where the scene went. But by this point I was so paralysed with fear, so terrified to utter a word, that I didn't really do anything. I couldn't abandon myself, because it wasn't an environment where you could make mistakes. Now I was at RADA, I didn't feel free. I couldn't stand up, I couldn't really go for it, I had no one to say, 'Okay, that didn't work, try something else.' It was just: 'You're wrong. You're rubbish. You clearly can't act.'

She stood me in front of the class, and said, 'You're shit,

you're shit, I just can't do anything with you.' I started crying. She looked at me wearily, and let out a sigh, almost like I'd inconvenienced her. 'Oh, she's crying. Okay, we may as well use these tears. Tell me about when you thought your father was going to die because he had a brain virus.'

Tears were rolling down my cheeks and my chest was heaving. 'Well, his head started hurting . . .' I began, recalling the awful day Dad had gone temporarily blind and been rushed to hospital, where they thought he had an embolism and was going to die.

Amanda Haberland, another girl in the class, stood up and said, 'This is wrong! You can't do this.'

But this teacher went on berating me and humiliating me, in class after class.

A few weeks later, we were asked to choose a song to sing and a poem to act out, and it had to be on a certain theme. The song I chose was 'Nothing' from the musical *A Chorus Line*. Narrated by a female character, it's about her experience of being in a drama class and sitting in a line with the other students pretending to be on a bobsled. Every day for a week the acting teacher makes them practise feeling the downward motion of the ride, the chill and the wind in their hair. 'You've really got to feel it,' he tells her.

Yet, although she digs deep down to the bottom of her soul, she admits to him that she feels nothing. Secretly she's thinking it's all bullshit.

The following week, she has to pretend to be a table, then an ice-cream cone, and really inhabit the roles. Again, she feels nothing, and the other students gang up with the teacher against her. Seeing the teacher and the course for what they are, she leaves and goes to another drama school. Six months later, when she hears that the drama teacher has died, she cries, because after digging deep down into her soul, she feels nothing.

We had an audience of all the teachers critiquing us and I sang this song to my acting teacher, and I really felt it. Then I performed my poem to her and my voice teacher.

The feedback was brutal. 'That was all wrong! You're breathing in the wrong place, because you were feeling the emotion, not the intention.'

They completely trashed me. I stood there, thinking, *I'm worthless, I'm nothing. I can't act. I don't even know why I thought I could. I just can't do it.*

Many years later, I saw on social media that a drama teacher had died, and her name caught my eye. I started reading it and, yes, it was my acting teacher and she had passed away.

As I read it, I thought, *Oh my God, the song has come true!*

It was insane. Life – and art – had come full circle. And yes, I dug right down to the bottom of my soul, and this time, I felt something. Relief.

I was still with Marc during my first year, but there was a huge frisson between me and Ryan, an American student. We had an understanding that we were both with other people and couldn't get it together, even if we wanted to, but of course that eventually went out the window.

Ryan was my buddy.

In one exercise where we had to improvise together, our acting teacher said, 'You have a very abusive husband, and now you have to sneak out of the house. You're escaping him.'

She wanted Ryan to wake up just as I was about to leave through the door so it would start a scene, but I begged him not to open his eyes, not to wake up, because I couldn't take another day of being vulnerable and then being told I couldn't act.

We started the scene. Ryan pretended to stay asleep while I got out of the bed, packed my stuff, went to the door. The teacher was so annoyed that he hadn't woken up, she took her socks off and started throwing them at him. They were hitting him in the face, and he still refused to wake up, just so I wouldn't have to start improvising. He basically saved me.

Matthew Rhys and Ioan Gruffudd really looked after me during my first year. Ioan had left the year before but was still popping in, and Matthew was in his third year. Everyone adored Matthew. He was fun, talented, just wonderful. Ioan was really handsome, and they were just these gorgeous Welsh boys.

Years later, I was in New York taking Dad there for his sixtieth birthday. We were walking through Central Park, and I was chatting away, being mouthy, saying where we needed to go. Then this really Welsh voice went, 'I know that voice,' and it was Matthew. I couldn't believe it. He was doing a play out there and we got chatting. It was mad bumping into Matthew in the middle of New York after all those years, but he was still the same old lovely Welsh boy.

Our dance teacher was the one person at RADA who I thought was sympathetic to me. So when we all sat round in a circle for our end-of-term reviews, I wasn't expecting her to say I wasn't any good.

'In class, you've just got this wall around you,' she said. 'You're bristling and your body language is saying, "Stay away from me," and so I'm scared to approach you.'

She went on to say that there was nothing she could really do with me. I was devastated. She was the one person who I thought understood me. *I've got no one*, I thought, *literally no one.*

Very early on at RADA, they decided I was too Welsh. My voice was too fast and too high. My voice teacher, Robert Palmer, had helped train Margaret Thatcher and he gave me the same kind of training, to bring my voice down and centre myself. The only way I could talk in RP was to sound very ordered and controlled. So for a whole term at RADA, I basically sounded like Margaret Thatcher. I couldn't find a way to make it natural. I went from being too Welsh and fast to suddenly sounding like Thatcher. It's no wonder I was told my acting was cold and detached.

When I tell my RADA stories to my friends, they always ask the same questions. 'Why didn't you drop out? How did you manage to keep going?'

Well, it was partly because I knew deep inside that I was an actress, that this was me, and it was what I was going to do. And it was also Mum and Dad's unwavering support.

I went through the same routine every day. At the end of lessons, I'd go back to the halls of residence. In the shared kitchen I'd make myself a chicken breast with sweetcorn and potatoes. After I'd eaten, I'd go downstairs to one of the phone booths in the hall, ring Mum and just sob into the receiver for hours. Every night, sobbing, and then going upstairs to sleep; every morning, getting up and doing it all again.

But I had a steely determination. And, however much the RADA experience chipped away at me, it stood me in good stead and made me tough. Being an actress is such a hard job anyway that you need to be prepared. You can go for round after round, and then they turn around and just say, you haven't got the job. It's brutal, and you do need to be hard and strong.

There's a part of me, anyway, that doesn't care what anybody thinks. That very much comes from my dad, who has a wild side and is always down by the sea and out in the countryside. The pull of nature and the elements is always there for us.

Even if he didn't sit on the phone to me every night, Dad was every bit as supportive as Mum was. He sent hampers full of treats, from Dime bars and Maltesers to Jeremy Beadle's *You've Been Framed* cassette tapes. Every single week for the entire time that I was at RADA he would send me his tips from work, around sixty quid. 'Don't tell your mother. She'd be furious,' he used to say.

I don't think either of us have admitted it to Mum, even to this day!

4

Oh, that's just Jo Page crying in the toilet: the RADA years, part II

At the end of my first year, I was giving out programmes at a Year Three show when I noticed a woman staring at me. She got up from her seat and came to talk to me. 'What's your name?' she asked.

We had a bit of a chat. 'Yes, I'm a student here,' I said. 'I'm in the first year.'

'Have you got an agent?'

I hesitated, unsure of what she meant. 'I don't think so.'

The following day I found a note from her in my pigeon-hole – the old-fashioned equivalent of sending emails and texts in the 1990s. 'I chatted to you when you were handing out the programmes,' she had written. 'I'm an agent and I'd love to represent you. Please can I look after you?'

I went to see a senior member of staff for his advice. 'I've just got this in my pigeonhole. What does it mean when someone says they want to represent you?'

He looked surprised. 'Well, if you want to go with her, then go with her,' he said offhandedly. 'It just means she'll look after you.'

It still didn't seem very clear, but I got in touch with her and said, 'Okay, you can look after me if you want to.'

I didn't tell any of the teachers that I had an agent. Maxine Peake had one as well, but we were the only ones, I think.

My agent kept sending me off on secret auditions. We weren't allowed to work, so I constantly had to lie to the teachers. It's weird. You go to drama school specifically to enable you to get work when you come out, but they don't want you to do any acting work while you're there, because they say you'll pick up bad habits. Yet surely the best way to learn to act is to go out and physically do it.

There was so much we weren't being taught. Not only did I not know what an agent was – until I got one – but I also had no idea how to play the game, or even what the rules of our industry were.

When I was asked to read a script for an audition, I didn't realise how important it is to be diplomatic. I was just being me, so I said what I thought. I even rang one big casting director who was expecting me in for an audition and said, 'Actually, I don't want to audition for this film. I think it's really badly written, and I don't want to be in it, so if you don't mind, I don't particularly want to meet for it.'

'Okay . . .' she said, and I could practically hear her eyebrows shooting up.

My agent phoned me the next day and went absolutely ballistic. 'What were you thinking? You do not speak like that to casting directors!'

'I've not spoken like anything,' I said. 'I've been honest.

I've said, "Thank you very much for the audition, but I can't make it." And also, "I don't want to rearrange the time, because I don't think the script is well written, and I don't want to be in it."'

'You said what?' she screeched. 'You can't say things like that!'

When my agent sent me to audition for the film, *This Year's Love*, I rang RADA and said there had been a gas leak in my flat and I couldn't come in.

I went down to Soho for the audition and I got the part. It wasn't a big part; I only had a couple of lines. But it was my first ever acting work and I was ecstatic about it.

When This Year's Love came out, my nan was the first to see it. 'Look, I don't mean to be funny,' she told my parents afterwards, 'but I can't see Joanna anywhere. I don't know if I've missed her bit because it was just so quick?'

Oh for goodness' sake, I thought. *I can't believe she's missed me.*

I went to see it the next day and waited expectantly for my scene to come up. *Here it is*, I thought, as, up on the screen, evening fell. Then, all of a sudden, it was morning.

I sat up in my seat. *Wait, where did my scene go?*

I was devastated. They'd cut it. My first acting work – and my first experience of (not) being in a film!

During my time at RADA, it was just plays, plays, plays. We only did one class of being filmed on a camcorder – one single lesson in two and a half years. I imagine it's completely different at drama schools now – there's such a huge focus on going to LA, screen tests and self-taping. But in the 1990s, it was all Chekhov and Brecht and no telly or film at all.

I had to do a Julie Christie speech from *Don't Look Now*, and they filmed me, and it was a close-up of my face. The man teaching us was Hugh Fraser, the actor who played

Captain Hastings in ITV's *Poirot*. I was really quite shocked when he came in and said that I was luminescent on camera, because I thought, *Jesus Christ, my face looks like a potato*. But the camera completely changes you.

I got one tip from that class: 'Don't move your head around a lot when you're acting on film, because the camera will be close in on you. Try and stay as still as possible, and don't put your arms into shot, because if that's going on, it's too much for the audience to look at.'

That was it. That's all I came away with.

I felt better about myself now that I had an agent, but RADA was as awful as ever. I was glad to go home for the summer after my first year. It was great to be back by the sea in Mumbles, breathing in fresh, salty air and walking on the beach.

We were set a big piece of homework to do over the holidays: we were given a character and told to write speeches in their voice, and then perform them. Mine was from a George Bernard Shaw play. I didn't have a clue what was going on in it. It was really hard to do research in those days, because I didn't have a computer with endless information on the internet. If I wanted to find something out I had to go to the library, and they didn't have a George Bernard Shaw section in the one in Swansea. My confidence was at such a low ebb that I couldn't motivate myself to do it. I didn't feel up to the task. *I don't want to write something for the first ever time, stand up, and act it out*, I thought, imagining the scorn and ridicule that would be piled on me. It just wasn't the space to do it in. I didn't feel safe. *I can't do any of it any more, so I'm just going to ignore it.*

I buried my head in the sand and refused to think about it. When I went back to London in September, I went with a heavy cold and a creeping sense of terror. *Jesus Christ, I've got to perform a monologue tomorrow that I'm supposed to have written!*

I could feel a panic attack coming on. My mind was whirling. *What am I going to do? I just don't know what I'm going to do!* I felt like I was going to explode with anxiety. I tied myself to the radiator in my room, hoping it might make me feel safer and more grounded.

I couldn't get calm, so I went to find Maxine in her room on the floor below. 'Help, Max, I haven't done it! What am I going to do tomorrow?'

She was in the middle of writing her speech for Elizabeth I. It was Elizabeth later in life, when she had a receding hairline, and Maxine had a yellow swimming cap on to give the effect of a bald head. So there she was, with her bald, yellow head, comforting me and trying to make me feel better.

When I went into class the next day and told the teacher I hadn't written anything, there was a big row and he really had a go at me. I mean, it was my own fault, I should've written something. But by this point I was so terrified of getting everything wrong, I couldn't even begin. He was so savage that I went to pieces. I rushed off and went into the bathroom next to room nine, and collapsed in a heap.

Later, one of my friends said they'd been able to hear my muffled sobbing through the wall.

'What's that noise?' somebody asked.

'Oh, that's just Jo Page crying,' the teacher said dismissively, not looking up.

That evening, I phoned Mum. 'I can't do this any more,' I wailed.

I was a mess, so Dad came to pick me up, and took me home. In my mind's eye, I can still see myself walking down the path to our house, hobbled and bent. I was so exhausted and ill, and just so beaten down.

I stayed at home for about two weeks. 'You know, you don't have to go back,' Mum said gently.

'I've got to!' I protested. 'If I want to keep my agent and if I want to work, I have to be in London.'

And I went, even though it was horrendous. It was tough for Mum, too, because I was back to the same routine of being on the pay phone every night, talking to her for three hours solid, crying hysterically, and saying on repeat, 'I hate it here. I just want to come home.'

Things improved when I went to a pet shop in Swansea, got a hamster, called him Tarzan, and smuggled him into my halls of residence. He had a little cage and I'd take him out and let him roam freely around my room. Then he'd disappear. *Oh my God, where is he?*

I'd hear him snuffling. Dad used to send me so much food that I couldn't eat all of it and used to chuck it in the suitcase under my bed, and that's usually where Tarzan would be. Once I caught him with nine Maltesers in his mouth.

Tarzan kept me company and Maxine would look after him for me when I went home for the weekends, which I did as much as I could. He was only small, but the effect he was having on my happiness and life was huge.

My agent had a Christmas party. I had no idea what to wear to an agent's Christmas party. So I went to Oasis and bought myself a black business suit, an orange lurex polo neck jumper and a pair of black court shoes. When I turned up, I remember her looking at me and going, 'Oh gosh ... oh ... you look ... nice,' and being really shocked. And then there were all these other actors in the business milling around.

There were people like Rhys Ifans there, in a pair of ripped jeans and a T-shirt, and Kellie Bright with her long, flowing blonde hair, in a dress. Everybody was creative and beautiful – just how you'd imagine actors to be – and I turned up in a pair of black court shoes and a bloody business suit.

The diploma course at RADA was all exercises to begin
with, but you finally start doing shows at the end of the
second year. My first play was an adaptation of *Dombey and
Son*, the Dickens novel. I desperately didn't want to be cast
as Paul Dombey, who is about eight years old, ailing and
wheelchair-bound, and who slowly becomes iller and iller,
then dies. Great! I wanted to play Florence Dombey, his
sister. A strong-willed, compassionate and resilient woman.
I waited with anticipation in the corridor as the cast list went
up. Searching ferociously, my eyes skimmed down the list
of everyone's names. Where was I? Page . . . Page . . . Page.
Found it. Paul Dombey.

So, I was given the role of a nineteenth-century con-
sumptive child. But actually, it turned out to be perfect for
me. Dressed as a little boy with my hair combed back, I
looked so pure and innocent that I could have walked into
any number of TV costume dramas. And it turned out to
be a blessing in disguise, because it attracted the attention
of a big agent.

I had already started thinking about finding somebody new
to represent me. As we were coming up to the second year
shows at the end of the year, I went to a photographer and
had some new head shots taken. Unsure of which ones were
best, I showed them to a senior member of staff, hoping he
would advise me.

'Out of these three photos, which photo do you think I
should put up on the wall for the agents?' I asked him.

He shrugged. 'In this photo, you look like the abused girl,'
he said. 'In the next photo you look like a social worker and in
the final photo you look like her mother. So it doesn't matter
which one you choose.'

That sums up what it was like for me at RADA.

'Can I talk to you about agents? Because I've been offered

two different agents and I don't know which one to go with,' I asked the principal.

'It doesn't matter. Won't make any difference,' he said. 'You're an ice queen. Can't get through to you, anyway.'

It didn't occur to him that he couldn't get through to me because the battering I got in his drama school had made me retreat into a shell.

One teacher tried to help me access my passion and sexiness by giving me the part of a sassy New York broad, trying to seduce and kill a guy on the subway. He'd told me to stuff my bra with cotton wool because big boobs would make me confident and channel Ruby Wax. *Please let me out of this room. This is torture*, I thought, as gibberish came out of my mouth, because I couldn't do a New York accent. *I'm completely flat-chested. I've got cotton wool in my bra. I'm straddling this big man, trying to seduce and murder him, whilst channelling Ruby Wax. It's too fucking much. I don't want to do it. Why can't I just be Juliet?*

Ryan tried to help me rehearse it. We'd recently got together, but it was very on and off. But I couldn't do it. I was too mortified. Yet I clearly was quite ballsy and sexy, because I remember drinking a load of White Lightning at a party with Ryan and having sex with him on top of the piano in room nine. Maybe it was my way of doing a dirty protest.

I was given some good parts in the plays, when the agents started coming. You might even have thought they considered me a decent actor − if they hadn't kept giving me the same sort of roles to play. It felt to me like they were saying, 'You can't do anything else, so this is the type of role you will play.'

I looked on enviously as other students were given a wide range of roles that showcased their versatility. Amanda was cast as a really old woman in one production, and then got the main part in a Brecht play; she was always wearing a wig or playing somebody completely different from herself. Lots of the students had that same diversity of roles, which was wonderful for them because, as an actor, you wanted to be stretched and challenged. Unfortunately, it worked against them in the end, because there was no clear direction for them in their casting, and the agent wouldn't know what kind of roles to put them up for. I remember one really talented student bursting into tears about it. 'I'm not going to get an agent! I've got to wear a wig again!'

We'd always thought that it would be the other way round and that an agent wouldn't take you unless they saw you playing different roles to showcase your abilities: 'I can play someone who is ninety-six; I can play somebody who's dying; I can play a thirty-five-year-old tomboy.' But it was just the opposite.

It worked in my favour to be typecast and always do the same kind of part. Although I don't think at the time they classed it as a good thing, it was brilliant for me, because it got the agents interested. I played Lily Smalls in *Under Milk Wood*, a budding actress in *Once Upon A Time In America*, Shelby from *Steel Magnolias*. They could see me walking straight into costume drama and playing the young ingénue.

With some actors they'd say: 'I can't see you being cast in anything now, but I can see what you're going to be cast in when you're forty-five, because you already fit the part, except you're too young, because you're twenty-three. When you get to forty-five, you'll come into your own and could do really well. But you won't last that long.'

No one at drama school is going to think, *I'll give it until I'm forty-five and then I'll eventually fit into the look I've got.*

In my case, I wasn't going to get cast as a seventy-five-year-old in the real acting world, so there was no need for me to try. An agent with Peters Fraser + Dunlop saw me in

Dombey and Son and decided I'd be great in costume dramas. He phoned the next day and said, 'I'd love to sign you.'

It was thrilling, because he looked after a couple of actresses that I really admired. As it happened, I went to meet him at his office on the day of the UK premiere of *Titanic* in Leicester Square. As I walked into the agency building, there were suits and dresses hanging up above people's desks, ready to change into, and a huge sense of excitement in the air. I straight away signed with him.

I still had the exact same ambition as when I'd applied to drama school: I wanted to be the next Kate Winslet. I loved costume drama and now I thought of myself as a serious, RADA-trained, classical actress. It didn't occur to me that I could be comedic or funny.

I think my drama-school teachers guessed I would go on to be typecast as the naive, blonde ingénue. It was basically the same role every time – lovely, blonde and sweet, with a little bit of bite.

That was my selling point. 'I can play a young girl but with a range of different accents.'

Saying that, when he saw me as Shelby in *Steel Magnolias*, my new agent said, 'That possibly has to be one of the worst performances I've ever seen. Your accent was terrible.'

'Oh my God, are you going to drop me?' I asked him.

He laughed. 'No, darling, of course I'm not, but that was one of the worst things I've ever seen.'

Actually, doing *Steel Magnolias* was one of the best experiences I had at RADA. It was all of us girls together and I'd begged to change acting teachers and my new one, Dee Cannon, was lovely – so gorgeous, so giving, so open. But it wasn't as easy in those days to work on accents because we didn't have the internet. Instead, you'd have to go to a lovely little theatre bookshop near Warren Street station, which doesn't exist any more. It was full of plays and cassette tapes. You'd find the tape for the accent, take it home, play it, and just listen to it over and over.

I phoned up my first agent to tell her I was leaving. I still hadn't learned how to be diplomatic and didn't make any attempt to choose my words carefully. 'Hi, another agent has asked to look after me,' I said, 'and I'd like to go with him, because he's really nice.'

She could barely contain her fury. 'That's it?' she said. 'That's all you're going to say?'

'Yes, I like him, and so that's what I'm going to do,' I trilled. 'Thank you very much for looking after me. Bye!'

I cringe when I think about that phone call. For someone who prided herself on being polite, it was actually pretty rude, but I just didn't realise it at the time.

In my second year of RADA, the vice principal picked me to represent the college at a Buckingham Palace Gala. Me and Sally Hawkins went. I played Phoebe in *As You Like It* – not the whole thing, just a bit of it. She played Rosalind. Afterwards, we met Prince Charles and Princess Margaret. He was charming. He talked about when he was at university in Aberystwyth and chatted in Welsh to me. He was a lovely man.

After that, I remember running around the corridors in Buckingham Palace and nobody stopping us – me and Sally just running around. Exploring. I stole a white napkin with Buckingham Palace on it for Mum and Dad, then spied through the thick velvet curtains of the throne room and spotted Judi Dench.

I didn't know what to wear for meeting royalty. I couldn't afford anything and Auntie Kirsteen very kindly gave me the money to buy a dress; I went to Harrods and bought something beautiful – a long, dark velvet and chiffon blue dress, with a wide neck, which was shaped like a column. I've got it in the dressing–up box now for the kids.

My new agent started sending me to auditions straight away. I had to do them all in secret. One day, I was told I had an audition with Tim Roth. He was casting for *The War Zone*, with Ray Winstone. It was the part of Ray Winstone's daughter, who's sexually abused throughout. It was utterly horrific and I don't think I could've gone through with it even if I'd been cast.

My agent said, 'Make sure you're dressed like a schoolgirl.'

I dressed as much like a schoolgirl as I could, and I went and met Tim Roth. He was really sweet, really nice and ab-solutely nothing but professional.

When you went to these appointments, you just kind of assumed and hoped everything would be fine. Another time, I had to get on about five different tubes to the back of beyond and go into a casting director's house. You turn up, go and do it, and just keep your fingers crossed that you're not going to be assaulted. The number of times you went into hotels, said, 'Hello, it's Joanna Page, here to meet so and so,' and then waited. Someone would meet you, take you up to a room, and you'd go in. It was always just men in there. Male director. Male producer. You'd sit down, they'd film you, and you'd have to read the scenes – and you just hoped nothing bad would happen.

If you're in that situation, you want to get the job. You're there with figures of authority and people that you admire. You're frightened of them. In that situation, if something happens, women often freeze. It's not, 'Fuck off, what do you think you're doing?' You freeze, because you're utterly terrified.

I was lucky that nothing awful happened to me. I wonder whether I looked so young and scared that I seemed like too much of a liability. I think it was happening to other actresses, but nobody would say, so I never heard it from anyone directly. You wouldn't say because you knew you'd get fired or you wouldn't get the job, and because you were probably frightened by it all.

In my second year, I decided I wanted to be more independent. Me, Ryan the American, and Sophie, one of the very posh actresses, decided to move into a flat in New Cross, opposite the station. So we left our halls of residence on Gower Street and moved.

New Cross was awful. I lived next door to a drug dealer who had a snake in his flat. It was really horrible, but I discovered Greenwich and used to go down there a lot. We had mice because Sophie used to eat in her bedroom and would forget to take her plates back to the kitchen. She was very posh but never cleaned anything. One time she told me she was lying on her bed and suddenly felt something land on her stomach – it was a mouse. We had mice all through the flat.

I remember standing on the toilet seat, screaming, while a mouse ran around the corridor and jumped down the stairs. It was filthy. Dad used to come and visit with Mum. We had an electric meter, and he would top it up and then go through the entire flat, cleaning everyone's bedrooms and bathrooms. Ryan had his own bathroom, and me and Sophie shared one. Dad would clean everything until it was spotless. Then Sophie and Ryan would come in and mess it all up again.

Halfway through my third year, I landed two jobs at once. First I auditioned for a part in the long-running ITV series *London's Burning*, and I got the part, which was incredibly exciting. But then a casting director at the National Theatre got in touch to ask if they could see me for a role in *The Prime of Miss Jean Brodie*, with Fiona Shaw. I did a Juliet speech at the audition and I got a role in the chorus of schoolgirls.

As I was weighing up which I wanted to do, I thought back to my first term at RADA, when they took us on a day trip to the National Theatre and I sneaked on to the Lyttleton stage, bent down and touched the floor. 'I'm going to be here one day,' I whispered.

'What should I do?' I asked my agent. 'It's a bigger part in *London's Burning* and I've got lines and all of that, and I don't have any lines in Miss Jean Brodie . . . but it's at the National! It's with Fiona Shaw, and I'm on stage all the way through. I mean, flipping heck!'

'Darling, you must work at the National, obviously,' he drawled.

'Okay, that's what I'm going to do.'

So I left RADA early, having done two and a half years of a three-year course, to go and work at the National. Not a single teacher wished me luck. It's just mad to think that my acting career started at the Lyttleton. And it was amazing, just brilliant fun.

I went back to RADA once after that, at the end of the third year, to do my Tree, which is when you perform all your monologues for the agents to come and see you. Although I already had my agent and I was working at the National Theatre, I went back to do it anyway. It was a point of principle.

I pride myself on being professional. I'm never late. But when I got to RADA to do my Tree, we were told to go to the wrong place. When I got there, on time, someone said, 'Sorry, the plans have changed. Now you're going to be in such-and-such room.' So when I finally got to where the Tree was being held, I was five minutes late.

'Ah, you've decided to turn up eventually, have you?' said Nick Barter, the principal. 'Just because you're working at the National Theatre now, you mustn't think you're better than everybody else.'

Oh, my God, it just never ends, I thought. *If I'm in this building someone will be bloody awful to me.*

One of the girls on the course was really annoyed with me. 'You don't come and see us in the rest of the shows,' she complained. 'You've just gone and dumped all of us.'

'That's not true!' I said. 'I couldn't come. I've been working.'

I don't think I made any truly lasting friends at drama school, apart from Maxine. And by the end of my time there, I just wanted to get away and never see anybody from RADA ever again.

The worst came last, that day. I was talking to one of the directors after the Tree and his assistant joined us. The assistant turned to me with a self-congratulatory grin. 'I know what it is now,' he said, pointing a finger at me. 'I always thought you were shit! But it's not that, it's that you're *Welsh*.'

That was my last day at RADA.

Going to RADA changed me as a person but not as an actress. Even today, when I go on-set, I worry that I'm no good, or that I can't do it. Or I think everybody's talking about me and saying what a terrible actress I am. RADA gave me that paranoia. But I still have the same determination in me. I still know that this is what I love and this is what I can do. The words of the teachers might still echo in my mind: 'I don't know what to do with you! You're just rubbish!' But I can rise above it now. I can forget it.

If I went back to RADA now, as a woman in her forties, I'd be much more confident. If I felt I wasn't doing something very well, or if somebody said, 'That's rubbish,' I'd think, *Oh well, I couldn't give a shit – it's not going to kill me, is it? I've got to go home and do the tea in a minute.*

I was incredibly young, out of my depth – too young, I think, to go through all of this. But also it was good being so young, because I took on board a lot of things without realising it. Yes, I think the way that they taught and the atmosphere there were really really messed up, but in a way, I'm quite glad that it was so brutal – and, my God, it was tough to get through.

Because nothing will ever be as bad as that again. Knowing I managed to cope, even though it brought me down and made me feel awful, tells me that nobody can ever bring me down so far again. That's why reviews don't bother me at all, even when they're negative.

I just think, *Well, nothing can be as bad as what I went through at RADA.*

5

No nudity, ever

I was out. By the summer of 1998 I was working as a proper real-life actress at the Lyttelton Theatre. I'd walk along the South Bank to the National Theatre, go to the stage door, say my name and they'd actually let me in. I was in my element, a proper real-life actress earning £250 a week.

Along the corridor that led to the rehearsal room there was a long line of pictures of famous actors. At lunchtime you'd go up to the canteen and see actors from the other theatres having lunch. I was properly in the acting world. It seemed incredible.

Set in the 1930s, *The Prime of Miss Jean Brodie* is a play about an inspirational teacher at an Edinburgh girls' school and the intense bonds she forms with the students she has selected to be in her 'crème de la crème' group. Fiona Shaw was playing Miss Jean Brodie; I was one of the girls chosen to receive her special attention and tutoring.

At the first cast meeting, I sat next to Sarah Goodchild, who was the same age as me and also playing one of the girls.

She'd recently left ArtsEd, another performing arts school. Sarah and I clicked straight away and went on to be big buddies on the tour. We had no lines and were in the chorus, but along with everyone else we still had to improvise in rehearsals. We did something called 'hot seating': you'd sit in a chair while Fiona Shaw and the others threw questions at you, and you'd have to answer them in character. I had to do it all in a Scottish accent, which is one of the hardest, and it was dreadful.

Sarah and I had the sort of friendship where one of us would set the other off, and then we couldn't stop giggling. We were always trying to find things to make each other laugh. We were beside ourselves when we heard that Kevin Spacey was coming to the National to give a talk, while we were in rehearsals. This was the year *American Beauty* came out, and he was a massive star. All anyone said for the next few days was, 'Oh my God, Kevin Spacey's coming!'

The actresses playing schoolgirls shared a big dressing room. Each of us was assigned our own cubicle with a little bed and a brown curtain to seal it off. We were performing *The Prime of Miss Jean Brodie* 'in rep', alternating with other productions, so during your week on, you could spread out a bit and make yourself at home in your little cubicle, but when your week was up, you had to pack everything away and stash it neatly in a corner, clearing the space for the next performer to move in.

The day of the Kevin Spacey talk, Sarah came out of her cubicle holding up a couple of plasticky pouches. 'Look what I've discovered! You put them in your bra and they push your boobs up,' she said excitedly.

Bra inserts, aka chicken fillets, were a relatively new thing then. Sarah had found them among the belongings of the actress who was using the cubicle when she wasn't there.

'Stuff it, I'm borrowing them,' she declared. 'I'm going to wear them for the Kevin Spacey talk.'

An hour later, sitting in the auditorium, we were hanging on Kevin Spacey's every word when Sarah turned to me and said, 'See that girl sitting in front of us? I am wearing her boobs.'

That set me off.

We were young and naughty, always getting into places we shouldn't. When we were alternating in rep with a production of *Cleo, Camping, Emmanuelle and Dick*, a play based on the life of the Carry On star Sid James, we went exploring their set, which was a reproduction of a scene from the film, *Carry On Camping*, featuring a big caravan. While we were messing about inside the caravan, Sarah found some bits of costume belonging to the actress who was playing the *Carry On Camping* star Barbara Windsor, including her massive pointy bra and her wig. Meanwhile, I came across a lacy gauze dressing-gown and a Sid James–style flat cap.

Backstage that night, Sarah put on the Barbara Windsor wig and fastened the bra over her school uniform costume, and I put on the flat cap and negligée over mine. The next time we ran out on stage, still wearing our stolen props, we were supposed to come together to form a famous Goya tableau and pose like the subjects of the painting. I had to stand on a desk and Sarah knelt on a chair. We tried to freeze in our poses, but I was laughing so much that the desk and the chair started shaking, making the most hilarious squeaking sound; my face was frozen in a mouth open pose, and with the laughter and panic, I started dribbling. I had to get through the scene with a long line of spit dangling down my face.

In the classroom scenes, we sat at wooden desks with hinge lids, that we lifted in unison as we sang out to the audience. Before the show started, I would creep down and stick a picture on the inside of each desk lid, so that when the others started singing and lifted them, they would see a printout of my smiling face, or a cat, or someone's boyfriend, or anything else that struck me as funny. Or I'd sneak Sarah's clothing out of the dressing room and put her shoes inside the desk, which would set her off. I loved playing these pranks, but I was hopeless, because I used to give them away in advance by collapsing into hysterics; I was just so full of glee at the thought of making everybody laugh.

While we were having all this innocent, schoolgirlish fun, the show was attracting a number of dodgy audience members who flocked in to see a bunch of twenty-year-olds prancing around onstage wearing school uniform. I remember one night in particular loud whispers going around backstage, because a fella was sitting near the front of the stalls wearing a mac and holding a pair of binoculars. He was so unsubtle it was ridiculous – like a parody of the stereotypical seedy bloke in a mac.

We opened in London and then travelled all the way around the UK. The digs were dingy and the dressing rooms dirty, but it was so much fun. Saying that, Sarah and I had a mixed bag of adventures. One night, somewhere up in the north of England, one of the theatre staff asked us to a house party and we agreed to go. Why not?

When we turned up at the address we'd been given we could hear conversation, laughter and music from outside the house. We walked in expecting to see your usual kind of gathering – studenty types chatting and drinking, and maybe a bit of dancing in the kitchen. But when we opened the door, there were naked people everywhere. Someone I knew was standing right in front of me with her knickers round her ankles. I caught her eye – and straight away wished I hadn't. We had walked into a full-on orgy.

'Oh my God, oh my God! Fuck this for a laugh,' we shrieked, and turned around and walked straight out again. Back at our digs we collapsed into bed, aching with shocked laughter.

When you arrived in a new town, they'd give you the digs list and you'd phone up random people and see if they had somewhere you could stay. They were usually people the theatre company had used before, sometimes over many years, and often it was a couple with a spare room in their flat or house. At the start of the tour, Sarah and I made a pact to stay in the cheapest places we could find so that we could save up our wages and splash out on staying at the Caledonian Hotel when we got to Edinburgh. But sometimes, when you arrived in the dark to a stranger's house, or when the bed was lumpy and the room cold and damp, I wondered whether it was worth the sacrifice.

Well, it definitely was. Our dressing room in the theatre in Edinburgh was so grubby that you could actually see the fleas jumping off the carpet, but we didn't care, because by night we were living in five-star luxury at the Caledonian Hotel – and it was well lush.

When I came out of the run of *The Prime of Miss Jean Brodie*, my agent phoned to tell me about an audition for the part of Dora Spenlow in the two-part BBC One drama, *David Copperfield*. He sounded very excited. 'It'll be on at Christmas,' he said. 'It's going to be the jewel in the BBC Christmas Millennium crown.'

At first, I didn't realise how big a deal this was. It was just another audition. I took it in my stride and thought, *Fantastic, a chance to be in a costume drama!* Life was great.

Dora Spenlow is David Copperfield's first love.

Sweet-tempered and childlike, she is the daughter of his employer, Mr Spenlow, a lawyer. But after David and Dora marry, he realises that she is strangely immature and not very suited to being a wife. He goes on loving her, but she is more interested in playing with her dog, Jip, than anything else. A year after their wedding, she has a miscarriage, becomes ill and dies.

The part of Dora suited me. She's young and innocent, with nothing sexy about her at all, and I went along to the audition thinking, *I've got this.* I was so new to the business that I had no idea how long the casting process can be. It went on for ever: I went back seven or eight times to read for the director; I read with three different Davids and did my dying scenes over and over again.

I was quite close to getting the part when one of the team got in touch with my agent and said, 'We're worried that Joanna's not pretty enough. Can you please tell her to put some make-up on before she comes in for the next audition?'

I didn't wear make-up, because I was no good at applying it. I was so young-looking that I'd never really had to bother. The only cosmetic item I owned was my mother's small compact, which contained three colours of eyeshadow – sparkling white, soft green and purple. Whenever I needed to doll myself up a bit for a job or audition, I would dab a combination of these colours on my eyes, usually starting with the white, fading into the green and then finishing with the purple.

On seeing the results of my efforts, my agent urged me to go to a beauty counter at a department store before the audition. 'Ask them to do your face up for you,' he said.

No, I'm not going in looking like a bloody clown, I thought, and did my own thing with my little compact.

My agent phoned after the meeting. I had passed the pretty-enough test but there was another hurdle to jump. 'They absolutely love you, but they're worried about your accent,' he said. 'It's got to be perfect, so I'm going to make you an appointment with a friend of mine, Joan Washington. She's the best dialect coach in the country and will be able to get you up to scratch.'

So off I went to see Joan Washington, who lived in a beautiful house in south-west London. I was always amazed by posh English houses – I'd been to one or two belonging to friends at RADA – and what struck me more than anything was the way the rooms interconnected. You never seemed to go into a room and come out of it by the same door. Instead, you'd leave by a different door, and then – maybe – the next door you went through would lead you back to the room where you started, although you could never be sure. Joan Washington lived in that sort of house. It blew me away. My little rented studio flat in Swiss Cottage was lovely, and had its own kitchen, but there was a shared toilet and I'd seen a spray of blood up the wall two days earlier.

Joan showed me into her office, where the walls were lined with books. She sat behind a big, elegant desk and I sat in an elegant chair next to her. Bright daylight streamed into the room through a huge arched window and I could see out onto a massive expanse of front lawn.

Feeling slightly overawed, I began practising my RP accent with Joan. All of a sudden, I saw a tall man with dark hair walking up the path leading to the front door. *It looks like Richard E. Grant*, I thought.

And then I realised, *Oh my God, it is Richard E. Grant!*

I'd seen and obviously loved *Withnail and I* when I was an acting student, it was a rite of passage, and now, Richard E. Grant was walking up the path to the house I was sitting in. I didn't go to pieces, though. I went on focusing on my vowels and inflection.

The next thing I knew, he'd come into Joan's office. I looked up.

'Hello,' he said, and I said, 'Oh, hello!' as casually as I could, like this was an everyday occurrence, and I hadn't just stepped out of Swansea.

My agent hadn't thought to mention to me that Joan Washington was married to Richard E. Grant. And here he was. While he and Joan chatted away, I was in turmoil, thinking, *There's a proper actor standing in this room, a real actor, a film star!*

When he left, I carried on practising Dora Spenlow's accent as if nothing unusual had happened.

I met Richard E. Grant again in December 2024, when we were contestants on a celebrity Christmas episode of the BBC's *Wheel of Fortune*, along with the lovely DJ Tyler West. As I stood next to Richard, who is one of the nicest men I've ever met, I couldn't help thinking how life comes full circle: *This is just so bizarre. All those years ago, I was sitting in your wife's office trying to perfect my accent for an audition, watching you walk up the front path, thinking, Oh my God!, and now I'm flipping standing next to you on* Wheel of Fortune.

As a dialect coach, Joan Washington was every bit as brilliant as everybody said she was. She helped me polish my RP for the next audition and later my agent phoned up and said, 'You've got the part of Dora because you are a–dora–ble.'

I was over the moon. *I can't believe this!* I kept thinking. It was a pinch–me moment and I couldn't stop smiling for days.

Then the nerves set in.

I was frightened about doing telly. That one lesson on filming at RADA definitely hadn't given me enough to go on and I was worried my acting would seem over the top.

All I could remember was the tip about keeping your head still and not moving your arms. *I don't know what I'm doing, and I don't know any of the technical terms because I've just not been taught it*, I thought, in a panic.

I was nervous about acting alongside people like Maggie Smith, Bob Hoskins, Nicholas Lyndhurst, Zoë Wanamaker, Imelda Staunton and Ian McKellen. Oh my God! I had total imposter syndrome. On my first day I met little Daniel Radcliffe, who was playing the young David, and I was fine chatting to him, because he was ever so sweet and lovely. But I felt very tense about working with the rest of the superstar cast. I kept having to push down all the horrible things that had been said to me at RADA; I was constantly thinking, *I really have to concentrate. I can't be rubbish, I can't!*

I didn't socialise with the others: I turned up on-set, did my part and left. I didn't go to the bar; I didn't talk to anybody. When the day was over, I would go back to my room, go over my lines and go to bed. David as an adult was played by Ciarán McMenamin and I was so reserved that we barely spoke off-set. He probably thought my standoffishness was because I didn't like him, or because I thought I was better than everybody else. In reality, I was just scared to my bones.

I spent a lot of time thinking about the exercises we'd been taught at RADA. You'd be given three character-istics – for example: 'I'm selfish, I'm forthright and I'm determined.' You'd plan what you were going to do as your exercise – maybe it would be 'getting ready to go out for the evening' – and then you'd have to get up in front of everyone and portray your three characteristics within that context.

Even though I spent a lot of my time at RADA flailing, I found when I was preparing for the part of Dora that I had absorbed a lot of what I'd been taught. Finding the character-istics; discovering your character's motivation; and learning lines by physically getting them into your body – by walking around and marking the different punctuation and thoughts – was really helpful, and I still use a lot of it now.

Playing Dora was my chance to prove myself out in the real world. My accent had to be perfect, so all my waking hours I worked on it furiously. On top of this, I had to sing a song in French at Dora's birthday picnic, with a perfect French accent. Actually, that bit wasn't so bad because I'd had to learn poetry and songs in Welsh for the Eisteddfod. But I also had to learn to play the guitar, the first instrument I'd played since being told in junior school that I was no good at the violin and I'd never play an instrument again.

I put all my energy into the work, and it was worth it, because *David Copperfield* was an utter joy to film – although it was overwhelming at times. I remember shaking with nerves before a scene with Bob Hoskins, who was just the most talented and amazing actor. We were doing a dinner party scene and it went on so long that my head was aching. I was hungry and needed some food. There was a massive joint of meat on the table that was greased with honey to make it look succulent, and someone kept coming in with a flamethrower to keep the honey moist. By the end of it, all I could smell was burnt flesh, my head was thumping and I thought I was going to throw up. Bob Hoskins was pissed off.

We were being delayed by an actor who kept asking what his motivation was in the scene. Bob Hoskins said, 'Your motivation is that it's half past six at night, and we all wanna fucking go home.' Well, it did bring a smile to my face.

Maggie Smith was ferocious. I was just in awe. One day, some of the assistant directors were trying to hurry her along. She stopped them in their tracks, told them to shut up, and said they were all 'clockwork cunts'. I thought that was quite wonderful.

We went all over the place on location. One of the absolute highlights came when I met Nicholas Lyndhurst in Norfolk. It absolutely blew me away, because I'd grown up loving *Only Fools and Horses*. I was straight on the phone to Mum: 'Mum! You're never going to believe it! I've just met Rodney!'

I also learned a few tricks of the trade, like keeping the dog playing Jip close to me at all times by holding sausage meat in my hand. They always say, never work with children or animals, and this little porker was a right diva. He nearly took my finger off – he bit into it so hard that I screamed out.

In one scene, I had to encourage the dog to jump over a pile of books, but he wouldn't.

'Just lift him up,' the trainer said.

I tried it, but he was on a lead and it was yanking on his neck. 'I can't do that,' I said. 'It's choking him.'

The trainer did not seem to get it. 'Just lift him up and pull him over,' he said.

'I'm sorry,' I said firmly, 'but we'll just have to find another way to do the scene.'

Mum read the reviews of *David Copperfield* when it was aired and she insisted on me reading them, as well. They all seemed to say what a wonderful costume drama it was, with so many great moments. And one said that Dora Spenlow's dying scene was a classic moment in a production littered with memorable scenes. *Oh my God, that's me!* I thought.

By now I was going out with Chris, a boy I'd fancied all the way through my time at West Glam. He was English, with a London accent, which seemed exotic, and had more of an edge than my other boyfriends. He was a brilliant actor, and when we went on holiday with my parents, everybody thought I was the girlfriend, and Chris was part of the family, because he was blond and good-looking, and got on with my parents so well.

Chris often used to stay with me in Swiss Cottage. It was an eventful time. I used to find plastic tubing in the toilet, and I would leave notes pinned to the door asking everyone to be a bit cleaner. One day, I walked in to find a man lying unconscious in the empty bath, fully clothed, with a tube wrapped round his arm. He'd been shooting up heroin. I didn't realise it at the time, but the front door of our shared house could be forced open quite easily, and the local drug addicts had figured that out. They were coming in, going upstairs, and using our shared bathroom to shoot up.

Soon after that, new landlords took over the building. They did a full check of the flat and discovered that my gas fire had been leaking carbon monoxide the entire time I'd been there. We were lucky to be alive. We moved out straight away. They were also putting the rent up, and when I said I was going to leave, they refused to give back my deposit.

So Dad and I decided to spite them. I'd been a really good tenant, but we cleared the whole flat out, sold all the furniture, and when they started phoning for the keys – because it had a massive fire door – my dad went to a river in Swansea and threw them in. When the landlady asked where the keys were, he told her, 'They're in the same place as my daughter's deposit.'

Chris and I moved in together to a flat in Willesden Green and then to Clapham Junction. It was around this time that I decided I wanted a dog. Mum said, 'A Jack Russell would be perfect for a flat without a garden.' Not bothering to do any research, I went with it.

One of Mum's customers had just had pups. We went to visit, and the man said they'd all gone. But suddenly, the older dogs parted and this little Jack Russell walked between them, settled at my feet and stared at me. 'Who's that?' I said. 'She's Sally, the pick of the litter. I'm keeping her for my wife.' I begged and begged, and he said no. But later that day he rang, and said, 'It's the Grand National today. If you give me fifty quid, you can have her.' I was there in a shot. I brought Sally home and renamed her Daisy. She had an eye infection, an ear infection and a cold. I took her to the vets, then nursed her like she was my first baby.

After *David Copperfield* had wrapped, my agent phoned and sounded me out for a new job. I had always tried to stand firm about what I would and wouldn't do. 'I'll never do nudity.' I'd told him on the day I signed with him. 'Never, ever. I don't see the need for it.'

Every time it came up, I said, '*Literally* no nudity. Don't even ask. I think it's uncalled for.'

Now he broached the subject again. 'Darling,' he said, 'they want to meet you for the part of Eve in *The Mysteries* at the National Theatre. It's a huge theatrical event that they're putting on for the Millennium. But if you're playing *Eve,* they would expect you to be *naked.*'

'Okay,' I said, without a moment's hesitation. 'I'm absolutely fine with that.'

'Are you sure?'

I was relaxed about Eve's nakedness because it was innocent. I've streaked up and down the Mumbles seafront enough times to not be worried about my body, but it was just the having to be naked and sexy that terrified me.

Tony Harrison's gritty adaptation of the medieval mystery plays of York and Wakefield, the cycle known collectively as *The Mysteries*, tells the story of the Bible, from the Creation to the Final Judgement. There are three plays – *The Nativity, The Passion* and *Doomsday* – and they were first performed at the National Theatre on Easter Saturday, 1977 – less than a month after I was born. Afterwards they went into the repertoire of the Cottesloe Theatre until 1985. Now, in

December 1999, they were coming back, with the original director at the helm, Bill Bryden, and many of the original cast, too, which was very male-heavy, as you'd expect from a production based on Bible stories.

The cast included some great actors – legends like Jack Shepherd, who was nearly sixty then, and William Gaunt, who was sixty-three. Some were older – in their seventies and eighties. The other actresses included Sue Johnston and Cathryn Bradshaw, who had been in *Oranges Are Not the Only Fruit*; and there was also Linda Thompson, a singer and original cast member.

Doing *The Mysteries* was an amazing experience – completely chaotic, but unforgettable and totally brilliant. It was the first time I'd worked in a production where the director didn't sit you down and talk to you about the play. Bill Bryden's approach was different: you'd turn up and mark something through, or talk for a bit, and then he'd say, 'Right, everybody down the pub!'

If you wanted to get any notes, you had to go down the pub. But I was still too shy to socialise. I was scared I'd be mute around a load of older men drinking. So I'd go home to Clapham and learn my lines without getting involved in that side of things.

I didn't have to do anything naked until towards the end of the rehearsal period. Then, suddenly, it was, 'Right, we're going to run through the Adam and Eve stuff now, but in the rehearsal room, with all your clothes off.'

'Okay,' I said.

Just before we got started, Sue Johnston popped her head in, and asked very casually, 'You guys okay if I sit in and have my lunch while Jo's doing this?'

Bill nodded.

'Absolutely fine with me,' I said.

I didn't question for one minute why she wanted to be there, but looking back now, I imagine she was probably checking in on me, making sure I was all right. It was just me, the actor playing Adam, our stage manager and a male director in the room, so it was quite an odd situation to be in and unlike anything I'd done before. 'Take off your clothes, lie down, and then just grow up out of the ground,' Bill said.

Aside from the fact that he was a massive drinker, Bill never did anything to make me feel uncomfortable, and with Sue sitting there, calmly eating her sandwich, I felt surprisingly relaxed about being stark naked and growing out of the ground in front of him.

One of the essential elements of rehearsing a play is to decide on the precise movements and positioning of the actors on the stage during a performance, which is known as 'blocking'. We didn't block much of the show in advance because Bill always wanted a drink at the pub. But when we got to the technical rehearsal and started focusing on the lighting, sound and stage changes, he knew he had to stick around. He was never without a can in hand – usually Tennent's Extra or Special VAT – and he drank steadily throughout. He'd last about half an hour, start to get angry, then scream, throw down his can of beer and burst out of the room. Ten minutes later, he'd come back and pick up where he'd left off.

We rehearsed *The Nativity*, which opened with the story of Adam and Eve, and then *The Passion*, where Jesus is crucified. So far so good, and not too many technical problems. But for *Doomsday*, the final play, me and the actor playing Adam spent most of our time inside a massive metal ball, using pedals to make it move, and it wasn't easy to control. This was the promenade production at the Cottesloe, and the audience could walk wherever they wanted to, while Adam and I were hurtling around in this big metal ball, barging through everybody. That rehearsal was pretty hit and miss, because we hadn't done much practice.

For the opening scene of the show, Ian (who played Adam) and I would stand naked together in a tin bath and get doused in cold water. Then we'd slather ourselves in mud, teeth chattering, lie in an empty pond and have soil poured over us until we were completely covered, apart from our mouths. A few leaves would be scattered on top.

They would push us onto the stage and then Jack Shepherd opened the show as the serpent. The audience would be looking around expectantly for Adam and Eve's entrance – and then all of a sudden, you'd see the soil trembling, and an elbow coming out.

We'd start growing out of the ground, stark naked, covered in mud. It was just mad, but quite beautiful. One matinee, we had a boys' school in. Ian and I slowly started appearing out of the soil, and there was silence. All these little boys just standing around in a circle and staring. Mid-scene, one of them pointed at Ian and said, 'Miss, he's got a dirty willy.' It was hard not to react, but we just had to carry on.

We'd do the whole scene, with the apple and the serpent, and then run off. The audience would part for us, intimidated by our nudity, and then we'd streak through the corridors of the National, laughing and screaming, have a shower, put our clothes on, and then get back on for Noah's Ark.

And you know what? Even though I got hypothermia halfway through, it was so much fun.

The days when we performed all three shows back to back were pretty intense. You'd start at half past ten in the morning with *The Nativity*, going straight through without an interval; at lunchtime, you'd move into *The Passion*; and by the evening, you were performing *Doomsday*. Later in the run, over Easter when the weather was better, we started doing it outside on the South Bank, which was incredible. It wasn't just a show – it was a landmark event.

It was a very masculine atmosphere and everyone got a load of ribbing from the older men in the cast. One day, they put some condoms in my bag. I went home, saw them, and thought, 'The little shits, look what they've done!'

It didn't bother me, but I went in the next day, pretended to cry and said my boyfriend had found something in my bag and dumped me.

They were really worried they'd ended my relationship, but then I turned around laughing, called them motherfuckers, and warned, 'Don't mess with me, because I will get you back.'

In one scene, we were supposed to be gutting some fish – real, smelly, slimy, proper fish, not props. 'This is disgusting!' I said, picking up a large herring.

'Why don't you like holding it?' one of the actors asked. 'Is it because it feels like a penis?'

'No,' I said. 'It's because it's a fucking *fish. I don't know what penises you've been feeling, but I've certainly never felt a penis like this!*'

Another moment came just after I'd performed naked as Eve for the first time. 'I thought your boobs would be bigger than that,' someone commented. I chose to ignore it. They should see them now! Forty-eight years old and four kids down. Massive. But honestly, everything about that show was surreal and the women were completely outnumbered, so I suppose a few odd things like that were inevitable.

At the end of the run, I was in my dressing room, sitting in my little cubicle, wearing just my pants – no one else around; I was completely alone when a big-name theatre director came into the room. He'd seen the show. He strode towards me telling me how wonderful he thought I was, and made as if to come into my cubicle. Quickly, I grabbed the curtain that sealed it off from the rest of the room and wrapped it around me, to hide my body. The curtain was attached to the ceiling and I ended up looking like a caterpillar. I was wrapped so tightly I couldn't move. He stayed for a while, put his arms around me, kissed me on the cheek, but then it all got a bit awkward, because it was clear there was no way this caterpillar was being unwrapped. He said his goodbyes and left.

It took me back to an experience I'd been through with a fellow actor the previous year. Turning up to rehearsals one day, I found him outside the theatre visibly shaking and crying. 'Oh my God, what's happened?' I asked. He'd been rehearsing with an older male actor who'd stood behind him, bent him over, shoved his hand between his legs and groped him. I asked him what I could do to help. But he didn't want to report it. He didn't want to get fired. So he wiped away his tears, put the smile back on his face, we walked straight back in and carried on like nothing had happened.

Now, when you start a job, there's a number on your call sheet you can phone anonymously to make a complaint if you feel that you're being bullied, or something inappropriate has happened. However, as an actor, you're often too scared to report someone you're going to work with the following day. It's hard enough to get a job as it is, so you're desperate to hold on to it. But on each and every new job I do now, I see the new generation of women coming up. Actors, costume assistants, camera crew. There's more of a feeling of empowerment and safety in our working environment than I ever had. There will always be certain men in the business who will carry on saying and doing what they want, unrestrained, but at least it's a start.

The first part of *David Copperfield* was shown on BBC

One at 7 p.m. on Christmas Day, 1999; the second part was on Boxing Day. I watched the whole thing with Mum and Dad, back in Mumbles. There was this one moment when the actor playing Ham Peggotty picks up young David – Daniel Radcliffe. He effortlessly puts him on his shoulders and carries him along the seafront. The actor seemed so rugged and manly to me, and he had this really lovely gentle quality about him. I suddenly blurted out, 'Oh my God, Mum, I want that man to be the father of my children!'

Meanwhile, up in Bradford in Yorkshire, James Thornton, the actor who played Ham Peggotty, was also watching with his parents. And it so happened, that when I came on-screen, he turned to his mum and said, 'Who is this girl? She's lovely – I want to meet her.'

We hadn't met on-set because we didn't appear together in any scenes, sadly. What's funny is that James assumed I was English, because Dora speaks with a perfect RP accent. He also thought I must be as sweet and reserved in real life as Dora is on-screen, so I must have done quite a convincing job of portraying her, because he thought I was just being myself.

But because he had all these assumptions about me – that I was posh, English and perfect – he decided I was out of his league. I wouldn't even entertain him. Maybe he could be my bit of rough for an evening, but there was no way I'd go out with a big, bluff Yorkshireman like him.

Little did he know that I'd already noticed him – and was already smitten. Before *David Copperfield* was aired, I'd seen him in *The Lakes*, the Jimmy McGovern drama series on BBC One, where he played the arrogant and awful brother of the main girl; and I'd seen him in *Playing the Field*, the BBC One Kay Mellor series about a female football team, where his character, Scott Bradley, is a fireman and the local football coach. You couldn't miss him, because he was always appearing in these irresistibly sexy outfits: leathers on a motorbike; in a fireman's uniform; or sports gear. Basically, if you walked into a shop and asked for a brochure on strippers, he'd already covered three themes. Fireman, Biker, Footballer. I thought he was absolutely gorgeous.

But he was just a man I fancied off the telly. I never imagined our paths would cross.

6

Club Tropicana

First it was, '*Literally*, no nudity!' Then it was, 'Okay, but only because it's Eve.' And then, before I knew it, I was on the phone to my agent agreeing to play a prostitute and do a sex scene in *From Hell*, a fictionalised account of the Jack the Ripper murders, starring Johnny Depp and Heather Graham.

From Hell was a 20th Century Fox film. I went up for the part of Ann Crook, an ex-prostitute who is in a secret relationship with Prince Albert, the heir to the throne. Amid a spate of murders of young women in London's East End, Ann is kidnapped and lobotomised soon after giving birth to Prince Albert's child.

A huge team of people came over from Hollywood to hold the auditions and I did round after round of interviews and readings. When at last I made it to the final stage I was called to a meeting at a casting director's house, where I met a producer from 20th Century Fox. Thank God she was American, because although I'd learned the lines and thought about the part, I'm not sure my Cockney accent was anywhere near accurate. I hadn't studied it properly; I was just sailing along, hoping for the best. And I got the part.

I had also just won the role of Zoe Cazalet in a BBC One TV drama, *The Cazalets*, a six-episode series following the life of a family from 1937 to 1947. Although I had to do RP again to play Zoe, I loved and clicked with the character, who was well rounded and had more agency than your usual period-drama female. *The Cazalets* turned out to be a lot of fun to make. But what's funny is that Paul Rhys, the actor who played my husband in the series, also played the doctor who did the lobotomy on my character in *From Hell*. So when the filming schedules overlapped, I went from kissing to being mutilated by the same actor.

Apart from the sex scene, which loomed up ahead of me like a terrifying trip to the dentist, filming *From Hell* was an incredible experience. It had a cracking cast of women and I spent a lot of time with the other actresses who were play-ing prostitutes – Samantha Spiro, Annabelle Apsion, Katrin Cartlidge, Susan Lynch and Lesley Sharp.

And then, of course, there was Johnny Depp . . .

It was filmed in Prague and it was the first time I'd worked abroad. I was driven straight to the set from the airport. When we arrived, I was shown past some offices and the hair and wardrobe departments, and we came to a wall. From the back it looked like it was propped up by a million matchsticks balancing on each other, but when I walked round the corner, suddenly I was standing on a cobbled street in the middle of nineteenth-century Whitechapel. The directors, Alan and Albert Hughes, proudly showed me around. They spotted a figure in the distance, chatting to someone. 'There's Johnny,' they said, calling out to him. 'You've got to meet Johnny.'

I had never taken much notice of Johnny Depp before. I don't like pretty boys and hadn't watched his films. But when

I saw this fella turn around to face us, I don't think I've ever seen a human being more attractive or physically perfect in my life. He was playing a policeman who was trying to find out Jack the Ripper's identity, and he was wearing a white shirt, a black jacket and a jet-black wig that set off his features in quite a startling way. As he walked towards us – and it seemed like he was moving in slow motion – we locked eyes. I was mesmerised. Johnny Depp was absolutely stunning.

He came over to say hello. As we chatted, I was thinking, *Oh, my God, this is just absolutely insane.*

Later, I went off to film with him.

It was the scene where I was crouched in the corner having just had the lobotomy done; I started really getting into it – and then I farted.

Johnny Depp made a face and burst out laughing. 'Who farted?'

I was too embarrassed to say anything, so I just kept quiet, looking around the room with an enquiring expression on my face. Who was it? Who had dared to fart? Afterwards I wished that I had just said, 'It was me!'

That night, some of us went out for a meal together. At the table, I was told that the empty seat next to me was being kept free.

Okay, I thought.

While we were having a drink and chatting before we ordered our food, I heard the door open and people saying, 'Come in, come in!'

I turned around to look. It was him, without his wig. To my surprise he had hair like Jennifer Aniston's – caramel-coloured with lots of highlights and so long that it came down to below his shoulders. He came and sat next to me, and quite clearly wanted to talk to me, but I couldn't think of anything to say. I came up with something about the importance in the film of them putting a fake mole on the right side of my face. He was probably wondering what on earth I was talking about.

I can't cope with this, I thought, turning to talk to someone else. *You're too good-looking and I genuinely can't speak to you because of it.*

Towards the end of the night, he tried to talk to me again and we had a good chat. By now the only people left in the place were Johnny and his bodyguard, Lesley Sharp and me.

'Can we give you a lift back to the hotel, girls?' they asked.

'Yeah, fine,' we said.

As they were dropping us off, Johnny got out of the car and came over to me. He slid his arms around my waist. I was completely thrown by this. I didn't move; I literally had no fight in me. Beneath the orange glow of a street light, he very slowly leaned down and kissed me. I could feel myself melting as he gently pressed his lips on mine, first on one side of my mouth and then on the other.

The spell was broken when he got back in the car and they drove away. I rushed up to my hotel room, picked up the phone and screamed, 'Mum! Johnny Depp just kissed me!'

What I found strange was that you had no control over the effect his beauty had on you. I can't imagine how you could ever have a relationship with him, ever sit on the toilet having a chat or cutting your toenails or flossing your teeth. He was dazzling.

Heather Graham was playing Mary Kelly, a stunning young prostitute who grows close to Johnny Depp's character. One night we went round to her flat because she wanted to cook for all of us girls. She had just started going out with Heath Ledger, who was filming *A Knight's Tale* in Prague at the same time, and when we turned up, all of us British women – the prostitutes – were basically fighting over who could say hello to Heath first and give him a kiss. He was so beautiful and lovely, and he and Heather made a picture-perfect Hollywood couple. As if to prove this point, Heather had a Polaroid camera and kept taking photos of the pair of them together during dinner, and sticking them up on the wall. Unfortunately, the chicken she cooked for us was underdone and on the way home we had to pull over for one of the actresses to throw up in the street.

From Hell was a pretty grisly film. I remember going out on-set one day and seeing Lesley and Katrin, both incredible actresses, getting ready for a scene. Katrin was holding her script up in front of her and wouldn't put it down.

'What's behind there?' I asked, curious.

She lowered the script to reveal a prosthetically slit throat stuck onto her neck. I gasped. It was horribly realistic.

I had my bald cap made before we started filming. First, I had my hair slicked down with grease and they covered my entire head in green jelly. I had straws sticking out of my nose so I could breathe and then came the Plaster of Paris. It was like I'd been buried alive, but you've just got to keep calm. After the plaster sets, they cut you out of it and make the mould for the bald cap.

They took a sample of my hair to match it with a wig I'd be wearing. In the meantime, I decided, on a whim, to go into the hairdressers and dye my hair red. Just before I flew to Prague, I thought, *Oh my God, I'd better go back to my normal colour otherwise it's not going to match the wig!* Luckily, I got a good match, but the hair people were absolutely horrified when I told them what I'd done.

There was a great atmosphere on-set, and we all made friends. My only run-in was with the costume department over a scene in the workhouse after Ann's lobotomy. They wanted to put me in a pristine wedding dress and have me looking like a perfect porcelain doll, but the make-up artist and I thought this was ridiculous considering what she's been through. On our own initiative, we put scars and bruises on my face and white contact lenses in my eyes. I was already wearing a bald cap, so by the time we finished I actually looked like I'd been through a lobotomy. Using the make-up, we dirtied up the wedding dress, too.

The costume designer had a fit when she saw me. 'What have you done to your costume?' she shrieked, because we'd really messed it up. She was absolutely furious, but I argued that it was a more authentic look for a post-op woman who has been dumped in a workhouse, and I was allowed to go on and film the scene as I was. Looking back, I can't believe I did that.

Heather Graham did a double take when she saw me. 'Why have you let them do that to you?' she asked.

'Because it's brilliant!' I said. 'It's much more fun than looking perfect and beautiful.'

The day of the sex scene arrived. According to the script, Ann has sex with Prince Albert two weeks after giving birth to his baby. She's riding on top of him and, as she nears climax, milk starts leaking from her breast.

I'm not bloody doing that! I thought, as I was reading it. I rang my agent and told him so.

It was so unrealistic. I mean, now, as a forty-eight-year-old woman who has given birth four times, there is no way in hell I would be riding on a man two weeks after giving birth. And if I did start lactating, I'd say, 'Get me a fucking bottle, we are not wasting this.' But this was a Hollywood sex scene.

Since giving birth, I've lactated everywhere – and it doesn't even shock me any more. My most adventurous lactating was dressed as Elizabeth the First. I was all done up, wig, gown, in my caravan with my bodice open, feeding. Oh yeah, and also as Elizabeth the First, running away from a Zygon, whilst trying to keep my breast pads in. My most panicked lactating was spraying milk across a cafe in Oxfordshire while Eva was crying. I got to the middle of a packed table, got my boob out, and before I could get her on, the milk just sprayed across the cafe. I remember standing up and saying, 'Come on, Mum, we're going,' and marching out. My strangest lactation was dressed as a Victorian prostitute simulating a hand job. Halfway through the scene, my fellow actor offered up, 'You know, she lactates!' to the director.

These days, lactating is like a walk in the park for me. But at twenty-three, I was very clear about it. 'I am not doing this.'

Every sex scene I've done has been an utterly horrific experience for me. I am rubbish at being sexy on camera because it makes me feel deeply uncomfortable. Yet I was often cast as someone alluring and attractive in my twenties. More often than not, when I was sent a script, I identified with the main character's kooky best friend. That's much more how I saw myself.

Filled with dread, the tension mounting, I sat in hair and make-up all morning having corkscrew curls put in my long blonde hair. When at last it was done, I had my body spray-painted for an all-over skin tone, put on a tiny thong and was sprayed again, with a glycerine solution that looked like sweat. Now it was time to start filming.

The fella who was playing Prince Albert, Mark Dexter, was also playing alongside me as my love interest in *The Cazalets*, which was yet another crossover between the two jobs. I was doing a sex scene with him in *From Hell* and falling in love with him in *The Cazalets*, while my husband in *The Cazalets*, Paul Rhys, was the awful surgeon in *From Hell*. A very odd threesome.

It was a closed set. We went in. I had to sit on top of Mark and they put up sheets around us for privacy. We had a chat with the directors and everybody cleared the set. As soon as they said, 'Action!' I was supposed to take my gown off and start writhing.

'Action!'

I couldn't move. I was paralysed by fear. As the seconds ticked by, I desperately wished I'd rehearsed how I was going to play the scene. Then it came to me. *Imagine you are riding a horse*, I told myself. *Aim for a slow trot on a horse.*

'Cut!' they shouted.

'You've got to be sexier. We need more oral,' the director said.

'What! What do you mean: "more oral"?' I asked in horror.

'You're not making any noise. You need to be moaning and groaning.'

They gave me loads of notes. 'Okay, I've got it,' I said.

You know when someone gives you a load of notes, and you nod your head saying yes, yes, as if you've taken everything on board, and then you don't do any of it? Well that was me.

'Action!'

I went back to riding the horse but I still couldn't do the noises. Committing to opening my mouth and letting out a groan was just too much to bear. Apart from the odd muted squeal, I couldn't make a sound.

Then the Wham! song 'Club Tropicana' popped into my head and started going round and round on an endless loop. I couldn't think about anything else except the drinks all being free. It must have been triggered by stress, but I really didn't care, because it seemed to be working. As I was singing the song in my head I was riding the horse in the same rhythm.

In the middle of riding her lover, my character is pulled away and kidnapped. Imagine being thrown over someone's shoulder while wearing a thong, and carried out of a closed set and into a big hangar, full of a hundred people. To my dismay, the monitor was there and everyone was crowded around it, watching closely. That day I learned that a closed set can actually be pretty public.

When I went to the screening of the final cut of *From Hell*, I was really nervous about the scene coming on. And then it started, but something wasn't quite right. I realised I could hear moaning and groaning, but it wasn't my moaning and groaning, it was somebody else's voice! – they'd had to dub somebody else over me because I couldn't make the noises. I've seen *From Hell* once, and I've never seen it again. There is something quite bizarre about sitting in a theatre with your boyfriend and watching yourself pretend to have sex with someone else.

This was life before intimacy coaches. You just got on with it. You had a quick chat with your director and fellow actor, then you blocked it, you got into costume, they said action, and you started kissing. And then what would be, would be.

I remember being taken by surprise while filming a romantic scene with a lover in a TV drama. It was a bedroom scene and we were supposed to sit on a bed and kiss. I was wearing a gorgeous, flimsy negligée with very thin shoulder straps and, because I was so flat-chested, a wardrobe assistant had sewn in bra inserts so that it looked like I had more of a bust. But these chicken fillets were so heavy they pulled on the flimsy fabric, and if my straps were untied they'd drop like rocks to my waist, leaving me completely exposed.

We started rehearsing the scene. The actor and I were kissing and falling back on to the bed. Before we went to do a take, the director took the actor off into a corner of the room and the pair of them started whispering together. 'Yes, okay,' I heard the actor say.

When they came back, the director shouted, 'Action!' and the actor and I started kissing, as rehearsed. We fell back on to the bed, then suddenly he started trying to pull my straps down.

Oh my God, what's happening? I thought. *I can't get my boobs out on the telly!* I knew if he managed to untie my straps my chicken fillets would fall to the ground and that would be it, they'd be out!

I was lying on my back, and the only way to stop him was to reach behind my head and grab on to the bedpost as if in ecstasy, making it impossible to pull my straps down. I threw my arms above my head, grabbed on to the bedpost, and suddenly realised he'd started thrusting on top of me. *Oh my God, we're pretending to have sex!* I thought.

Bear in mind, we'd not rehearsed this. We'd not even spoken about it. It's written in the script that we simply kiss. But now, I'm lying down, holding my arms up in the air so that my boobs don't come out, and I've got an actor thrusting away on top of me having sex, I had no idea where his hands were going next.

I didn't feel I could say anything. It wasn't that I was scared, I just, didn't say anything. I carried on filming the scene until the director said, 'Cut!' And I did it again and again, without complaining, until we went on to the next scene. Nothing more was ever said about it.

I was travelling back and forth from Prague to England filming *From Hell* and having a fantastic time on *The Cazalets*. I loved playing Zoe, a young, flighty socialite who marries Rupert Cazalet, and Paul Rhys was a delight to work with.

While Rupert is off fighting in the war, Zoe goes for a

dinner date with this other fella, who's a doctor, and he takes advantage of her. In the scene, there's a moment where she's fighting back to stop him and I thrust my head forward so violently that I chinned the actor in the face.

Zoe finds out she's pregnant and goes ahead and has the baby, but during all of this, Rupert goes missing in action and we don't know what's happened to him.

Paul Rhys and I went on *Richard & Judy* to promote the series. I was bricking it because I had no experience of doing press and it was very alien to me. Sitting opposite Richard and Judy was like looking at Mickey and Minnie Mouse. It was insane – they were as familiar as cartoon characters.

We started chatting, but I was still very nervous, and I think Paul was nervous too. We were talking about the wonderful actress who plays Steven Dillane's daughter in the series. 'She's only just starting out and her range is incredible. It's been so great working with her . . .'

Richard leaned forward and asked, 'What's her name?'

I looked at Paul and he looked at me, and we had to say. 'Oh dear, we've forgotten!'

'Paul, what has happened to Rupert?' Richard went on. 'What year is it now? Is it after the Battle of Britain?'

We hesitated, and then Paul said, 'For goodness' sake, Richard, I don't know. It's only acting.'

I'd been saving up for a couple of years and now I could put down a deposit on a tiny little house by Wandsworth Common. It was a new-build that had been split into four, so it was one corner of the building. You walked in through a small garden. Inside, there was a tiny living room and a small conservatory extension. There was a winding staircase, and upstairs there was a toilet with a slatted door, and a tiny bedroom.

Chris and I split up. It just wasn't working any more. I

started seeing an assistant director, Tom, who was quite posh, English, and a proper grown-up. Tom had his own house – I stayed over once and was terrified to see a framed tarantula on the wall, which he said his dad had brought him back from abroad. Tom was really lovely, but he was balding and used powder on his head. He didn't wash his hair much, probably to make it easier to style, and he was also really short. In bed, if I cwtched under his arm, his feet would only reach my shins. I found that a bit off-putting.

Everything with him felt very adult: he liked cooking roast dinners together at the weekend, and I wasn't used to that kind of grown-up life. I completely ruined it the day he came round and we had a big pork roast and loads of fatty potatoes. After eating, we were cwtched up on the sofa about to watch a film, when my stomach started gurgling. All that fat. 'I'm just popping to the loo,' I said.

The toilet was upstairs, just past the winding staircase, with a flimsy little slatted door. There was no privacy. I went up and basically exploded. I tried to be quiet, clenching my bum, but in the end it just went. It was mortifying.

When I finally came downstairs, he had his coat on. 'I think I'd better go.' I begged him to stay, but he said, 'No, I'd really like to go.'

He left, and later texted saying he was going away on holiday and would see me when he got back. I texted back saying I'd see him soon.

About a week later, completely out of the blue, Maxine Peake phoned me up.

'Hiya Jo, I'm in this play at the National and I'm working with this fella who says he's in love with you.'

'Yeah? Who is it?'

In the background, I heard a man shouting, 'Tell her it's Ham Peggotty!'

I was stunned. *I can't believe it,* I thought. *It's that actor I fancy off the telly. The one who carried Daniel Radcliffe on his shoulders along the seafront.*

'He'd like you to come and watch the show,' Maxine said. 'He wants to meet you.'

'Okay, yeah!'

It was September 2000. The show was *The Cherry Orchard* by Anton Chekhov, starring Vanessa Redgrave, Roger Allam, Corin Redgrave, Ben Miles and Maxine. I'd actually auditioned for the show myself and done a dreadful meeting with Sir Trevor Nunn, absolutely bombing because I'd been so nervous around him.

Ham Peggotty – James Thornton – was playing Yasha and was every bit as gorgeous as I'd remembered. There was a group of girls in the audience who clearly thought so too and they were screaming for him to come back on after the curtain call. When he obligingly ran back for another bow, I thought, *God, he's a bit full of himself!*

After the show, I went backstage to the green room bar. Maxine was there, and she introduced me to James.

'You look different!' he said, when he saw me. Those were his first words to me.

I did look different. I'd had a long blonde wig on when I was filming *David Copperfield,* and for *The Cazalets,* which was set in the 1940s, I'd had my hair cut into a short bob. The next shock for James was that I sounded different, too. He thought I was a posh English girl like Dora, and my Welsh accent came as a surprise.

We got talking and hit it off straight away. He was wearing a grey wide-neck top and he had a lovely neck. And his forearms were really strong.

'My real name is Russell,' he said.

'What! Russell Thornton?!'

He explained that it was James Russell, but he'd had to change it because of another actor having the same name. The village he comes from in Bradford is called Thornton, so that's why he chose it. After going on to another bar, he drove me home. He parked outside my house, waiting for me to invite him in.

We sat in silence for a couple of minutes, both waiting. In the end, I just had to say to him, 'Do you want my number, or what?'

He turned to me and smiled. 'Well, I was hoping ... I mean, can I come in for a coffee?'

I liked his self-assurance. It was understandable, because he was single and very attractive. But I wasn't going to stand for any of that. I was going to make him work for it.

I smiled back. 'No. If you want my number, you can have it, but you're not coming in.'

'Okay.'

He phoned me the next day. We spoke for two hours and it was like we'd known each other for ever. He was telling me all about a flat he'd just bought in Dulwich, and how there was a shed in the back garden where he was going to put his drum kit and other stuff.

No, I was thinking, *when I move in there with you, I'm going to knock the shed down so we've got more space in the back garden for Daisy.*

We hadn't even been on a date, but already I just knew.

We went out for a drink and started to get to know each other. As we talked, we realised that we'd very nearly met when I was in drama school. James had also been at drama school in London, and he was in the same year as Jo, an actress I knew from the National Youth Theatre of Wales. One night, Jo had invited me to a house party over in the flat James was sharing with a friend of hers, but because I was just so shy, I'd chosen not to go. If I had, I would have met him there. But it wasn't meant to be.

We could also have met when the production team put on a special screening of *David Copperfield* for the cast and crew, in London. I hardly ever go to screenings, but James was there, and afterwards he was looking around trying to find me. I must have seemed quite mysterious.

We talked all night. Never running out of things to say. Then he asked me back to the flat he was renting in Putney until he could move into the one he'd bought in East Dulwich. *All right*, I thought. As soon as we got back he offered me a drink and a massage. I will take a massage from anyone if offered. You will not get any sex, or a return massage; all I will do is lie there and try and get the longest massage out of you that I possibly can.

I whipped my top off and lay on his bed on my stomach in my bra. 'I can't properly massage you with this on,' he said.

'Tough. You'll have to work round it,' I replied.

Within a week he'd moved his entire belongings into my house, and never went back to his flat.

Tom came back from holiday and sent me a text message saying, 'Hi, I'm back. Can we meet up?'

'Sorry, met someone else,' I texted back.

I was pleased that I'd moved on; he had poo-shamed me.

James and I settled into a very natural life. We knew it was love and instantly started living together. He would go into my garden with his saw and nails and hammer and build boxes for me to put my plants in, while I would cook for us and keep house. Then we'd settle down together and watch *Survivor* on the sofa.

James adopted Daisy and she went from being anxious and overprotective to really mellow. I was terrified when they first met because I thought, *For God's sake, please don't bite him!* But there was something about his calmness and deep, soothing voice that made her roll on her back so he could tickle her tummy. Like mother, like daughter!

I'd had a few other boyfriends, but James was my first love. I could sense it was different with him, and I felt differently, so I decided, *I'm just going to be myself. If I don't like something, I'm just going to come out and say it, whatever it is. I don't care if it's something unreasonable, I don't care if it's something stupid – I'm just going to say how I feel. And if that's the wrong thing to do, or if means him deciding, 'Well, I don't like that, I'm not going to go out with her any more,' then, so be it. I'm not going to pretend to be anything that I'm not. I'm just going to be me.*

And that's the way it has always been between me and James.

We had quite a fiery time together in the early days. Eventually we moved into James's flat in East Dulwich and one of our first big arguments was over something that came to be known as the 'gnome pig'. I saw it on a trip to the garden centre with James and straight away said, 'Oh my God, that's incredible. We have to have it.' It was a life-size gnome, which was as tall as my hip, sitting on the back of a large pig, holding the pig's ears in the air with a gleeful almost psycopathic grin on its face. It was right up my street.

'There is no way in hell I'm having that in my back garden!' James said. 'I've just put on an extension. I'm doing up my flat. If you think I'm going to have that stood in the middle of the garden after all the work I've done, you've got another think coming. There's no way.'

'How dare you try and control me!' I retorted. 'If I want that pig, I'm going to buy that pig.'

'Our relationship is over if you buy that gnome pig,' he declared.

'That's absolutely fine. Let's split up. It's over. I'm getting the gnome pig. You're not telling me whether I can buy something or not.'

I took it home. We continued to argue. I kept it in the house for a bit, and then we obviously made up. Eventually, it went into the garden. And it's moved with us, from house to house to house.

There are a lot of similarities in the way we were brought up. James is the only other person I've met whose mum forced him to take Virol, a thick, black syrup made from malt extract that was used as a nutritional supplement. Mum gave it to me to try to enhance my appetite. I absolutely hated it, so she'd hold down my arms, wrap me in a towel and spoon it into my mouth. I remember running away from her, round and round our back garden in Treboeth, yelling, 'I'm not taking it.'

James and I share the same likes and dislikes and agree on the way that we want to live. And luckily, over the years, we've grown together.

I've always said he's quite Heathcliff-ish. He's a Scorpio and can be very brooding, and he's sexy. But he can also be gentle, sweet, loving and fun. He's got thick, dark, curly hair and a really strong roman nose. Couple that with a broad chest and a big heart, well, I think I hit the jackpot.

Over the Christmas 2002 holidays, we went to stay with my parents in Mumbles. I'd gone berserk buying presents that year, and it was also the year I decided to cut my own fringe so short that I looked like a monk.

By four in the afternoon on Christmas Day, we still hadn't eaten anything because we were busy opening presents. I'd bought James a camera, but he seemed agitated, and so did Dad. Mum was being normal. Dad hadn't told her that James had asked him for my hand in marriage the night before. Mum and Dad loved James, so Dad said, 'Yes, of course!'

James was so tense. We were still opening presents when his family from Bradford phoned and said, 'Hi, how's it going? What's happened?'

'Everything is fine,' he said. 'We've not opened any presents. We haven't done *anything*. We've only opened a camera.'

'Oh, okay, bye.'

At half past four, he said, 'Look, let's go across the road and I'll take some photos of you with the camera.'

Bear in mind, it was half four: we hadn't washed, we hadn't eaten. I'd cut my fringe that day; I had a red jumper on and my hair in bunches.

We crossed the road and stood under a tree on the grass bank opposite my family home. 'Stand here and close your eyes,' James said. He handed me a Bonio. 'Hold this.' Then he said, 'Open your eyes and call Daisy.'

I called Daisy and she came running towards me. It was a miracle, because she's obsessed with water, and if she sees it, she's gone. The fact she didn't run into the sea . . . Goodness only knows how that didn't happen.

Round her neck she had a pouch with feathers on it. I unzipped it and there was a wooden ball inside. I took the ball out and it broke open to reveal an engagement ring.

James went down on one knee. 'Will you marry me?'

'Yes, yes, of course I will,' I said, excitedly.

Daisy was eating the Bonio, and Dad was watching from the window. Mum didn't have a clue what was going on. The neighbours in the big white house nearby saw what was happening and said, 'I think James has just proposed.'

We went back into the house and Dad was ecstatic. Mum was in shock. We phoned Nan and her boyfriend, Tim, and they came straight down. Mum managed to turn the Christmas cake into an engagement cake, and we sat down and celebrated. We were over the moon.

7

The naked one from
Love Actually

There seems to be a particular kind of sod's law when it comes to auditions: if you go in behaving as if you don't want the job and you don't need the job, you end up getting it. The opposite happens if you really, really want it – and even when the rules don't apply, it's never a simple process.

I did lots of plays when I first came out of RADA. Theatre was my first love and I was ambitious to play classic roles. So when my agent's assistant sent me to do an audition for *Three Sisters* by Chekhov in 2002, I was really excited. 'It's at the National Theatre,' she said. 'Imogen Stubbs and Samantha Bond have already been cast.'

When I was offered the part, I thought, *One hundred per cent I want to work on this!*

But in the days and weeks that followed I was a bit puzzled that there was no advance press about *Three Sisters* coming to the National. In the meantime, my agent sent me to meet the eminent writer and director, Dr Jonathan Miller, who was directing a play called *Camera Obscura* at the Almeida Theatre in Islington, London. Normally, I would be horribly nervous about meeting someone as clever and distinguished as Dr Miller, but knowing I'd got the part in *Three Sisters* meant that I was really relaxed about getting the job.

When I walked into the audition, he said, 'Can you do your New York accent for me?'

'No, I can't,' I said. 'I haven't really worked on it. I'm just going to do her Welsh. Because, to be honest, I don't think I'm going to be able to do this show. I've been offered *Three Sisters* at the National, and I think I'm going to do that. But I thought I'd like to come and meet you.'

He didn't bat an eyelid. 'Okay, fine,' he said.

I read for him and when I got back home, the casting director phoned up and offered me the job.

I phoned my agent, and I said, 'It's great about the Almeida, but I'd prefer to do *Three Sisters* at the National. Only, I'm not seeing anything about it, which is weird.'

'Darling, *Three Sisters* is not at the National Theatre, it's at the Nuffield Theatre in Southampton,' he said.

'What do you mean? Your assistant told me that it was at the National.'

'No, darling. She got it wrong.'

Turns out, she'd been getting a lot of things wrong recently. She didn't last long.

'Well, that changes everything,' I said. 'I don't want to do *Three Sisters* at the Nuffield when I thought it was going to be at the National. I'm going to accept the play with Jonathan Miller.' (Luckily I went on to work with the wonderful Imogen Stubbs another time.)

And that's how I came to do *Camera Obscura* at the Almeida, working with this great director, Dr Jonathan Miller. But I did it with the awful sense that I'd only got the job because I'd said I couldn't do it, and I kept thinking, *What if he finds out it's not true? What if he says to me, 'I don't remember seeing* Three Sisters *at the National? It hasn't appeared.'* I was worried he might think I was some weird liar or fantasist.

Rehearsals went well and I was loving being part of the company. But I was still very young and probably not as well behaved as I should have been. *Camera Obscura* was about a reclusive invalid in his dying days, played by Peter Eyre, who lies in bed all the way through the show. One by one, each of the supporting cast come on, chat away to him, do a bit of a monologue and then go off.

We were performing in the Almeida Rehearsal Room, which is a relatively small space with fifty seats. When you were on stage you could feel the audience's breath on you, you were so close to them. Which was slightly awkward and off-putting as my character had to lie on his bed and fake an orgasm. During a performance early on in the run, I was running up and down the corridor backstage, messing about and being quite noisy, when all of a sudden someone said, 'Peter is complaining about the noise! He's stopped the show.'

Oh my God, it's for me! I froze in horror. *Jesus Christ, I've stopped a show at the Almeida.*

What made it worse was that James and my parents had come to watch me that evening. I thought *Oh my God, they're going to think that I'm awful.*

But – fortunately for me – I was not the guilty party. There was another culprit. Apparently, the show had started and Peter was in the swing of it, when a woman sitting in the front row started coughing. She coughed and coughed and coughed. Eventually, Peter stopped speaking and turned to look at her. 'Are you just going to cough all the way through?' he said. 'Because you are ruining the show.'

'I'm so sorry. I'm just not very well,' she said hoarsely.

'Will you go outside, please?' he said.

She shook her head and started coughing again.

'No? Then I'm stopping the show. There is no point going on.'

He summoned the stage manager and the play was suspended.

After a short break, the coughing woman got a glass of water and left. I think she was mortified, and we restarted the show from the beginning. But for my parents, there followed a tense couple of hours. Sitting up front with James, they were so nervous about making even the slightest noise that they didn't dare move a muscle for the entire performance.

As an actress, you will say almost anything to get the job, but there was one thing I couldn't lie about when I auditioned for *The Lost World*, starring Bob Hoskins, James Fox and Robert Hardy. I was called up for the lead female part, but when they said I'd have to be filmed with a real tarantula on my back, I said, 'No, I'm sorry, I can't do it.'

So they let me read for the other female part instead, which was much smaller, but I loved doing it because Matthew Rhys played my fiancé. I'd idolised him since meeting at RADA and I got to kiss him next to the big dinosaur in the Natural History Museum, in the middle of the night!

Usually, in an audition, I'd say whatever they wanted to hear. You want me to ride a horse? I can do it. You want me to do acrobatics? I do it in my spare time. You would say yes to everything, get the job and then desperately have to cram whatever skill you'd lied about into the short space of time you had before filming started. Then hope for the best.

In late 2002, my agent put me up for the role of Rosie, a ship's Operator Mechanic, in a Carlton TV series called *Making Waves*, all about the Navy. One of the producers asked, 'Are you sporty?' and I didn't miss a beat in saying, 'Yes, I'm very sporty. I play football and everything.'

The producer smiled approvingly. 'Your character fights another Wren in a charity boxing match. How would you feel about boxing?'

'Yeah, I'd be absolutely fine,' I said. 'I wouldn't be worried about that at all.'

This was stretching it, because I'm the least sporty person I know. At school, I ran away from the hockey ball after someone slammed me in the face with the stick. I threw up when I had to do cross country and I used to just carry the ball for the netball team because I was never allowed to play. I'm all yoga and dance.

Making Waves was mainly filmed on board HMS *Grafton* and other warships, and also at the HM Naval Base at Portsmouth in Hampshire. It was really good fun because it involved throwing yourself into all sorts of weird situations.

For one scene, we had to pretend we were going onto another warship to save a load of crew members in distress. A little powerboat took us all the way out to sea, where two huge grey warships were anchored in deep, dark, choppy waters. A sailor threw a long rope ladder over the side of one of the ships and – I can't believe they would do this with a load of actors that can't be trusted – we had to climb all the way up the side of the ship until we were high enough to be hauled up and over the top.

We were terrified. One of the actors, Lee Boardman, was climbing up just before me. 'Is it safe? Is it safe?' he kept saying.

He sounded like Laurence Olivier in the movie *Marathon Man*, when he's torturing Dustin Hoffman and saying exactly those words: 'Is it safe? Is it safe?' We teased him endlessly about it afterwards.

A few days later, we filmed another dramatic rescue scene where we had to board a warship that had been set on fire. They put me in yellow rescue gear and covered my face, neck and arms in a protective gel used by stunt men in fires, and I had to run right up close to the flames on the ship.

In another stunt, a group of us were in a room that was slowly flooding up to the ceiling and we couldn't escape. It was one of those edge-of-your-seat, 'Will they make it?' scenes and really good fun to do. We wore wetsuits to protect us from the cold, and at the beginning of the day, when they let a load of water into the room, the stunt coordinator said, 'I recommend that you wee in your wetsuit first of all, so that you get yourself warm.'

We were in the water for the whole of the day and I weed in my wetsuit seven times. By the time I came to unzip it, I smelled like a tom cat who'd been spraying himself up a wall.

As you'd expect, there were a lot of male actors in the cast, and sixty real-life Royal Navy sailors had been deployed to play the ship's crew. All through filming, you could sense the clash of egos, with all of the fellas together. When the actors were hanging about waiting for the next scene, hands in pockets, the proper Navy were forever coming over, slapping at their hands and telling them off.

The male actors didn't like it.

There was a slant to some of the writing and directing that didn't sit well with the women in the cast, either. One day we were given a scene that had just been rewritten. 'We're going to film it just with the girls,' they said.

I was taken aback as I read it. 'This is rubbish,' I said. 'Who wrote this?'

'I did,' said one of the producers, who was standing nearby.

I instantly apologised, but it didn't change how I felt about the scene, which opens with the Wrens in combats and Doc Martens, sitting on the floor and playing cards together. An alarm goes off, a signal that it's time to get ready for training, and now we've got to remove our boots and strip off our clothes to our underwear, put on our new uniform and run out the door. That's it. The whole scene is basically a group of Wrens getting undressed and dressed again.

We weren't happy, so we spent the whole of the scene until they shouted, 'Cut!' undoing our boot laces and chatting. Not one of us took our clothes off.

I didn't like feeling objectified and was worried about how they were going to film the boxing scene. 'Can you make sure that I've got long shorts and a T-shirt on, just so I feel comfortable?' I said to the wardrobe department. 'Don't worry, we'll look after you,' they said.

But when I turned up on the day, they had these teeny-tiny shorts, little baseball boots and a white vest with crisscross lace seams at the side, so my bra was showing underneath it.

We filmed the scene in a working men's club on the Isle of Wight. I'd been rehearsing with a female Thai boxer, but I was too embarrassed to make the aggressive breathing sounds that a boxer does. The producers were using about a hundred real-life sailors as extras spectating the match and they encouraged them to behave as if they were having a night out on the booze. My opponent and I had to get in the boxing ring and fight each other in front of all these rowdy, shouting sailors.

My friend Diane was playing the Wren with the task of sponging my character's face when I was sitting down for a rest between rounds. She'd never done it before, and when she plunged her enormous sponge in the bucket of water she forgot to squeeze it out, slamming it in my face, and completely drenching me. So now it looked like a wet T-shirt contest. I was soaked through, and my white vest and tiny shorts now clung to my skin, but I had to carry on.

Although I tried, I just couldn't manage to be aggressive enough or make the right noises. But midway through the match, when my guard was up, one fist in front of another, my opponent hit my glove, which hit my other glove and I punched myself in the face. The shock of it triggered a surge of adrenaline and fury. *Not my face!* I raged silently. *Do not let her break your nose or do anything to your face.*

I put my guard up again and started fighting back with a vengeance, and all of a sudden I was enjoying myself. We filmed all day and I kept up a barrage of punches and coun-terpunches, jabs and hooks, and I found it exhilarating. When it was over, one of the male actors climbed over the ropes, lifted me up in the air, put me on his shoulders and walked me round the ring in a victory lap, while hundreds of sailors cheered. It felt amazing.

You'd expect a drama about the armed forces to feature some seriously macho characters, or it wouldn't be true to life. I'm quite tough and, if some of their behaviour occasionally spilled over when we weren't filming, I was prepared to let it go. But there was one fella on the job who was constantly making sexually aggressive comments, and none of the women liked it. So my heart sank when I was told I'd be filming an all-day scene with him and two guest actors.

About an hour into filming, he started saying offensive stuff at me. Before long he was chanting about all the dif-ferent things he wanted to shove up my arse. 'I'm going to shove this up your arse! I'm going to shove that up your arse!'

It went on for the entire day.

Now, I'm a really strong person. I can give it back and be quite mouthy. But something about this behaviour stopped me in my tracks and I found I couldn't respond. All day long I felt mute and helpless, humiliated and embarrassed.

When we had finished, I went to my trailer and asked to see a producer. 'I don't quite know how to explain what has happened today, because I don't actually know what the words are for it, but I think I've been sexually bullied,' I told him. 'There's no other way I can think of to describe it. And you need to know that I do not want to work with this man again. If we go to a second series, I am telling you now, I will not do a second series with him. I will not work with him again.'

He could see how upset I was. He didn't push back or try to argue. 'I completely understand,' he said. 'We really want you for a second series and I promise you that you won't have to work with him again.'

I honestly loved filming *Making Waves* – the good times far outnumbered the bad. But you couldn't escape the tough-guy tension that simmered among certain members of the cast and you couldn't help wondering when it would boil over.

Things came to a head when we did our press call and were sitting on round tables talking to various journalists. Two of the male actors were sitting opposite one another and they started bickering. Then, in front of all of the press, one of them launched himself over the table and grabbed the other, and the punches started to fly. It turned into a full-on fight on the floor and it was just mad. Everyone was staring down at them, thinking, *What the hell are you doing?*

Making Waves was set to be screened in the summer of 2003 but only reached the screen in 2004. 'What's the problem with it?' everyone was asking.

James and I watched the first couple of episodes on the sofa at home. It was a bit of a letdown, to be honest: the acting was good and you could see how the different characters and plot possibilities gave it the potential to be a long-running series, but there was something about it that didn't work.

The following week, I had a phone call from the producer. 'I've got some news,' he said.

Before he could go on, I said, 'You're axing it, aren't you?'

'Yes, regrettably, we are,' he said. 'The ratings are way down and so we're not going to show it beyond the third episode. The rest of the series won't be screened.'

So my boxing scene wasn't shown, but neither did anyone see me say the worst line of my career. In the sixth episode, my character Rosie propositions another sailor with a flirty look and says, 'Do you want to come and help me look for the golden rivet?' It's a saying based on the naval myth that the final rivet hammered into a ship is always made of gold, and it's a prank to get the junior sailor to bend over while looking for this non-existent rivet. I'll leave the rest to your imagination.

Fitting real life in with acting was hard. I'd been suffering with my wisdom teeth for quite some time and I decided to have them all removed. We'd been advised not to do it in RADA because there was a possibility that it would kill the nerves in our tongue, making part of it go numb. Personally I think they were being slightly overdramatic.

I had them all taken out and a few days later I was called up to audition for *Ready When You Are, Mr. McGill*, a film with Bill Nighy, Tom Courtenay and Amanda Holden. I went along in agony. One of the extraction holes hadn't sealed up, so it was just an open socket.

In order to get through the night before the audition, I took so much ibuprofen and paracetamol that I'm lucky I wasn't taken into hospital. I ended up getting a huge blistered rash on my back and still spent the night in pain.

The next morning, I was completely off my head on

painkillers and had to hold onto the wall as I went into the TV studio to meet the director and read for him. Everything was floating around me and I had no idea what I was saying, but apparently I told them all about my wisdom teeth in great detail. I then had to guide myself back out of the room by holding on to the walls again.

But, I got the job!

Babs, my character in *Ready When You Are, Mr. McGill*, is Welsh, and my father was played by the wonderful Alan David, who also played one of Doris's boyfriends in *Gavin & Stacey*! She's worried because she's doing her first sex scene in a film and she's got to be topless, and she spends the whole of the film trying to get out of it by making herself sick.

Bill Nighy is playing the director in the film, and he was just really lovely and softly spoken, exactly how he comes across.

Bill gave me some advice I've never forgotten: 'Never reveal your age. Don't let them know how old you are, because they can pigeonhole you and it'll affect your casting. Just be mysterious. Don't let them know anything about you.'

I cocked that up quite early on and every time somebody mentions my age or asks how old I am, all I can think of is Bill Nighy, and how I didn't take his advice.

Life as an actor can chop and change at the drop of a hat: I went back to the theatre and was touring with Jonathan Miller's production of *Camera Obscura* when my agent phoned and said, 'I'm sending you the script for the new Richard Curtis movie.'

What? Oh my gosh! I thought.

Notting Hill had just come out and it was massive, so I was flabbergasted that I might have a chance of getting a part in a Richard Curtis film.

I loved the script when I read it. When I got to the final

page, I said, 'It's going to be a brilliant film, but I pity the poor sods who are going to be playing John and Judy.'

John and Judy are professional stand-ins who meet while doing the sex scenes for a film, and they have to appear completely naked and simulate sex positions while chatting away about unrelated things.

Meanwhile, I was up for the part of Sarah, whose devotion to her mentally ill brother prevents her from getting it together with the guy she fancies. I wasn't sure the role was quite right for me, but I carefully picked an outfit, learned the lines and made sure I was word perfect before I went to the audition.

My agent sent me to meet Richard Curtis in *the actual* Portobello Road in Notting Hill, near the 'blue door', which is where his office was. It all looked very familiar as I made my way from the station. *It's like I'm in the film*, I thought. *This is amazing. I just can't believe it.*

There were *Notting Hill* movie posters on the walls of the office as, terrified, I was shown in to meet Richard. I'm very good at selling myself in an audition, but this time I was really scared, probably because I knew I wasn't right for the part.

I did my best. They phoned afterwards and said, 'We love her. We think she's really funny. But she's too young to be Sarah. Will she come back and read for Judy?'

'Judy?' I screeched to my agent.

It put me in an instant quandary, because it's so amazing on the one hand to know that Richard Curtis likes you and you've got the chance to be in one of his films. But on the other hand, it was the part that had really shocked me.

'Martin Freeman from *The Office* is playing John,' my agent said.

I felt myself waver. 'Okay, well, he can't be a pervert because he's just been in *The Office*, so that makes me feel better. All right, I'll go and meet them again.'

I went back to Notting Hill to audition for Judy; I read the lines and it went really well. My agent phoned and said, 'They love you. They want you for the part.'

I still felt worried. Even though I'd recently played Eve naked and done a sex scene in *From Hell*, I was worried about being fully nude in a Richard Curtis film.

I phoned Mum. 'Oh, for goodness' sake, Joanna, just imagine you're on holiday and you're sunbathing topless,' she said, to my utmost surprise.

'But, Mum, I've never sunbathed topless and I never would.'

'Just do it! You'll get to be in a Richard Curtis film.'

'All right, I will,' I decided. If Mum was not remotely worried or bothered, then maybe it was time to relax a bit. I accepted the job.

The read-through of the script was one of the most terrifying experiences of my life. The entire cast was present, so all I could think was: *Oh my God, there's Hugh Grant. There's Martine McCutcheon. There's Emma Thompson. There's Alan Rickman. There's Liam Neeson and there's Claudia Schiffer – she's so gorgeous.* Everybody was there.

I sat down feeling pretty nervous – I'd say it was an eight or nine out of ten. Then Richard came up to me and turned the dial up to a hundred. 'The American girls aren't here today,' he said. 'Can you read their lines at the end?'

I nearly had a heart attack. These were the sexy American girls who get together with Colin, played by Kris Marshall.

'Yes, of course, I can do that,' I said, swallowing hard.

I spent the next two hours of the read-through panicking. *Should I put on an American accent? Should I do it Welsh? I can't be sexy – oh my God, this is really awful. I've got to be a sexy American girl in front of all these actors.*

When it came to it, I tried to do a sexy American accent

and Richard openly started laughing. 'That has got to be the oddest American accent I've ever heard in my life,' he said.

And this is all happening in front of Liam Neeson! I thought in disbelief.

When we'd finished the read-through I went straight to the toilet. But the chain wouldn't flush and when I opened the door to come out, Emma Thompson was standing there.

'Hello, Joanna, it's so lovely to meet you,' she said warmly.

'Hello, Emma, it's lovely to meet you,' I said. 'The toilet won't flush, but I've only done a wee.'

Imagine that: you meet one of your all-time idols and those are your first words to her!

Martin and I rehearsed our scenes in a village hall just outside London. He was nice and pleasant, and I went in very open and friendly. That's my approach whenever I go onto a job: *We're all working together – let's all get on with each other.* Even if you're both going to be naked.

The day of filming arrived and my driver taking me to set was very chatty. 'Apparently there's a couple who are taking all of their clothes off today,' he said gleefully.

I looked at him deadpan. 'Yes, I am one of them.'

Before I went on-set, Liam Neeson very sweetly took me aside and gave me a pep talk. 'You stick to your guns about what you are and aren't going to do,' he said.

It was very kind of him, but it was also a shock to be up so close to Liam Neeson and all I could think was, 'My God, he's attractive!'

Just then, I saw Claudia Schiffer walking past my trailer looking absolutely gorgeous and, of course, fully clothed.

Once she'd gone, the costume people came in with the underwear. In my panic, I put my thong on the wrong way round. Once I'd got it on the right way round, they stuck it with tape, and started cutting the sides off. All I had was the tiniest triangle at the front and the smallest sliver of material at the back. Martin wore something that was like an olden-days coin pouch: open it, put everything in, draw it tight.

As soon as someone shouted 'Cut,' at the end of a scene, the costume girls would run straight in and cover me up. They were amazing and made the job so much easier.

Filming went very smoothly and, when it came to it, I didn't find it difficult to act the part of Judy with Martin at all. We were acting out sex scenes, but we weren't trying to be sexy, which is the bit that I'm dreadful at. Judy is such a sweet character and the storyline with John is lovely, funny and innocent.

Love Actually was released in November 2003, but I couldn't go to the premiere because I was on the Mumbles seafront all day filming *Mine All Mine*, an ITV drama written by Russell T. Davies and starring Griff Rhys Jones. We finished filming at about half past seven at night, and James and I drove to London to go to the premiere party. It worked out well, because I didn't really want to sit through the film with the rest of the cast looking at my bits and bobs. I just got to go to the party afterwards.

I didn't see it until I introduced it at the Cardiff Film Festival later in the month. I sat in the front row with James and my parents, and that's been the only time I've ever seen it. But last Christmas, as I was flicking through the channels, I saw it was coming on and instead of panicking and switching over, I thought, *Sod it, I'm going to put it on and watch it.* Suddenly I remembered what a lovely film it is. So moving and funny and heartwarming, and I was very proud to be in it.

Granted, I was watching in the afternoon, and my scenes with Martin are usually censored in the pre-watershed cut of the film. But I think it would have been fine even if John and Judy had popped up.

What's funny is that Mum and Dad always say, 'It's not Christmas until we've watched *Love Actually*.'

And I think, *Do you mean, It's not Christmas until you've watched me on-screen in the nude?*

James and I got married two weeks after *Love Actually* was released, on the only day I was allowed off from filming *Mine All Mine*. My hen do was just brilliant and so Swansea-ish. I'd just finished a day on-set and was at home in Mumbles with my parents when the door went. It was my cousin Claire, Sarah – my soon-to-be sister-in-law – Sarah Goodchild, some of my other friends, lots of Mum's friends and some relatives. They had a stretch limo.

They put a veil on me with porn playing cards and condoms, handed me a whip and a massive chocolate willy, and shoved me in the car. They drove me into town.

I drank so much that by the time we got to Ritzy's nightclub, I was going around forcefully slapping everyone with the whip. I had to be told, 'Will you stop hitting people with the whip? It's not funny. It's genuinely hurting people.'

Then I had to go in filming the next day.

8

In a foreign land

I went straight back to work the day after my wedding to James. It wasn't what I'd hoped for: we were married in Swansea, and *Mine All Mine* was set in Swansea, so you'd think the two would somehow dovetail. But we weren't even filming in Wales the day after the wedding – we were filming in Manchester. So instead of kicking back and basking in the glow of my joyful wedding with my wonderful new husband, I was driving up the motorway in absolute floods of tears, regretting every mile that took me further away from him. And instead of heading off on honeymoon, I was about to spend a week in a Manchester hotel with a bunch of actors. I cried for the entire drive. I just wanted to be with James.

Despite the heavy schedule, *Mine All Mine* was great fun to film. I was playing Candy Vivaldi, the youngest daughter of Max, a taxi driver who believes that Swansea was built on land that historically belongs to him. Candy was happy-go-lucky, selfish and spoiled, a really fun part. Griff Rhys Jones played Max, and the rest of the cast was amazing, including

Ruth Madoc playing my grandmother, and Siwan Morris as my sister.

It was a very busy show. At one point, Candy was auditioning for *Pop Idol*, and I had to learn an entire Diana Ross song, 'The Happening', go into a studio and record it. The lyrics and the music still sit in my head and haunt me now. Candy wasn't supposed to be good. It didn't need to be perfect, but at the time, I wanted to get everything right. I practised every day for a month.

It was such a busy time: as soon as one job finished, another came in, and then another. And one thing you quickly learn as an actor is to say yes to anything good that comes along, so I wasn't complaining (apart from that week of my wedding, anyway). I knew I was lucky to be non-stop working.

Soon after *Mine All Mine* finished, I was cast in the much more serious and dramatic BBC series, *To the Ends of the Earth*, which I was very pleased about – even though my part, Marion Chumley, was another sweet-natured child-woman, who captures the hero's heart before she's even said a word. I had to play her with a posh, plummy accent.

'My acting doesn't feel completely truthful when I'm putting on an accent,' I complained to my agent.

'Life is never perfect, darling,' he soothed.

'I know it isn't,' I said with a sigh.

There are times, though, when you appreciate your life more than you could ever have imagined. You have a defining moment when you think, *I will never take anything for granted again*. Maybe it wears off, but something inside you has definitely changed, all the same. And I had one of these moments when I was about to start filming *To the Ends of the Earth* in South Africa, where it was being made.

I flew out to Durban on my own. The rest of the cast had already been there for a while and were off working on

location when I landed. It was a fantastic bunch of people –
Benedict Cumberbatch (playing the hero), Denise Black,
Charles Dance, Jared Harris, Cheryl Campbell and Sam
Neill, among others. I was looking forward to going into
rehearsals. But for the first couple of days I had nothing to
do but hang around my hotel.

I started missing James like mad, and got quite homesick,
I felt so very far away from him. I missed him so much
that I ran up a huge phone bill calling him. We didn't have
smartphones in 2004 and long-distance calls cost the earth,
especially when you insisted on talking to the dog every
night, like I did.

By the third day, I was starting to get restless.

I'd been told, 'You must have a driver and a chaperone with
you at all times. It's not safe.'

That's silly, I thought. *I'm not going to be told what to do; I'm
not a child.*

I went down to the hotel reception. 'Could you order me
a taxi to take me to a shopping centre nearby please? Or just
somewhere I can wander around for a bit?'

The hotel concierge frowned. 'It really isn't safe without
someone to chaperone you,' she warned.

'I'll be fine, honestly,' I insisted.

So off I went in this taxi and was dropped off at a big shopping centre. It was fine at first: I wandered around for a bit,
looked in the shops, got something to eat. But then, at around
half past five, the sun started going down – and everything
just changed.

It was like a switch had been flicked. There was a shift in
atmosphere. A strange tension filled the air. I realised I had no
idea how to get back to the hotel. I didn't have the number for
my chaperone. I didn't know the area. I was completely alone.

I've got to get back, I thought.

Aged about three, rocking a pageboy
haircut and a showbiz smile.

Auntie Iris, the queen of am-dram. Her
big cupboard full of costumes at the top of
the stairs ignited my passion for dressing
up and being someone else.

Nan and Gramps, my maternal grandparents:
he was strong, ballsy and forceful; he had his
faults, but a lot of charm, which I think you
can see in this photo. When they were happy,
they had a lovely time together.

Nana and Grandpa Page, my dad's parents:
the first time I slept over at her house, Nana
sat up all night by the side of the cot and didn't
stop staring at me. When she died, Grandpa
Page would come and watch me once a
week at my swimming classes.

Me and my brilliant mum, Sue, and dad,
Nigel: a really happy threesome, in Auntie
Iris's back garden on a fab retro sun lounger.

At Gwyrosydd Junior School, being a witch and probably reciting a poem at the same time, in one of the school Eisteddfods on 1 March for St David's Day.

Aged eleven, very proud of being head girl: smart, studious and pleased with my Princess Diana haircut.

Aged fifteen and head girl of Mynyddbach Comprehensive School for Girls. My one rebellion was to wear my tie the wrong way round so that it was skinny, which I thought was very cool and trendy.

Fifteen years old, busily emoting and enjoying the drama during a production at West Glamorgan Youth Theatre Company. I loved being dramatic and serious.

At Bonham Carter House next door to RADA, where I lived in my first year at drama school, surrounded by cuddly toys and the pictures that had been on my bedroom walls in Swansea. Smiling, but inwardly terrified and wanting to go home.

The first head shot I had taken when leaving RADA in 1998, aged twenty-one. I have absolutely no idea why I was wearing my dad's big, baggy, blue cotton shirt, but it looks good.

Aged twenty-two, walking around the streets of London with my then boyfriend, Chris. I obviously had a bit of an attitude, thought I was cool and was trying to channel Kate Moss.

1998: appearing in my first film, *Very Annie Mary*, playing a bedridden twenty-one-year-old. It was brilliant to act with the dog, which lay on the bed for every day of filming.

Setting off for my first ever day of filming on *Very Annie Mary*, feeling independent, in control and professional. I was driving myself to work and my mum had given me a briefcase to keep my script in – very much a working woman.

Playing Zoe Cazalet in *The Cazalets* at my lover Roddy's bedside, busily emoting again and enjoying playing the more serious side of my character.

This was just after I'd finished filming my lobotomy scenes with Johnny Depp. I can't believe I'm standing next to him with a bald cap on and grisly scars, but it was brilliant fun and he was lovely.

With the adorable Martin Freeman on *Love Actually*, filming our scenes outside as John and Judy. What a delight he was to work with.

With my gorgeous, big, strong man: young, happy, not a care in the world and falling madly in love. 'Ham Peggotty' and 'Dora Spenlow', at my house in Wandsworth.

Our first dance to Barbara Streisand's 'Evergreen' at our wedding in 2003. Looking adoringly at each other, with Richard Curtis's penguin, which he kindly gave to me as a present, looking on just behind us.

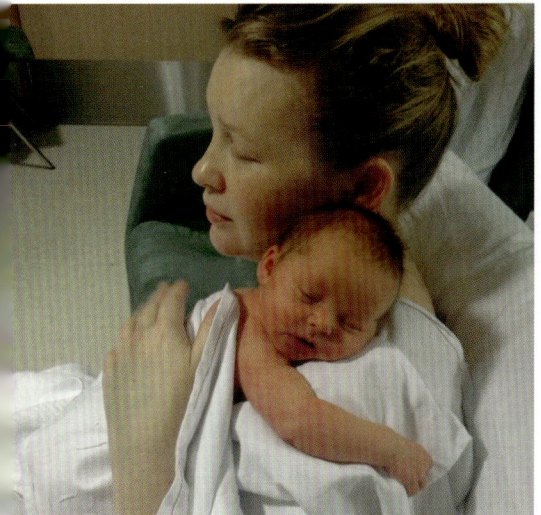

Literally just after Eva had been born – she just loved going on my left shoulder from the start. I'm content and happy – while obviously in pain and constipated – and in a bubble of protective love.

Mix *Doctor Who*, Queen Elizabeth, Zygons and breastfeeding a six-week-old baby, and this is what you get. I'm laughing hysterically; inside I'm dying. I certainly don't look like the Virgin Queen and I'm barely keeping it all together.

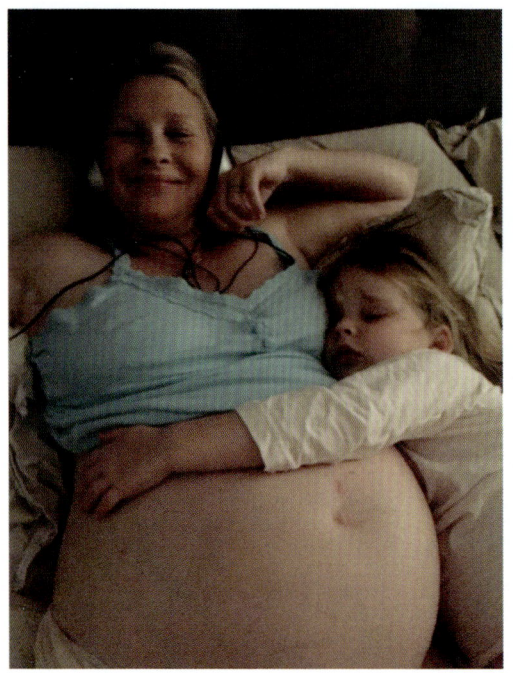

Pregnant with Kit and having a mid–morning nap with Eva, who loved cuddling into my belly and wouldn't sleep unless she was attached to me.

My gorgeous, wonderful, adorable boys, Noah, Kit and James, looking like they've broken into the house and they're about to attack me.

Laughing with Boe, my fourth baby, with a pair of Kit's underpants on my head. This is what life's all about; this is when I'm at my happiest.

My life: Boe, Noah, Kit and Eva, all showing their personalities …

My proud mum on Barry Island, pointing out her twenty-nine-year-old daughter on the side of Marco's Cafe.

Me and Melanie Walters, who plays Gwen, my mum, on our first day of filming the 2018 *Gavin & Stacey* special, which we were all so surprised about because there had been a gap of about ten years.

Filming the Christmas dinner scene for the 2018 Christmas special. It was the first time we filmed in a studio, but it was necessary because there were so many points of view and angles for the camera.

This was my first day on set for the 2024 *Gavin & Stacey* finale, filming with Ruth Jones. James Corden was on set as well and it was really lovely.

Still my first day at the slots on Barry Island, chilling with Ruth Jones, having a coffee and a gossip. Even when we were just sitting and chatting in between takes, we had to watch what we said, in case we revealed anything about the plot.

Our last day filming on Trinity Street in Stacey's family home. I'm arm in arm with Melanie Walters, and we're walking all the way up to the top of the road, where there were crowds of fans behind barriers.

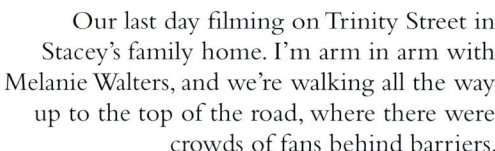

Just after we'd finished filming the stunt where we burst through the hedge on the *Gavin & Stacey* Christmas finale in 2024. We were excited because we were near the end of filming but also having lots of fun.

I went to find a taxi outside the shopping centre. There were men everywhere: cars pulling in, people offering lifts, all these drivers touting for fares, and I didn't know whether any of them were licensed taxi drivers or not. *I'll just have to risk it*, I decided. *If I don't get in one of these cars now, I'm going to be stuck here all night.*

I walked up to a driver and said, 'Can you help me, please? Can you take me back to my hotel?'

He smiled. 'Yes, of course. Get in.'

I got in. I sat in the back. He drove for a while and then he started saying he wasn't going to take me back to the hotel, after all. He said he was going to drive me somewhere else. He wanted me to take off all my clothes and he was going to take photos of me.

My blood went cold. Most of the time I think I can get myself out of any situation. But this was different, completely different. I had no control over any of this, and even if I managed to get out of the car, where would I go? I wanted to panic and scream, but I thought *No, stay calm. Make him laugh. Keep it light. Joke along with him.*

So I pretended not to take him seriously. I treated his suggestions like jokes and said something stupid and cheeky every time the conversation became menacing. Inside, I was feeling utterly terrified, but I tried to act like it was all a bit of harmless fun.

Somehow it worked and eventually he drove me back to the hotel. The feeling of relief as I got out of the car was overwhelming. I ran inside the hotel to the reception and breathlessly told them what had happened.

They looked at me in horror. 'You have no idea how lucky you are,' the concierge said.

When you come that close to disaster, you see life differently. I was already homesick and now my love for James and Daisy the dog – and Mum and Dad – multiplied by a hundred.

I had the most wonderful time on that job. Going whale watching in between filming. Rehearsing scenes and having lunch with little monkeys trying to steal our food. Sharing a flat with Charles Dance, and Sam Neill taking me to see the All Blacks play rugby. It really was a wonderful experience.

I finished on the job and flew back home before everyone else, and it was shortly after that I found out that Denise Black and Benedict Cumberbatch had been kidnapped and robbed at gunpoint in the middle of the night. They'd escaped to safety, but only after having the most terrifying experience. It was then that I truly realised just how lucky I'd been.

I carried on working and going to my auditions, when all of a sudden, one day, my agent called and said, 'You've got the main part in a movie.'

'Really?' I didn't remember meeting for a film or audition-ing for it. 'What is it?'

'It's a road movie and it's being filmed in Slovakia and Brussels. It's got German backers and they want you for it.'

It didn't make sense. I wondered what had prompted these German backers to cast me as the female lead in a film with-out even meeting me. At first I thought they must have seen me in something on the BBC, because the BBC was known internationally for making prestige TV. I'd just done *To the Ends of the Earth*, but they wouldn't have seen the Stephen Poliakoff drama I'd just filmed – *Gideon's Daughter* – because it hadn't aired yet. So maybe it was *Love Actually* that had caught their attention?

'Are there any nude scenes?' I asked my agent.

'No.'

'Has anything else come in?'

'No.'

'And it's filming in Slovakia and Brussels?'

'Yes.'

'Fine. I'll do it.'

Life began to feel a bit like a fairy tale. And like a princess choosing a prince from among her suitors, my first task was to read with three different actors, and see which one I had the most chemistry with. First up was a talented young actor who had worked on a couple of TV series I liked. The second was a very good-looking actor-director, but I didn't particularly gel with him. The third was a familiar TV actor, really sweet and really lovely, yet not quite right, either.

I was happy with the first fella and made sure I put that point across. He was the youngest of the three and, in fairy tales, it's always the youngest brother who turns out to be the good one. He was cast.

The plot of the film seemed a bit of a jumble, but I expected them to smooth it out as we went along. The disaster-prone leading man is trying to get rich quick and win back his girlfriend – me – and has a series of crashes and capers across Europe that involve a car, some jewels and a dead comedian. In the end they get back together. To be honest, a lot of the time I didn't really know what was going on.

Off I flew to Slovakia to film, where I met the rest of the cast. Some of them were German movie stars and clearly very famous and highly rated; there were also a couple of British actors who tended to stick together and take it all less seriously.

We were staying in a hotel in the middle of nowhere, deep in the Slovakian woods, and the first thing you saw when you arrived was a sign saying, 'Beware of bears.'

'Do not go into the woods because there are many dangerous bears there,' the hotel staff repeatedly warned us.

The food was awful. We were there for ages, and one by

one we had a breakdown over the food. There was nothing fresh and everything was out of cans. 'I can't eat this any more!' we'd wail.

The film opens with me waking up in bed next to a one-night stand. 'We need someone to play the guy in bed with you,' the producer said. 'Would James come over and do it? It's just a cameo: you chuck him out of bed in the morning, walk out of the flat, get into your Mini, and drive off.'

James was fine with it and came over to Slovakia to pretend to be my one-night stand. It felt really weird being in bed with my husband on a film set. He had to look as if he was naked lying next to me, so they put a flesh-coloured thong on him. I had to wake up, turn and look at him, groan and say, 'Oh God.' Then I was supposed to kick him out of bed and he'd run down the corridor, with his bum on show (but wearing a flesh-coloured thong), hiding his willy with his hands.

The merging of two worlds was too much to bear. It was hilarious. I was at one end of the corridor and he was at the other end, standing with his hands clasped around his willy, trying to hide it, sort of talking to himself, getting psyched up in order to be able to shout and run down the corridor. It was the funniest sight I'd ever seen. I was in hysterics, not taking any of it seriously, while James was having a mini meltdown, realising that when he'd said yes to this favour, he never imagined it would be standing naked in front of his wife and a camera crew, holding his willy.

We started the scene. I shouted at him, he shouted back, ran down the corridor naked and out the door. The last thing you see of him is a flash of his backside.

That, I think, is the last time we've ever filmed together.

A few days after James went back to the UK, a new

version of the script came through, which is not unusual on a film. I glanced through it but didn't really pay that much attention. Things constantly change on film sets and you're always getting little pink pages through with all your amendments.

A few days later, we were rehearsing a scene in a futuristic office with glass walls and doors, when one of the producers said to me, 'We're going to be doing your shower scene later today.'

I looked at her, puzzled. 'There is no shower scene.'

'Yes, we have now added a shower scene,' she said. 'You're naked in the shower and your boyfriend walks in and you have a chat with him.'

I shook my head. 'I'm not doing that.'

The producer pursed her lips. 'Well, the director is going to come and talk to you. Because you *are* going to be in the shower. You *are* doing the scene.'

I panicked and rang my agent. 'They're telling me I'm doing a nude shower scene. Please can you call them and tell them it's not happening!'

I was sitting in the office rehearsing my lines, when I suddenly looked up and saw the director storming towards me through a series of glass doors, absolutely fuming.

'Don't worry. I'll look after you,' said the actor playing my boyfriend.

The director burst in, shouting, 'What do you think you're playing at? You *are* going to be doing this scene.'

'I'm not doing it,' I said, quaking slightly. 'It wasn't there in the script originally. We've not talked about it. I don't want to do it.'

He was insistent. 'You *have* to do it!'

'No, I'm not taking my top off. I'm not being naked in a shower.'

A row ensued. The actor tried to calm the situation down. The director stormed out again.

Eventually, we agreed that I would stand in the shower wearing shorts and a vest. I'm not sure it was staying true to my character to take a shower in shorts and a vest, but that is what I did.

At one point, the strap of my vest slipped down slightly, and the director said excitedly, 'Yes, that's it! That's what we want.'

When we came to do another take, he said, 'Make sure the strap comes down.'

That's fine if you want a bit of slipped strap, I thought. *At least I'm not naked.*

We were in Slovakia for months and the only way to pass the time was to try and have a laugh. But me and a couple of the other actors eventually started going stir-crazy out there in the middle of the woods. There was nothing to do and we got so bored that we started looking for something – anything – to make life interesting.

We even went so far as to get into a hired car and drive out into the forest, taking a load of bananas with us. After all these months of living with warning signs about bears – and after endlessly talking to each other about being attacked by bears – we decided to go actively looking for them.

Deep in the woods, we stopped, wound the windows down and started throwing bananas out of the car. 'Bear! Bear! We're here!' we yelled. We had finally lost our minds.

We were crossing over from Hansel and Gretel into horror-film territory now. We'd all freaked each other out because the hotel where we were staying in Brussels resembled the one in *The Shining* and downstairs in the lobby area there were big green goblin statues, placed artistically around.

One of the British actors was especially bothered by them. He shivered at the sight of them.

As the days went on, I had an idea for a prank. I started collecting a few of these goblin statues and storing them in the cupboards in my room. One day, while the British actor was working, I got hold of his room key, took all the goblins I'd gathered, and placed them around his bedroom in spots where you couldn't quite see them – until you *could*. I was hoping that he'd catch a glimpse of something out of the corner of his eye while he was in bed; he'd turn his head, see a weird goblin peering out at him from behind a curtain and totally freak out.

When I went on-set later, I told the others what I'd done. Meanwhile, the British actor was completely oblivious, happily chatting away without a care in the world while we were all in fits of giggles. What was so funny was that the actor thought that *he* was making us laugh with his witty repartee, but it wasn't that, it was the thought of how he'd react when he got back to his room, jumped into bed and noticed a goblin looking at him from behind the curtain. It was a good prank because the anticipation and laughter lasted for hours – and the trick paid off, too. After working all day, this poor actor flopped into bed without noticing the goblins, only to have a complete fit in the middle of the night when he woke up and saw them watching him, grimacing faces staring through the darkness.

I don't know what happened with the German-backed film after it went into post-production. First it had one title, then another. It came out in Europe, but not in the UK, and there wasn't a UK screening. It was just one of those weird jobs that you do and then forget about, and so it shall remain nameless here. I've got it on DVD in the house somewhere, but I've never watched it. I can't. Because it's all dubbed in German!

I came back to London and did the play *What The Butler Saw*, and then waited to see what would come in next. I'd gone from job to job since I'd left drama school; there was always a steady flow of work. I was lucky.

But suddenly the jobs dried up.

It came as a massive shock. *What's happening?* I thought anxiously. *I've lasted all this time and always worked, so what has changed?*

No one could say.

The Stephen Poliakoff drama, *Gideon's Daughter*, with Bill Nighy and Miranda Richardson, was screened in February 2006. It was a glossy, critically acclaimed production and I had a lovely time playing the part of Diane, an It girl with the most fabulous wardrobe. I got to meet Miranda Richardson! I worked with Tom Hardy. I had to be on my toes because Stephen Poliakoff could drop anything on you at a moment's notice, and you were expected to be able to deal with it. One day, I was sitting in the make-up truck when he walked in and announced he'd written an A4-page monologue for me. He handed it to me and said I needed to learn it now, because we were filming it straight away. So I did.

I carried on pottering along, but soon everything started to slow down.

I was all right money-wise. I was living off my savings – and Dad was still secretly sending me the tips he was given at work in the garage, even though I told him not to – but instead of doing something useful or fun with my free time, I sat at home with my stomach in knots, worrying that my acting career was over. So many actors I knew had gone through this same torture. Some people I'd been at RADA with had given up on acting altogether. Now I was reaching a point where I was also thinking, *I can't do this any more.*

I had to take charge of myself. As I was passing a shoe shop in East Dulwich with James, saying, 'I'm going mad. I need to do something,' I noticed a sign in the window: 'Sales assistant wanted', and I walked straight in.

'Hiya, I'd be really interested in applying for this position,' I said. 'I'd love to sell shoes.'

They offered me the job on the spot and I started work a couple of days later. And so began some of my happiest times, strangely enough. All of a sudden, life seemed much simpler. Instead of flying off abroad or driving to Manchester and Edinburgh, and instead of getting up at dawn to go on-set, or spending evenings and matinees in the theatre, I was trotting along the road at nine-thirty every morning, carrying my sandwiches in a lunch bag, dressed in a lovely smart outfit, on my way to work in a nice shoe shop.

And I really did like spending time in the stockroom. Crocs had just come in: they were delivered loose and I used to chuck them all into the gigantic cardboard box out the back – the one I was inside when my agent rang to tell me about the *Dirty Dancing* job. Whenever someone came in looking for a pair of Crocs, I'd have to jump into a sea of plastic shoes and try to find them. It was fun.

I have so many lovely memories of that summer, of James, and of Daisy. But it was awful not to be working – awful to be always waiting for the phone to ring. The tension gnaws away at you and makes you jumpy, and the endless audition process for the part of Baby just made it worse. And when I didn't get it – after all the effort I put in – I absolutely bombed.

What I didn't realise was that the biggest job of my life was just around the corner. And if I'd been Dirty Dancing right then, I'd never have been able to do it.

9

Gavin & Stacey

I'm always going to be British, but if somebody asks me, 'What are you?' I will always say, 'I'm Welsh.'

Because I am – I am Welsh. It's a feeling, it's a spirit and it's a passion and you share that passion with the whole of your country. There's a strong, hot, fiery, dragon-like spirit in you when you're Welsh, and it gives you strength and makes you feel like you could go anywhere and take on the world. It's a shared history. It's the way you've been brought up. It's your identity.

Coming to England was strange for me, because England is completely and utterly different. The way people are, the way they talk, even their houses – it's all different from the way I grew up in Wales, where there's a spirit and earthiness, a feeling inside my gut.

Looking back, I find it so strange that the thing that makes me unique, and makes me *me* was what they wanted to strip away from me when I was at RADA. Yes, of course you've got to be able to do accents if you want to play different characters, but they were going for my Welsh identity, trying to annihilate it, and it must have been so deep-rooted in me that it was just impossible to take it away from me.

Take the women in our family, for instance: they are very strong, and when you've got them all together, it's non-stop talking. Gossiping, finding out who's died, who's done this, who's done that: 'You'll never guess what they've done!'

James found it strange when he first met them all, because he's quite quiet. He would just sit there, looking exhausted. 'You all talk so fast,' he'd say. 'And I don't understand what you're saying. And you just don't *stop*.'

And so when I started reading the script for *Gavin & Stacey*, my feelings of recognition were off the scale. There were so many echoes of my own experiences; everything about it felt familiar. *This is my family! This is me. This is my life*, I kept thinking.

Even if you've never watched it, you'll probably know that *Gavin & Stacey* is a comedy series about two families and their friends who meet and mingle when Essex boy Gavin Shipman and Welsh girl Stacey West fall in love. Gavin lives with his mum and dad, Pam and Mick, in Billericay; Stacey lives with her widowed mum Gwen in Barry Island – with her protective Uncle Bryn across the road. Their respective best friends, Smithy and Nessa, are perpetually popping in.

The show follows key moments in Gavin and Stacey's romance, from their first meet-up in London to their wedding and beyond, and the events and relationships that take place among their friends and family amid the swirl of it all, including a love–hate bond between Smithy and Nessa. There's loads of comedy in the characters and how they interact when they get together – and they are drawn with such affection, tolerance, quirkiness, love, struggle and honesty that the whole thing feels very real and genuine.

I couldn't believe it as I was reading the script, because my mother *is* Gwen, Stacey's mum: she makes omelettes all the time, and she looks like Gwen, as well. And in the script Stacey's Uncle Bryn gives her a rape alarm before she goes to London to meet Gavin, and my Uncle Anthony gave me a rape alarm before I went to drama school in London.

I am Stacey, I thought. *I've got to get this part. In fact, if I don't get this part because some fucker who's got famous parents gets it, or some celebrity who is not even an actress gets it, then that's it, I am done. This is my last shot.*

Gavin & Stacey was written by Ruth Jones and James Corden, who also star in the show as Nessa and Smithy. I first met Ruth Jones when I went for my initial audition for the part of Stacey. I'd just been watching Ruth in the brilliant show *Nighty Night*, which was written by Julia Davis – who later went on to play Dawn in *Gavin & Stacey*. Oh my God, I was starstruck by the pair of them. I just loved the dark humour. I thought Julia Davis was out of this world. You could see she played everything on the edge – she's so dark, not afraid to go there.

Ruth, playing Linda, was just so funny and odd. When I found out I was going to be meeting her, I thought, *I can't believe this. She's Welsh, for starters, and I've just been watching her on telly!*

I got down to Spotlight and went into the toilets. I was putting a bit of make-up on and doing my hair when Ruth walked in. 'Oh my God, it's so lovely to meet you,' I said.

Her face lit up. 'Oh my gosh, Joanna, it's lovely to meet you too.'

I told her I thought she was amazing and brilliant. I can't remember what else I said – I must've been nattering away about something. Then she said, 'Okay, I'll see you in there,' and I went, 'Okay, bye.'

She was lovely and friendly and everything I hoped she'd be. But also completely different from the character of Linda. She'd totally transformed herself. As she did again when she went on to play Nessa. Ruth is smart, really intelligent, very pretty and beautiful, gentle and funny, and she's just a really sorted woman. Meeting her, I realised what an amazing actress she is.

Apparently, she then went into the audition room and saw Chris Gernon, the director, because James Corden was away in America doing *The History Boys* at that point. She said to Chris, 'I just met Jo Page in the toilet. She is Stacey.' Which was good.

I then went into the audition room and met Chris and Ruth, and Ted Dowd, our wonderful producer. Apparently – I don't even remember this – all I did was talk non-stop about my *Dirty Dancing* audition, how it had gone wrong, how I'd booked myself into the Savoy, how I'd been crying and was really upset about all of it. I eventually stopped talking, and then I left.

Chris turned to Ruth and said, 'We've just found Stacey.'

Originally, Stacey was supposed to have a Cardiff accent and be a lot rougher, like Nessa, Stacey's best friend. When I went back in for my recall, Ruth asked, 'Can you do a Cardiff accent?'

Oh my God, I don't know what a Cardiff accent sounds like, I thought. *I don't have the internet. I don't have a computer. What am I going to do?*

The one time I get to audition for something Welsh, and I still can't do my own accent!

So I didn't do anything. I just decided to do a really Welshy, valley sound. I had to go back in and do a chemistry test with Mat, to see how we gelled together and if it worked between us, and I started doing everything in this weird, exaggerated accent. Ruth asked me to come outside for a minute. 'What are you doing?' she asked.

'I'm trying to do a Cardiff accent,' I said.

'That's not what a Cardiff accent sounds like. Just go back in there and do your own accent.'

So I went back in and carried on reading with Mat in my normal accent.

It was clear from the start that we had great chemistry. We did the scene from the first episode, in the nightclub, where we're talking over the music and then end up kissing. It was all really natural. We just gelled. It worked.

After that, I said goodbye to Mat. He was staying in to read with another girl who was trying out for the part. She had a Cardiff accent and a different take on the character. It was between her and me. After he read with her, they decided there and then that it was going to be me.

It's funny, because all through the years I'd often had to work so hard to get into a character, but Stacey came easily. I don't think I was what they were looking for, but the sweetness worked – and with all my non-stop chatting, they felt I was right for the part.

That's why Stacey is from Swansea, rather than Cardiff – and it's why Gwen and Uncle Bryn don't have the Cardiff accent, either. Melanie Walters, the young flame-haired actress I saw all those years ago in *Educating Rita* at the Swansea Grand Theatre, was cast as Gwen, my mum, and Rob Brydon, the actor, comedian and writer of *Marion and Geoff* and *Human Remains*, was playing my Uncle Bryn.

I could have worked harder on my Cardiff accent and I would probably have mastered it, but I wouldn't have enjoyed playing Stacey half as much. Doing an accent can often spoil this wonderful passion I have, that I completely give myself to, because it's like trying to wade through treacle whilst doing it. I can't let myself go and be free and really embrace acting and being in another world, because there's a barrier there and I'm not able to fully get to the truth of what I'm doing. So when I got *Gavin & Stacey*, it was a joy because I realised I could be truthful in my acting.

The first series of *Gavin & Stacey* was commissioned by BBC Three. It was edgier and more raunchy when we first started, before it went over to BBC One. In the first series, we had someone saying fuck, and there was a blatant sex scene at the wedding. I liked it that way – I liked Stacey's sweetness, and vulnerability, but she was earthy and rough and had a strength and quirkiness to her which was so much fun to play.

All the way through my career, I'd been the ingénue who never wanted to be the ingénue. Stacey and I are very similar, from our families to our personality, and I was over the moon because I knew her so well.

I didn't really think about being comedic. I was never thinking, *You've got to be funny*, or *This is a funny line*. To my mind, I play her quite seriously, because that is just her, and she is being serious most of the time. She's just this lovely character who falls in love and throws herself into everything. It just so happens that, because of the way her part is written, it ends up being funny.

Ruth and I really bonded in that first series. She made me laugh, we'd talk and gossip – it was like finding the most wonderful friend and we'd chat away endlessly. There's an out-take of the two of us on the coach as we were being driven around Leicester Square. You can see we're clearly gossiping – I'm just going, 'Yeah, and then she came in and she said . . .' Then you see me look up and Ruth says, 'Are we filming?' And Chris Gernon says, 'Yes, we are.' I say, 'Oh, right,' and just slip straight back into character. But every time the camera stopped, Ruth and I would go straight back to gossiping and laughing. I love her so much.

When we filmed the scenes in Leicester Square, which were the only scenes we've ever filmed out of Cardiff, we got mistaken for a couple of prostitutes. Ruth was enraged and turned to the men, declaring, 'We are serious actresses.'

Sometimes there'd be scenes with Nessa, and if there was a pause or she was just looking at me, especially when Nessa was pregnant and there was a long moment while she was having a scan or lying on the bed, we'd stare at each other and collapse into fits of giggles. I couldn't stop laughing.

I first met James Corden at a costume fitting. I'd already got the part, and he'd just come back from America. We had the most brilliant costume designer for the first series; she had loads of old clothes and she completely understood Stacey's world: living in Barry, not much money – she totally got the vibe. I loved all my costumes and the way I looked.

James came into the office where I was trying on outfits. He was really charming, sweet and polite – a bit like Rob Brydon when you first meet him. And then, over the course of filming, Rob and James both turned into your brothers – older and younger – just constantly taking the piss out of you the whole time.

Ruth and James have always been a joy to film with. It's never felt like I was working with the writers. They didn't get involved in directing. They just let you do your job. We've never changed a word of the script – it's always been so good that you don't need to. I've always acted exactly what's written and they've never tried to direct me – that's always been left to Chris Gernon. She's the only one who's ever come up to me and said, 'Why don't you try this?' or 'Maybe Stacey's feeling like this.' But Ruth and James – when I act with them, they're just Smithy and Nessa. The atmosphere on-set has always been relaxed, laid-back and really good fun.

There was one time in the first series when Mat was meant to be filming, but he was ill and was sent home. I had that day off, but I got a call saying, 'Mat's been sent home. We're coming to pick you up. Ruth and James are going to write a new scene.'

I remember being brought to set and sitting down for my hair and make-up; Ruth was on one side of me, James on the other – and they started writing a brand-new scene over my head. I think it was a scene where Stacey goes to visit Nessa at the slots and it was amazing to see. Right in front of me, they just made it happen. They bounced ideas off each other. Ruth would come up with something, and James would say, 'Oh yeah, and add this,' or 'Put that in.' It was incredible to see a scene come to life like that, in real time, and then go and film it.

It's brilliant rehearsing with them too. They both do other characters when we're reading through scenes. James usually does the women – does a brilliant version of me, Welsh accent and all – and Ruth will cover the other characters.

Everybody loves each other. There's a warmth that you don't always get. It's also really interesting watching how James and Ruth work together. They just know when something isn't working, and they'll change it quickly or add something in.

As an actor, you feel completely free. There was one bit, in an early episode when Stacey is saying goodbye to Gavin at the train station. I say, 'I love you,' and then I just make a little noise. A sort of emotional screech.

'Keep that in,' Ruth said. 'It's mad, because it's just something Jo Page would do.' So we kept it in. That sort of spontaneity, that freedom – it just makes everything feel alive. You always feel totally free to be yourself and make it your own.

At first, I was quite nervous around Mat Horne, because I knew he'd done stand-up and been on *The Catherine Tate Show*. He was quick and witty, very dry, and constantly took the piss out of me, but he was an utter joy to work with. I was just a classically trained actress and hadn't ever really thought about my comic timing or anything like that. I was just playing Stacey as I'd play any role, I didn't think about being funny.

The whole of the first series was fantastic. It was an absolute ball. Everybody seemed to be perfect for their roles. When I met Alison Steadman, who was playing Gavin's mum, my heart wouldn't stop racing. *She's played bloody Beverly*, I thought. *She was Candice-Marie in* Nuts in May.

I've always tried desperately to be professional and cool when I've met and worked with my idols. I've just put my head down and got on with the job. But it was hard to be massively relaxed around Alison Steadman, because I was completely awestruck. Then came a moment when we were doing the 2018 *Gavin & Stacey* special, when Alison was in the bar with me and Mat, and we started quizzing her about *Nuts in May*. She told us all about the song she made up for it. She talked about the improvising and how they did it, and then she sang the 'zoo song'.

I came out of my body. I was completely blown away. Mat and I spoke afterwards and said, 'Oh my God, we've just sat in the bar and Alison has just sung us the song from *Nuts In May*! This is incredible!'

No matter how much you all get used to being a family, there are still those moments that stand out and make you realise as an actor how lucky you are!

I tease Rob Brydon – Uncle Bryn – and say that the only time he's ever truly been polite to me was when he didn't know me. We turned up for the first day's rehearsal, and he sat next to me, and I said, 'Hello, I'm Jo, nice to meet you,' and he said, 'Hello, I'm Rob, lovely to meet *you.*'

And I've never seen that person since!

Working with Rob was the best fun ever. To be able to be in a scene and watch this man bring the words to life was such a privilege. I'd forget I was acting with him because I'd enjoy watching him in the scene so much. His ability to flip from making me howl with laughter to making me cry in the scene when he reads my father's letter to me in my wedding car was astounding.

My mum's favourite bit of casting, though, was Larry Lamb – Gavin's dad – who was a very young sixty years old when we started filming the first series, and very dishy.

We filmed in Cardiff and Barry and the surrounding areas. After a day's filming in Cardiff, we would go to the bar at the Park Plaza Hotel. Next to the fire there was a big chair where Alison would sit drinking gin and tonics. She named it 'Ali's Parlour'. The rest of us sat on the sofas around the fire. All evening, we would just talk and talk, and tell stories and laugh. It was unlike any other job I've ever done in my life, and I can't imagine finding that camaraderie and feeling of family ever again.

Mel, who played Gwen, was forty-seven when we did the first series, a year younger than I am now. She was coming back to acting after taking time off to look after her little boy, who must have been about seven, and she was so, so nervous. During the first series, she was always in the corner, wringing her hands, doing mouth exercises or trying to calm down.

One night Steve Coogan was coming to visit, because he's the Creative Director of Baby Cow, the production company for *Gavin & Stacey*, and we'd filmed all day, and we'd all done our close-ups, apart from Mel. She was the last one to do her close-ups – and that's when Steve Coogan showed up. I was laughing so much because it was awful: she was terrified, as I would have been in her position. She had to do all of her close-ups with Steve Coogan sat behind the camera, watching. *Oh my God!* I was thinking as I looked on.

I didn't escape unscathed, though, because we all went out to a bar afterwards and did karaoke, which is my nightmare. Mat was badgering me to sing 'Islands in the Stream' with him. I caved in and we did it. I was horrific. The crew was filming me and I couldn't get the right key – I was either too deep or too high – and this was all in front of Steve Coogan! *This is so embarrassing*, I thought. *He's never, ever going to hire me for anything.*

For the whole of the first series, there was this awful smell in Stacey's house, which in real life belonged to a woman called Glenda. The smell just got worse and worse, and no one could work out what it was or where it was coming from. We just had to get on with it and keep filming. It was only right at the end of the shoot that somebody discovered that they'd accidentally unplugged Glenda's fridge-freezer right at the start of the shoot. All that time, everything in the freezer was slowly rotting.

We were working long hours and sometimes exhaustion tipped us over into hysteria. After one very long day, we were upstairs filming in Stacey's bedroom – Mat and me, and a couple of the others. We were all exhausted. Mat was messing about, trying to keep us all going by making us laugh. He opened a chest of drawers, assuming that everything in Stacey's bedroom was props and, seeing it was full of knickers, he pulled out a pair and put them over his head like a balaclava, with his eyes showing and the crotch over his face. Then he started jumping around and showing off, making jokes about Stacey's knickers.

'Mat, I don't think those are set dressing,' I said.

'What?'

He instantly pulled them off.

Somebody came in and said, 'No, those are Glenda's knickers. We haven't bothered taking any of her stuff out of the drawers.'

The trauma as he realised he'd been wearing Glenda's knickers over his face is one of the funniest things I've ever seen. It still makes me laugh to this day.

We shot the wedding-fair scenes at a hotel, and then suddenly there were whispers going round that the Welsh rugby team were staying there. They'd been out training and had come back to the hotel, wanting to know what we were filming.

'Can we meet them?'

This was early days, so no one knew who we were or what we were filming, but they all agreed to meet with us. They'd just been training and you could feel the heat coming off them. We've got the best photo ever of the cast with the Welsh Rugby team. All the women's faces are lit up, beaming, eyes wide, full of glee. We literally look like we're glowing. And all the male cast members look emasculated – completely serious, not smiling at all.

The day we filmed Stacey's hen party, for the scenes that appear in episode five of the first series, has to be one of my favourite days of filming. We were all dressed up as schoolgirls for starters, and they got a real-life stripper. I turned up on-set feeling really excited. I couldn't stop telling people how thrilled I was that I was going to have a real-life stripper, because I'd never experienced a stripper before in my life. He was dressed as a policeman, and his name was Toyboy.

I went on-set and Chris started directing us. She turned

to Toyboy. 'Right, just do a brief sort of dance – whatever you'd normally do at a hen party.'

All the crew were there. Loads of the fellas were standing around by the cameras, watching. James Corden was there, as well.

'Let's just do a walk-through of it and see what happens,' Chris added.

And here's what happened:

Toyboy presses play on his boombox and 'Sex Bomb' by Tom Jones comes on. He gets me to sit on a chair and I'm just going with it, feeling quite relaxed. He takes off his policeman's helmet and plonks it on my head, and I'm laughing away.

All of a sudden, he's standing in front of me and he rips open his shirt. I draw back and say, 'Oh!' The crew start laughing. Toyboy gets out some oil, rubs it all over his chest, grabs my head and starts rubbing it against him. I'm thinking, *What's going on here?* but I'm completely swept up in it.

And then – out of nowhere – he jumps in the air, lands in my lap, and starts humping me. Out of the corner of my eye, I can see James Corden behind the camera, having hysterics. Toyboy slides down me and onto the ground, starts humping the floor, then jumps back up. The whole crew are doubled up now.

Then he whips his trousers off. He's wearing a thong. It's only a walk-through, but he comes up close to me, whips off the thong, and he's standing there completely naked – and his actual real-life willy is right in front of my face.

End of walk-through.

I was hysterical.

'I think we can stop there now,' Chris said.

She approached him to give direction. He stood there

naked, expectantly. 'Do you want to put some clothes on?' she said.

'No, I'm fine. I'm used to being like this.' He wasn't at all bothered about being stood there naked in front of everyone.

'Okay, will you please go and put on some clothes before we talk this through?' she said. Once that was sorted, she said to him, 'So that's the general plan. What would you normally do at this point, at a hen party?'

'Well, normally I'd blindfold her and I'd put a dildo in her mouth.'

'I am not doing that,' I said.

We started filming the first take. Toyboy did the routine again, came right up close to me, willy there in full view, and I looked at it and thought, *Something's strange.*

After the take, he said, 'I'm just going to the toilet to get myself ready for the next one,' and wandered off.

I turned to Lindsay, the producer. 'There's something wrong with his willy. Something's . . . odd about it.'

We went to do another take and the producer – who was also an extra – came up to me just before the take and whispered in my ear, 'He's got an elastic band wrapped around it.'

They shouted, 'Action.'

So I've got that thought in my head now, and he comes over, does the routine again, rips off his trousers – and I swear, there's an elastic band wrapped around it. To keep the blood in.

I was astounded. Absolutely floored. I couldn't stop laughing. After each take, he'd head back to the toilet to sort out his elastic band, ready for the next one. What a pro.

In real life, I was exactly the same as Stacey in this scene: I was in utter hysterics and let the stripper do his thing, and I enjoyed every single minute of it.

Every day playing Stacey was fun. When the first episode came out, and I sat down to watch it, I remember thinking, *This is the best thing I've ever done. I can actually watch this.*

The show resonated with audiences and critics. It was praised for its dialogue and humour, its heart-warming story-line and its quirky but relatable characters. It's funny to think that the viewing figures came in at just under a million for the first series, which was considered great for BBC Three. Its reach quickly went far beyond those figures though and it broke through to a more mainstream audience. Twenty million watched the final special in 2024.

Every time I got an acting job, from me leaving drama school until she died, Nan would always say, 'Oh, it's not Welsh, is it?' And I'd have to say, 'No, it's not Welsh. I'm doing an RP accent,' or, 'I'm doing a northern accent.'

'Oh, thank goodness for that,' she'd say, because I think she thought Welsh was somehow not as good as anything else. Or that I wasn't properly acting.

When I got *Gavin & Stacey*, Nan said, 'It's not Welsh, is it?' And I had to say, 'Yes it is.' But when she ended up seeing it, she loved it, and thought it was great. People started talking to her about it and saying, 'We've seen your granddaughter in this, and we think it's brilliant.'

So the good thing was, her friends liked it.

Not long after *Gavin & Stacey* came out, I was offered a pantomime at the New Wimbledon Theatre. The production was *Cinderella*, with me in the title role and Gareth Gates as Prince Charming.

I had never done pantomime before. It wasn't 'serious dramatic actress' territory, but it was everything I'd loved doing when I was young. Dressing up as a princess, being in a fairy tale, singing, dancing, 'Yes, okay, I'll do it – but only if my husband can be in it with me.'

They agreed – and then I had to ask James, 'Will you do the pantomime with me, please? So that we don't have to be apart all over Christmas?'

James agreed to play Dandini, Prince Charming's best friend.

Pantomime has its roots in the sixteenth-century Italian *commedia dell'arte* tradition and has developed through the ages to take in loads of other theatrical traditions – from masques to music hall. It's spontaneous and chaotic and an utter joy to be in; I love the slapstick and familiar lines and characters, and the jokes that work on different levels. But of course keeping the balance between structure and mayhem is key to putting on a great show – and you need to be working with a really professional cast of actors to be able to achieve it.

Luckily, *Cinderella* had a fantastic cast and crew and I think we did a really good job, but pantomime is hard work and we had the occasional dip. And I'm afraid to say that there was one performance that very nearly fell apart.

We'd all been out the night before. Dressed up as pirates, we'd gone around Soho partying until the early hours, and then we had to go into work the next day. When I got to the theatre, my head was spinning and I felt really unwell. I was such a wreck that the stage hands had to put a bucket in the wings for me in case I was sick.

Because I was feeling weak, I didn't have my usual control when things went wrong – and things always go wrong when you're performing a live show, even if they're only tiny. Me being me, even the littlest mistakes can set me off giggling, and so I knew I was facing a risky couple of hours.

For the hundredth time, I wished I hadn't stayed up so late the night before.

The show started well. I felt a bit shaky inside, but I kept it together until the point in the show when the fairy godmother comes on, wearing a hooded cloak to disguise her identity.

I had to go up to her and say, 'Old lady, is something wrong?'

The old lady looks up at Cinderella from under her hood. Normally it would have been Louise Dearman looking up at me. But instead it was my husband. I found myself looking into the face of James bent over under the cloak trying to do an old woman voice – and that was enough to set me off.

I took a deep breath. *Don't give in to it*, I told myself.

I kept going. The next scene was when Cinderella meets Prince Charming for the first time and we duet in the love song. I was wearing my rags all trussed up; he was all dapper in his jacket and breeches. We were dancing around and singing, pretending to be completely besotted with each other. But, just then, over Gareth's shoulder, I caught a glimpse of the little Shetland ponies being ushered into the wings, in preparation for the transformation scene. They were so little and cute, but then one of them started pooing and the trainer who was looking after him stepped in it and slipped.

It started me and Gareth off laughing. It was really, really bad, because this was the big love-song scene in *Cinderella* and we were supposed to be singing our hearts out, and I couldn't stop giggling. To rein in my laughter, I tried focusing on Gareth's neck, and the top button of his shirt. But it just didn't work, I ended up gurgling and couldn't sing at all. I went mute and stopped singing and just stared at his chest, shaking uncontrollably.

Gareth carried on singing but you could hear his voice trembling, and then he started wheezing, and finally he stopped singing too. We carried on doing our dance routine. The pianist went on playing. All you could hear over the microphone was the pair of us trying to stifle our hysterical laughter like Muttley from *Wacky Races*. Then Gareth said, 'Come on. Pull yourself together,' and the microphone picked it up.

We finished the dance. I did an apologetic curtsy. He bowed, and then he said to the audience, 'I'm so sorry.'

We walked off stage to the biggest round of applause we'd had over the whole run of the show. When we came back on, everybody was cheering. What's wonderful about pantomime is that you and the audience are friends, and like good friends, this audience had forgiven us.

Gavin & Stacey seemed to have a similar connection with its audience and by then it had become a bit of a sensation. While we were filming the second series, I'd had a call from my agent, saying, 'You've all been nominated for the best comedy actor and best comedy actress newcomers at the British Comedy Awards.'

I was amazed. 'What, all of us together? The four of us, as one?'

'No, you have each been individually nominated – which means that you, Jo, are up for the best comedy actress new-comer award.'

I just couldn't believe it. Things like that didn't happen to me. So, to find myself doing this job and being nomi-nated at the British Comedy Awards for something that was so effortless for me – and for the show to win BAFTAs, as well – seemed unbelievable. It was so exciting to be part of this amazing drama that put Wales on the map. Would there be a third series? I desperately hoped so. It was my favourite job ever, ever, ever.

10

Fame

'When you're riding high in your career,' my agent used to say, 'your personal life hits the floor.'

That can't be true for everyone, I thought.

'It always seems to happen,' he'd say.

Fame crept up on me and I found it all quite strange. The attention started when the first episode of *Gavin & Stacey* came on TV. There was a big buzz around it and the BBC wanted to do a huge launch, so we did loads of press and a promo video. One evening I turned the telly on, and suddenly this show – and my first-ever lead role – was being reviewed on *Newsnight*, of all programmes, by Germaine Greer, who I'd idolised my whole life. I just couldn't believe that this incredible writer and feminist was discussing a show that I was in.

She then went on to say she thought it was quite twee, a bit like *The Good Life*, and that me and Mat were like Felicity Kendal and Richard Briers. Which, to be honest, I was quite pleased about.

I thought, *Well, if I'm going to be the next someone, I wouldn't mind being the next Felicity Kendal – she's got lovely hair!*

Suddenly you find yourself thrust into this whole other world: you're going to awards ceremonies and red-carpet events, ending up in places you never imagined existed. I couldn't believe it the first time I went into a gifting suite. These places actually exist, where you can walk into a room and take anything you want. There are freebies everywhere: handbags, silk scarves, shoes, dresses, cosmetics and food.

A woman came up to me wheeling a massive suitcase. 'You point to what you want,' she explained, 'and I'll put it in the suitcase for you.'

'Oh, you don't have to do that,' I said. 'I can carry my own suitcase.'

'No, that's not how it works,' she said. 'You wander around, choose what you like, and I'll take care of it.'

It felt bizarre to be walking alongside her, picking out nice things, while she dragged my case along behind me. But you get completely seduced by it and quite soon I was thinking, *This is amazing!* I left one gifting lounge with two pairs of very nice snow boots and a pork pie.

I remember doing an entertainment show and James came with me. We were sitting in my dressing room, I'd had hair and make-up done, and the female producer came in to say hello. Then she said, 'Just to let you know, when we're filming, the presenter can be very handsy with the women. I think he'll think you're very attractive, so he's probably going to start touching you, but that's just him. Just don't worry about it.'

'Okay, all right,' I agreed, but I was quite shocked.

Then we went on-set, and I sat next to the presenter for the segment we were doing. I was quite nervous meeting him anyway, but that doubled as I sat there waiting for him to spring on me. Just as the producer had said, he started feeling me up.

I slapped his hands off and said, 'What do you think you're doing? Get your hands off me.' I commented on his really thick hair and said, 'Jesus, I feel like I'm in Bristol Zoo, being mauled by the lions.'

He didn't touch me again after that, because I was quite mouthy with him. But it was just unbelievable that in those days you'd go on a job, and the female producer would go, 'By the way, you're going to get touched up in a minute, hope you're okay with that.' And you, as an actress, would go, 'Oh, okay then,' and just have to deal with it.

I went on all the panel shows. And they were an experience. It was quite scary, because everyone was expecting me to turn up and be funny and cracking gags and be Stacey, but she was just a character I played, those were lines I'd learned, so I had to just relax and trust in my own ability to be funny.

One time I went on and turned to a comedian and said, 'I feel like saying such-and-such. What do you think?' I was nervous about putting jokes across.

One second later, he said my joke.

What a shit! I thought. *You've just stolen my joke.*

Great things happened, too. While we were filming the second series of *Gavin & Stacey*, the producers managed to get us free tickets to go and watch Take That, who had just reunited and were performing in Cardiff. James Corden and I got there early and were put in a box in the stadium. One of Take That's people came up and said, 'Do you want to go and meet the boys before the show starts?'

'Oh my God, yes!' I honestly couldn't believe it! It was like a dream come true!

The pair of us were taken to their dressing room and told to wait in the corridor for a minute. Suddenly the doors burst open because the concert was about to start, and all the Take That boys came out. I was delirious!

I had just done a music video with Mark Owen, so Mark said hello when he saw me and was quite shy. He turned to the others. 'See? I told you I knew her.' The boys had apparently been saying, 'You don't know Jo Page from *Gavin & Stacey*.' And he was saying, 'She was in my music video. I've actually kissed her.'

I can't believe I'm talking to Take That, I thought. James did the whole of one of their dance routines for them and they loved it.

As I was walking to the stage with Gary Barlow, I thought, *This is the most unreal experience of my life.*

We walked all the way to the side of the stage, chatting to them. We said, 'Good luck, go for it, boys, we'll see you out front,' and left.

They went straight on stage. The concert started, and James and I went back up to the box and just sat there going, 'Oh my God, oh my God, that was amazing!'

But with fame comes harsher scrutiny in the media. When I was cast in the West End debut of Neil LaBute's comedy *Fat Pig* in 2008, a tabloid critic wrote a really nasty review suggesting I'd only got the part because of my *Gavin & Stacey* profile. For him, I hadn't existed as an actress before then – I was just a little Welsh woman who'd been plucked out of obscurity and plonked on a West End stage, and I was rubbish. It was such a lazy, condescending piece of writing.

He's free to have his opinion, but he's wrong, I thought.

People often think that the show that gives you your break is the first thing you've ever done. If only it was that easy! Most actors usually work for years in theatre, doing telly bits, all sorts of things, before – if they're lucky – they get their break. So it's quite frustrating to be written off as some young Welsh beginner who shouldn't be allowed on a West End stage.

Fat Pig was a smash hit. It starred Ella Smith, myself, Rob Webb and Kris Marshall and played to packed audiences at the Trafalgar Studios. Oh my God, it was such fun. When you're in a hit West End play it's like being in this amazing bubble. We just had a ball.

It was a tricky start, though. Kris Marshall had to miss the first couple of weeks of rehearsals because he'd been run over by a car and was still in hospital. Luckily, he got better in time to open with the rest of us and we went on to have a brilliant time working in the centre of London, right in the thick of things. James would often drive me to the theatre and drop me at the stage door, and be waiting for me after the performance, and most nights we'd go to the Groucho Club in Dean Street and get merrily drunk.

Fat Pig is a comedy critiquing our image-obsessed culture and prejudice towards plus-sized women. Ella Smith was playing Helen, a bigger girl, and Rob Webb's character falls in love with her. Jeannie, my character, and Carter, played by Kris Marshall, can't understand how he could love somebody who doesn't conform to 'normal' beauty standards.

During the run, I had the worst moment I've ever had on stage, while Rob Webb and I were doing a scene together. There was an understudy in place of Kris Marshall that night, which wasn't a problem until he came on, forgot where he was and in his panic skipped from the beginning of the scene all the way to the end of it.

Rob and I stood and stared at each other helplessly. *I've got nowhere to go*, I was thinking. *We're at the end of the scene and I don't know how to bring us back to where we should be.*

The silence seemed to go on for ever; stretching out time until it felt like a full ten minutes had passed since someone had spoken. The feeling of fear was overwhelming. There is nothing quite like drying onstage. You can feel the moment coming from a couple of lines previously, and the panic sets in. You continue acting in the scene, going through the motions, but in your head it's like a wildfire. Your brain is screaming, *What's coming next? What's my line? Oh my God, what do I do?* Then it comes to the moment when you're about to speak and you freeze in time and have no idea where you are, what you're doing or what comes next. Some actors manage to pick it back up and carry on; for others it can scar them for the rest of their career.

I was very close to turning to the audience and saying, 'I'm sorry, I've lost my place. I don't know what I'm doing. I'll just go and have a look at the script and come back.'

But then I came back to my senses, and we started making something up. Somehow we found our way back to the start of the scene and managed to pick it up and carry on.

Actors have a dread of drying on stage and if you have a moment like that and don't get through it, it might put you off going on stage for ever. So it felt freeing to have survived it. You realise it's not the end of the world. What's the worst that can happen? You turn to the audience and say, 'I'm sorry. I've completely forgotten it.' Then you walk off, find out what you're doing and walk back on.

In another scene, I had to slap Rob Webb, and we talked about it beforehand – should it be a big theatrical slap, or should I just slap him properly? He said, 'No, just do it properly. It'll look better.' It wasn't meant to be a huge dramatic fight or anything, so I slapped him properly across the face.

But one day, he was really getting on my nerves on stage – we'd been working together for a while – and I gave him a proper belter. Oh my God!

We stopped and looked at each other – we were so shocked. I hadn't realised how hard it was going to land and now there was a huge, flaming red handprint on his face. I remember getting off stage as fast as I could and hiding in my dressing room, in case he came in to shout at me, but luckily he didn't.

My publicist got in touch and said I'd been nominated for Best Comedy Actress in the *Glamour* Awards. I went with James and Mum and Dad. I loved being among so many fabulous women: Kate Beckinsale, Lily Allen, Fearne Cotton, Danii Minogue and Annie Lennox. David Gandy was there the second year I went. He was absolutely gorgeous!

I did a *Glamour* photo shoot beforehand, which was very exciting. I got to keep all the clothes, including a massive gold chain necklace with the Yves Saint Laurent YSL in chunky letters on it. Gorgeous for a photo, but I've never worn it in real life, I just couldn't. Day to day, or even to a party, I'd feel far too self-conscious with a huge YSL hanging off my neck.

Flash forward twenty years and my daughter Eva's getting ready to go to soft play. All of my old things are open to the kids – they treat it all like a fancy-dress box. As she's about to walk out the door, I turn to look at her and she's in the Isabel Marant trainers I bought in a moment of madness, but which have actually been the best value for money, and my massive gold YSL chain. She looked like Mr T from *The A-Team*.

'Get the necklace off, please,' I said. 'Go upstairs and put on jeans and a T-shirt.'

The *Glamour* stylist brought round a beautiful Matthew Williamson dress for me to wear at the awards. It was quite daring – short and split all the way down to the waist. I looked like a little blonde butterfly.

Before an awards ceremony, I'd have a make-up artist at the house, doing my hair as well, then I'd go all the way into town for a proper manicure. Now I think, 'What a waste of time!' I recently went to the BAFTAs and just filed my own nails and painted them pink. No one noticed.

'You need to get a fake tan,' the stylist said, and sent me for a St Tropez tan. For a St Tropez tan, you get painted with what I can only describe as gravy browning – a thick, dark brown substance all over your body. It stains your skin and it's streaky. Most people who have it done go home, wait twelve hours, wash it off and are left with a lovely glow. I had it done in the morning, and the awards were that evening after the show.

I had a matinee and evening show to get through, all while looking like my character was a cavewoman who had rolled around in mud before dressing up as a high-powered New York businesswomen.

Afterwards, I had a quick shower, did my own hair and make-up and jumped on the back of a motorbike that took me across town to meet James and my parents at the awards. Paul O'Grady was presenting. As I walked in, he said something lovely like, 'Yay, she's arrived.' And then he said, 'This whole evening was getting a bit snippy and sharp with the jokes. Thank God for a breath of fresh air.'

I walked up on stage, which was difficult as I'd been loaned a pair of Jimmy Choos and they were so high I couldn't straighten my legs properly. I accepted my award and said, 'I can't believe how many amazing women are here tonight. I'm so excited. This is fantastic.'

I was given a magnum of champagne because I'd won. That's four standard bottles in one, and my dad and James drank the lot. Mum and I didn't even get a glass.

Later on, Lily Allen was carried out of the awards in the arms of a security guard. Her dramatic exit and the press scrum around her meant that no one photographed me and Mum holding up my dad and James on the way out, and no one spotted how drunk they were.

'For God's sake, try and stand up straight,' I kept saying. 'There are loads of paparazzi outside. I do not want to see a story on the front of the newspaper about my husband and father crawling out of the *Glamour* Awards.'

We got them into the back of a car and sped off towards East Dulwich. Before long, James started heaving. I was stone-cold sober. I'd not really had a chance to have a drink, I was so busy looking after the boys. Even though I was enjoying everything – the dress, the laughs, the atmosphere – I was still me, I was still in work mode.

Earlier, we'd had to warn Mum about her behaviour. She'd turned up at the awards before me, with James and Dad, and was starstruck by all the celebrities. 'Oh my God, it's Kate Moss. Oh my God, it's Lily Allen.'

James looked over and saw that Mum had taken a notepad and pen out of her handbag and was writing things down.

'Sue, what are you doing?'

'I'm writing down all the celebrities' names so I can tell the girls in the office back home.'

'Sue, put the notepad away now.'

And now James was heaving. I was mortified. We had to stop at least once so that he could be sick. When we got home, James and Dad staggered towards the house and collapsed into the neighbour's hedge. We pulled them out, got them inside, and Dad went straight to bed. James walked upstairs, projectile-vomiting all the way.

That magnum of champagne was now spread across my stairway like it was some kind of modern art installation. We got him into bed and put a bowl beside him. Mum and I took our high heels off, got a bowl and a cloth and spent the rest of the night cleaning the stairs and walls – wiping down the sick, sterilising everything, scrubbing the carpets and spraying detergent on every surface.

When I finally finished, it was the early hours. I took off my beautiful Matthew Williamson designer dress, placed it carefully on a chair and went to bed.

And *that* was how I spent my evening on the night of the *Glamour* Awards 2008. The following year, I won the *Glamour* Magazine Best Theatre Actress award for *Fat Pig* and did it all again – this time in a fabulous Prada dress.

Gavin & Stacey was more popular than ever after the second series aired. A special episode was scheduled; the BBC wanted a third series and it was fantastic when James and Ruth decided they wanted to write it. I had other work and offers coming in as well – my career was flying.

So of course, as per my agent's rule about success, it had to follow that my personal life would break apart, and that's exactly what happened when my husband James decided to join the cast of *Emmerdale* in July 2009. He was cast as John Barton, an honest, hard-working farmer who is family-focused and quite fiery with it. The character was instantly popular and James enjoyed the camaraderie of working at *Emmerdale*. But we had to live separate lives and it was hard.

James started off living in Wakefield, where he rented the singer Jane McDonald's house, and he later moved to Leeds. He was up north solidly all week, coming home on a Friday and going back on a Sunday. Suddenly, I wasn't with my best mate, my soulmate, sitting and watching *Survivor*, eating our favourite pasta, him introducing me to olives and then me wanting olives in everything, cwtching up on the sofa – just us, cuddled up together. We spent so much time on the phone, feeling sad, missing each other. We just wanted to be with each other. It was awful.

So I was in this weird situation where there was all of this excitement surrounding *Gavin & Stacey* and everybody was talking about us, but I would go home after work and sit on my own watching telly. It should have been a time full of happiness and excitement. But it wasn't, because the one person I wanted to be with couldn't be there.

It showed us how strong the thread between us really was, because it was unbreakable, despite the distance between us. It was like that from the start – nothing could come between us. When we first met, although I'd seen him on TV and formed an idea of who he was, I didn't know who he really was, didn't know his personality. But there was just something about him – and before we'd even gone on a proper date, we were on the phone for hours, talking and talking.

We both felt that something. When you know, you know. *This is completely different to anything I've experienced before*, you're thinking. *I just want to stay up all night talking. I love everything about you. I don't have to try or pretend or be anything else. It's just all amazing with you.*

So being suddenly ripped away from that left us both with a desperate ache and longing. We started snapping and arguing when we were together, not because we were angry with each other, but because the situation was so frustrating and upsetting. You're like, *I've had enough now. I just want to talk to you and be with you.*

In the meantime, I was asked to shoot the December 2009 cover of *FHM*, a men's lifestyle magazine.

'It's their comedy issue, so it's not like doing a lads' mag cover,' Amy, my PR person, said. 'At the same time, I think it would be good for you to look sexy and gorgeous.'

As I'm not the sort of person who likes 'being sexy', I didn't think I was the sort of girl you'd put on the cover of *FHM*. But I said, 'Okay then, go on – stuff it.'

Altogether, 2009 was quite a year for me. I was also voted the sexiest woman in Wales in the *Western Mail* newspaper. I found out about it while we were filming the third and final series of *Gavin & Stacey*. Someone on-set told me.

'What? I had no idea,' I said.

It seemed so hilarious that I hunted down a copy, took photocopies and stuck it up on the mirror in the make-up truck.

'We're going to be adamant about what you will and won't wear for the *FHM* shoot – and what you will and won't do,' Amy said. 'We're going to stipulate absolutely no underwear, and absolutely no swimming costumes – nothing like that.'

Which all went out of the window – something I was becoming very used to!

We turned up at the studio and I was nervous. I'm not usually nervous on photo shoots: I can act, I can do poses; put a costume on me and I'm somebody completely different. But it's not the same when you're doing a sexy *FHM* cover.

When we walked in, there was a rack of clothing, but it was all bras and knickers. 'She's not going to be in her underwear,' Amy said.

They shrugged. 'This is what we've got.'

'Well, I just won't do it,' I said.

Another rack came out from somewhere. This had little dresses – much more suitable.

I went into hair and make-up and they made me look absolutely gorgeous. I put on big knickers and a slouchy vest for one shot, and a little bandeau dress for another. My hair was in a blonde bob. I felt bloody amazing.

Then I was put in front of the camera and I felt very stiff. It's difficult when it's just you and your body and you're expected to pull sexy poses. The fella who was directing the photo shoot was a real big bear of a guy. He had thick dark hair, a thick beard and a moustache; he was well built, older and very manly. He stood in front of me doing sexual poses and saying, 'Pose like this. Do this. Do that.' He looked incredible: he knew exactly how to align his body – which way to put his leg, how to shrug a shoulder, how to do a real doe-eyed sexy look. It was so peculiar to see this huge bear of a man doing the most feminine sexual poses I've ever seen.

I couldn't relax, so they opened a bottle of champagne and I proceeded to work my way through it. It was the only way I was going to loosen up. We carried on doing the shoot, and this man just stood in front of me posing while I drank a bottle of champagne and copied the moves he was doing.

Afterwards, I had to do an interview, and I found it just as peculiar as the shoot. 'What kind of man do you go for? What specifically do you like? What would you like a man to do?'

I found it hilarious. 'I don't go for any sort of man. Somebody comes up to me that I fancy, and if I like talking to him – that's what I go for.'

I put it down to experience. I've got the magazine at home and so have Mum and Dad. They've still got it pinned on the wall in the cupboard under the stairs.

Over Christmas 2009, not only was I on the cover of *FHM*, there was also a Christmas Eve special of *Gavin & Stacey* on BBC One and I was playing Cinderella at the New Woking Theatre with Michael Aspel and Jon Lee from S Club. So things were going quite well and from an outsider's perspective it all looked wonderful and amazing. *But it isn't amazing*, I thought, because I was desperately missing James. *It's not much fun at all.*

By the way, if you watch the *Gavin & Stacey* special again, you'll notice I have no voice in all of the bits in Marks & Spencer. I'd just come off the back of doing panto and when you go into panto, straight away you get ill because you're working with children. If you don't have kids yourself, you don't have any resistance to all the germs spreading from their coughs and colds. You get really sick, then you get a cold, and you're pushing and straining your throat every day, and then you lose your voice. And that's what had happened. I was growling like a bear.

One time I was hiding behind the set onstage with the ugly sister and he was coughing and coughing because he'd become so ill from being around all the schoolkids. He coughed into his handkerchief and brought up blood, and as I saw the bright red spray land in the hanky, I thought, *Oh my God. I'm going to catch this next.*

Then we both had to put a smile on our faces, walk out onto the stage and carry on acting.

Now and then I went to visit James, and we started talking about making a permanent move up to the north of England. James had grown up watching *Emmerdale* and the set was near his childhood home and his family. He was well suited to the role of John Barton and it was potentially a job for life. It made sense for us to settle near his work.

'Let's sell the place in London,' I suggested. 'Shall we move to Hebden Bridge? We can settle down there.'

'Are you sure?' James asked.

'Yes, I'll do the travelling instead. I don't mind.'

Hebden Bridge is a beautiful, vibrant market town in West Yorkshire, with a river running through it. We started looking at flats and houses and it was all quite exciting. But as time went on, I began to have doubts about moving. I was daunted by the prospect of living somewhere unfamiliar. And how much independence would I be giving up? I had visions of sitting in a flat on my own waiting for James to come home from work.

I changed my mind. 'I don't think I can live all the way up here,' I said. 'It's so far away from everything. So far from my parents. I'll just be stuck here. I want to be working, I want my own life.'

So we carried on being apart during the week and together at weekends – and we went on missing each other and arguing because of it. Long-distance marriage is impossible.

In February 2010, about nine months after James had started on *Emmerdale*, I was at home in East Dulwich, upstairs in the attic, when I had a phone call from him. As we weren't actually speaking, after arguing earlier in the day, I thought, *I'm not answering that!* So I didn't.

He left a message on the answer machine, saying, 'Hi, it's me. I'm just outside the supermarket on Lordship Lane. I've been run over. I'm in an ambulance. Can you come?'

I didn't think twice – I ran out of the house to the end of our road and there was the ambulance. I went straight over to it, opened up the back doors and saw James lying on a stretcher inside. 'Don't come in!' the paramedics warned me.

'I'm his wife!' I said, climbing in.

It's funny what shock does to you. I'd just bought James a lovely cream woollen cardigan, similar to one I'd seen David Beckham wearing. That was the first thing I noticed – there was blood all over it.

Lying on the stretcher, James told me he'd been crossing the road and hadn't looked before he walked out. A car was coming really fast down Lordship Lane and went straight into him. It hit him on the side; the force of the impact threw him up into the air and then he came down, boom, headfirst onto the windscreen, smashed the windscreen with his head and landed on the ground, breaking his leg. The car kept on going and disappeared up the road.

James said he somehow managed to stand up and start walking down the middle of the road, trying to find his phone. Blood was pouring from his head and people were shouting to him. Later, the car came back.

Somebody phoned for an ambulance. He'd split his head open, but he was walking around. When the ambulance arrived he found his phone and called me, and that's when I ran out to find him.

We rushed down to the hospital and they took him straight in. As I waited in the family room, someone came out to warn me that he might have sustained brain damage. It was terrifying. I was so worried for him. 'All his vital signs seem fine, but he landed on his head and smashed a windscreen, so we can't be sure how badly he's been injured,' they said.

They stitched his head up and then he went into surgery to have his broken leg seen to. For weeks afterwards, he had a full leg cast and was on crutches. When he went back to *Emmerdale*, they had to write into the script that he'd been kicked by a cow.

In the meantime, I looked after him and did everything for him because he couldn't do anything for himself. He literally couldn't walk. One time, when he was sitting on the toilet, I was on all fours in front of him, with his leg propped up on my back so he could go to the loo. I looked up at him and said, 'There are men who would pay a lot of money for me to do this!'

Soon after James had gone back to *Emmerdale*, a Kay Mellor script came in with a potentially interesting part for me. I'd always wanted to work with Kay, but her characters were usually all northern and got snapped up by northern actors. I was over the moon. Set in Leeds, the first series of *The Syndicate* is about a betting syndicate of five supermarket workers who win a significant amount of money on the Lottery. My character, Leanne, comes 'from somewhere else' and so I could be Welsh, which was amazing – at last! Working with Kay Mellor was like working with TV royalty.

So often I went for auditions and they'd say, 'That's absolutely brilliant! You're perfect for it. But can you do a different accent from your own?'

God, just for once, can I just not have my own voice in something dramatic? I'd think. And, in *The Syndicate*, I could.

Leanne was a great role, with real emotional heft. I was working alongside Timothy Spall, Lorraine Bruce and Matthew McNulty. My character has a secret: she has run away with her foster daughter to stop her daughter's birth mother, a drug user, from claiming her back. She's on the run, terrified, and falling in love with Matthew McNulty's character.

There's a big scene where I'm crying and admitting that I've run away from my husband, and it involves a very long monologue. Kay Mellor's granddaughter was playing my daughter and, as part of the scene, Kay wanted a shot where a butterfly lands on her granddaughter's arm. It took ages and ages to get this butterfly shot and meanwhile I was walking around with headphones on, listening to music, trying to stay in the mood and be ready to go. Half an hour before the end of the day, Kay said, 'Right, Jo, you can do your monologue now.'

I was a wreck by then, but I managed to get through it.

Around this time, James started getting restless at *Emmerdale*. Long-running dramas have rules that limit what other projects actors can be involved with and he wanted to be free to do his voiceovers and other acting.

Eventually, he decided he wanted to move on and do something else. And, after nearly three years of living apart, things had come to a head between us. 'We can't do this any more,' we decided.

We needed to be together. So James asked to be written out of the show and his character was killed off. It was such a relief when he came home.

Glad that we hadn't bought anywhere in Hebden Bridge, we picked up our life again in London, hoping we could go back to how things had been. Sometimes I think I would have been happy for James to earn the money and do his voiceovers while I had loads and loads of kids, worked in my shoe shop and enjoyed baking ... and we would have been fine. I'm not saying I didn't absolutely love the work I was doing in *Gavin & Stacey*, because I did. It's everything else that gets in the way and complicates things.

We had begun to think about moving out of London. We wanted a quieter life and to settle down. There was a hospital down the road from where we lived and you'd often get patients turning up, knocking on the door, screaming outside the house or asking, 'Does Stacey live here?'

It was starting to get a bit worrying. Sometimes I'd get followed down the road, which I didn't like. And then, one night, James and I were watching telly when suddenly we heard this weird banging. And it wasn't just one bang – it was over and over again. When we looked out the window, there was a fella smashing up our neighbour's brand-new Porsche with a huge bit of wood. Our neighbour was standing just a few feet away, watching in a horrified trance.

The fella set fire to the inside of the car and it went up in a fireball of flames and smoke. James and I ran outside and stood there in shock.

The police came. They dragged the fella away and put him in the police car. As they were shutting the door, he turned to the four of us – James and his wife, and me and my James – and yelled, 'I am the devil! You're all gonna burn in hell. I'm going to kill all of you.'

They drove him off and we were left thinking, *Yeah, this is all getting a bit too much now.*

11

Everything changes

All of a sudden, at thirty-five, I woke up one morning feeling unbelievably broody. It hit me like a wave. I said, 'Right, that's it. I want a baby. I need to have a baby.'

It was such a shift because, up until then, I'd never been interested in kids. I'd never looked at children and thought, 'Oh, aren't they lovely!' I just didn't connect. I think a lot of that came from being an only child. I was used to my own company. I hadn't experienced brothers and sisters, or having a newborn in the house. I was an actress, after all, and the work was my baby. I looked on children – especially groups of them in cafes and the like – as a bit of a nuisance. Loud and annoying.

I'd never pictured myself having children. Same as I never really wanted to get married. I wasn't that little girl dreaming of a white dress or a big wedding. I was always a bit tomboy-ish, and I was just fine as I was.

James says that when he married me, I made it clear that I wasn't interested in having kids. I couldn't even imagine it. But all the way through our marriage – the ten years we were together before we even talked about having kids – he kept thinking, *She'll want children one day.* He never pushed it, never said anything, just quietly hoped, God love him. And then, that morning, I proved him right.

We were still in East Dulwich at that point. 'I want to move out of London. I want to be closer to Swansea, closer to Mum and Dad,' I said. 'Because if I'm going to have a baby, I want to be near them.'

Finding Lavender Cottage in Oxfordshire felt like magic. It was absolutely gorgeous – a thatched cottage with two acres, a lovely little pond and two ducks we called Michael and Mabel. There was a field next to us, and all the cows would stick their heads over the fence. We'd feed them apples and talk to them. James was over the moon because he had a ride-on mower. It was the proper countryside dream and we absolutely loved it.

I got pregnant straight away.

I remember going into the downstairs loo, chatting away to James, not even telling him I was doing a test. I weed on the stick and carried on nattering, looked down, and this big blue cross came up so quickly, so strongly – I was in complete shock.

I shouted, 'James! Oh my God, quick, quick!' And he came running in, and we were both flabbergasted. We were staring at it, stunned – me in total disbelief that it had happened so fast, and him absolutely over the moon, but cautious too.

Mum had been telling me for years, 'You need to have children while you're young, because you don't know if you'll be able to have them later.' It was drilled into me that I'd probably have problems getting pregnant. So when I got pregnant so quickly, I was astounded.

I started looking everything up online, finding out what

to do next. Instinctively, I wanted to go to a birthing centre, be surrounded by doulas and midwives, fully embrace the hypno-birthing. But quite early on, I changed my mind and decided I was going to go private. I was scared of ending up in a hospital with no bed, or no room, and I had Mum's miscarriages and ectopic pregnancies in the back of my mind, so I didn't want to take the risk.

We weren't the kind of people who spent big money on cars or holidays. We barely even went on holiday before we had kids. As actors, we'd think, *We can't go away in case we get a voiceover, or a job comes in.* Now I look back and think, *Why didn't we just go travelling?* I think we only ever managed three holidays together; it was always work, work, work. And that work was unpredictable.

Stuff it, I thought. *All the money we haven't spent on holidays or cars, I'm going to put into going private, because that will make me feel secure and happy.*

I found a wonderful obstetrician on Harley Street, who I will call Samir. He delivered babies at the Lindo Wing at St Mary's Hospital. I thought if it's good enough for the royals, it's good enough for me. I went to see him when I was nine weeks pregnant, feeling nervous and out of place.

'Hello, how can I help you?' he said when I walked in.

'I read online that you delivered an eleven-pound baby naturally,' I said. 'I think I'm nine weeks pregnant, and I want you to deliver mine.'

He had the most calming and reassuring presence. 'Right, okay, let's have a look and see if there's a baby in there first.'

He gave me a scan, and there it was – I was clearly pregnant.

'I've decided I don't want any pain relief,' I told him. 'No epidural. I want it all to be natural.'

'Well, you're only nine weeks pregnant, so we don't need to think about any of that just yet,' he said. 'That can be further down the line, when you decide what you're going to do and what you're not going to do.' And then he added, 'Personally, I find writing birth plans a bit of a waste of time, because nothing ever really goes according to plan.'

It was all new to me, so I didn't know what to expect. But I was in full-on planning mode at the beginning, even though I had no clue what was coming.

Morning sickness hit and it was horrific. I reassured myself with the thought that it could mean it was a strong pregnancy. Even though there's no fact behind that at all, it definitely helped me endure it. I'd wake up in the morning and start being sick. And it wouldn't stop. I'd be sick through the day, into the evening – just this constant nausea. I'd walk around the garden, my mind in a fog, and lie out on the grass trying to feel normal. I had all sorts of herbal remedies; I wore sickness bands on my wrists; I honestly don't think I could have eaten any more ginger if I tried. Nothing worked – except nibbling on huge quantities of M&S Percy Pigs.

I started voicing a character in *Q Pootle 5*, an animated cartoon for children about aliens. I play Oopsy, a little pink alien. The first session was fab. The other actors and I were all together in the booth and it was brilliant fun. For the second session, I arrived with two Tesco carrier bags full of Percy Pigs and other sweets to suck on, and loads of cans of Coke to sip all day. When I told the producers I was pregnant a few weeks later, they said, 'We did have an inkling. It was either that or a hangover, because you didn't stop eating and had to go to the toilet all the time.'

I was kind of freaked out by the whole thing at first. I remember walking into Mamas & Papas in Reading, looking around and thinking, *No, fuck this.* I turned straight around and walked out. The whole thing overwhelmed me, and I stayed like that for a good few weeks.

By about twenty weeks, though, I started to settle into it. We'd found out the sex really early on – I'd had a blood test – so we knew it was going to be a little girl. Although, to be honest, I was fine either way. I think being an only child myself, and knowing Mum's history, I thought, *You're lucky to get one healthy baby, whatever the sex is.*

Mum was over the moon it was a girl. I think she had this vision of me dressing her up in all these pretty outfits. But in reality, all I ever put Eva in were white babygrows, because they were easy to clean and to get on and off.

I was still really struggling with the morning sickness, but feeling better about the pregnancy, so I went back to Mamas & Papas and bought a soft little Shetland rocking horse. You could press its ear and it made clip-clopping noises. It was just this sweet little thing the baby could sit on. I took it home and put it in what was going to be the nursery, and that was it – I didn't buy anything else until right at the very end, because I had this feeling that buying things too early might jinx it. No clothes, no baby stuff. Just that one little pony in the corner of the room.

Everything seemed to be going well until I went in for my twenty-week scan. The sonographer was scanning away, all very casual. 'Yeah, everything looks absolutely great. Baby's looking lovely.' Then she paused and said, 'Have you been bleeding?'

'No, not at all.'

'Good. Well, just so you know, if you do bleed and it's bright red shooting down your legs, you need to call an ambulance straight away and get to hospital. If it's more of a brownish blood, that's old blood and it's okay – don't worry about that.'

'Hang on . . . what?' I said. 'Why are you saying this? Why would I be bleeding?'

'Don't worry, just go upstairs now and see Samir. He'll talk you through it.'

I was absolutely beside myself, thinking, 'What the hell's going on?'

Samir read through the notes and said, 'Okay, don't panic. At the moment, your placenta is lying low and growing over your cervix. What we hope is that as the pregnancy progresses, the uterus will grow and the placenta will shift with it and clear the cervix. If that happens, everything should be fine.'

'And what if it doesn't?'

'We don't need to think about that yet. Just focus on the week you're in. Don't go too far ahead.'

'Please, just tell me,' I said. 'If the placenta is covering the cervix, does that mean the baby can't come out? Will the baby just stay in there and die, or something?'

'Oh my goodness, no, not at all. It just means you'll need to have a C-section.'

'Oh! Is that all? That's absolutely fine.'

I think he thought I wouldn't take it well because I'd been so adamant about wanting everything to be natural. But when you're suddenly faced with something serious like placenta previa, you're not about to get upset that you won't have a vaginal birth. Or I wasn't, anyway. All I cared about was that my baby would be okay.

'Here's what we're expecting,' he went on. 'Because the placenta's covering your cervix and the baby's pressing down on it, as things progress and the pressure increases you'll probably start to bleed. We're hoping to get you to about thirty weeks – thirty-two would be ideal – but you'll most likely have some bleeds. Probably around three and, after the third one, that's when we'll need to deliver the baby.'

I sat there thinking, *Oh my God!* It was so much to take in. Nan, who'd been a hospital matron, understood how serious it was. Apparently, she said quietly to my mum afterwards, 'It's quite worrying. She's probably going to haemorrhage.'

They were really worried, but no one told me just how serious it was at the time.

'The first two bleeds should stop on their own and we'll keep them under control,' Samir said. 'But that third one will likely be big, and when it happens, we'll need to get the baby out.'

He told me not to think too far ahead. By that point I had about a million books and was reading everything I could get my hands on, obsessing over every little thing I was eating – what was healthy, what nutrients I needed, what to avoid. I was trying to do everything right.

But when the morning sickness hit, all the careful planning went out the window. Suddenly, none of it mattered – the nutrition, the green veg, the perfectly balanced meals. I was simply trying to survive the day sustained by a can of Coke and a bag of Percy Pigs.

'Forget being healthy,' I decided. 'I'm vomiting in public, into a bag, in front of everyone. I just need sugar and something fizzy I can keep down.'

I took Samir's advice about the books and binned them. 'I'm going to be like a cow in a field,' I said to myself.

You never see a pregnant cow freaking out about what to eat or reading pregnancy books. She's just standing there, chewing some grass, totally in the moment. Not overthinking, not planning, not panicking. Just pregnant and present. So that's what I decided to be – pregnant and present.

I told everyone around me, 'I'm not talking about it. I'm just getting through it, week by week.'

Around week twenty-six, the sickness finally lifted. Thank God. It had felt like having the flu constantly – aching shoulders, heavy limbs, total exhaustion and constant nausea. But then, almost overnight, it just stopped. And I was starving.

All I wanted was fatty food. Nando's. Spicy chicken. Chips. Burgers. Anything greasy. I was drinking pints of milk. I was like Christian Bale bulking up for a movie role: I didn't stop eating.

Around week thirty, the day before Christmas Eve, I woke up in the middle of the night feeling a bit off. I went to the loo and looked down. My knickers were full of brown blood.

I know now how much you can actually bleed during pregnancy without it being an emergency, and that brown blood means it's old blood. But back then, I was totally panicked. I shook James awake: 'I'm bleeding!' He leapt up.

We phoned Samir's office and I was told to come into the Lindo Wing the next day. Samir was away on holiday, so I was seen by Guy Thorpe-Beeston, who I later found out assisted in delivering Prince George. That's my weird little claim to fame: the man who delivered the future king of England had his hand up my vagina. My friends all found it hilarious.

'Yes, there's been a small bleed, but everything looks fine,' he said. 'You're not bleeding now, but we'll keep you in overnight. I'll check on you in the morning, and if everything's still okay, you can go home.'

So I stayed in and it was honestly one of the loveliest Christmas Eves I've ever had. My parents and James came to visit and brought me a big box of Roses; I had the TV on with carols and hymns playing late into the night. You could hear babies being born on the ward – and the odd scream, which was slightly off-putting, admittedly – but then you'd hear the babies crying, and it was actually really beautiful.

Everyone went home, and I lay in bed with my little baby

in my belly, and I felt so peaceful. We'd already decided on her name – Eva Page Russell. Eva because we loved it, Page after my maiden name, and Russell, of course, was our married name.

So that was my first bleed. I stayed overnight, was looked after and everything was fine. Guy came back to check me over on Christmas Day, said, 'You're good to go,' and I went home.

Two weeks later, I was back home, in bed again, and I woke up in the middle of the night needing the loo. I went to the bathroom, looked down and – oh my God – it was everything the sonographer had warned me about. All I could see were bright red lines, shooting from my groin down to my ankles. So fast you wouldn't believe it. Line after line of blood, just pouring. At first I froze – and then I started screaming for James.

He came running in, saw the state of me, and phoned for an ambulance. I didn't know what to do, so I lay on my back and shoved my legs in the air, thinking, *Right, that'll hold the baby in.*

I remember seeing the blue lights of the ambulance as it pulled up outside the house. I jumped to my feet, yanked on a pair of leggings, shoved a towel down there and sprinted for the back door. I was huge by then – I wasn't one of those women with a tidy bump. I was five foot one and a half and round. But adrenaline kicked in, and I bolted down the stairs and straight into the ambulance.

They were trying to calm me: 'Slow down, slow down – it's okay.' But I was in and already handing over my notes.

As we were racing down to the Royal Berkshire Hospital, the paramedics were chatting away, trying to keep things light – asking me if there'd be more *Gavin & Stacey*, talking about *Emmerdale* with James. Paul Daniels was mentioned. Anything, I think, to keep me calm. And it worked – for a bit.

About halfway through the journey, my blood pressure dropped. I started shaking uncontrollably – not just trembling, but properly shaking, like I was having a seizure. I couldn't stop. I just lay there, shivering violently.

One of them said, 'You might be delivering this baby as soon as we get there.'

When we arrived, they rushed me straight in on a gurney. I was taken into a room next to theatre. It was a Saturday night and there were loads of junior staff around, buzzing in and out. There was one student doctor, bless her, who looked like she was about to faint.

They scanned me and confirmed that my placenta was covering the cervix and wrapped right round the front of my bump. The student doctor was panicking, properly freaking out. I could hear her saying, 'I can't do it. I can't operate. I'm not qualified to do this. I can't cut through. She's just going to bleed.'

Another voice – maybe one of the senior midwives – was saying, 'He's in bed. You need to phone him and get him here now.' I think they were talking about the consultant.

I turned to James and said, 'Just phone Samir.'

We were two hours away from the Lindo Wing, out in the middle of Oxfordshire. My plan at the beginning – actually, my *idea* of how it would all go – was that my waters would break and I'd say, 'Oh gosh, we've probably got about thirty-six hours now before the baby comes. Let's calmly get in the car, drive down to Paddington, park up, and then I'll go in and have the baby.'

That was the fantasy.

But babies don't come like that.

That's when I realised: forget having a bloody birth plan. There *is* no plan. The shit hits the fan and you just deal with what's in front of you. You don't get choices, you just react.

I was still haemorrhaging, like properly pouring out blood. It was terrifying. James phoned Samir and told him what was going on. Samir said, 'Don't let them operate. The bleeding will stop.'

James was panicking. 'She's losing so much blood! She's bleeding out.'

'It will stop.'

Meanwhile, they were prepping me for theatre. I was gowned up, lying there, still bleeding. James was gowned up too, trying to lighten the mood – typical him – by sneaking gas and air off the wall. He was off his face, giggling away, until one of the midwives caught him and told him off.

Then, just before they took me in, they examined me again and the bleeding had completely stopped. They scanned me, checked the baby – heartbeat perfect, everything fine. It was like nothing had even happened.

'Okay, we're not going to operate. We'll just monitor you now.'

They moved me up onto the ward and said, 'We want you to rest and do absolutely nothing.'

I stayed there for about three days. There was no more bleeding and everything calmed down. I was examined regularly by anyone and everyone.

'We've just been watching *Love Actually* in the staffroom,' one of the nurses said.

'By the time I leave here, you lot are going to have seen *literally* every inch of me,' I giggled.

They decided to transfer me to London, so off I went to St Mary's for about a week.

And that's when I met the most wonderful girl – Eleanor – who was in the bed opposite me. She had a similar situation to me, except she wasn't allowed to move *at all* – not even walk around – because she had a weak cervix and had to stay in until the baby was delivered.

We hit it off and instantly started talking about baby names. I said that I was going to call my baby Eva Page Russell. I must have mentioned Daisy, my little Jack Russell, at some point, and Eleanor, whose husband was Dutch, said, 'You know, in Dutch, the word "Madelief" means daisy.'

What a lovely name! I thought. *I'll call her Eva Madelief Russell.*

It felt like it was meant to be, even though I've got no links to anything Dutch, aside from Eleanor! Daisy was basically my first baby and I was carrying all this guilt worrying about how I was supposed to look after a baby and a Jack Russell and love them both the same. So it felt like a way to include her, to connect her to the new baby.

So Eva became Eva Madelief Russell.

Eleanor also said that if she had a son she was going to call him Kick. I thought that was a really cool name. At the same time, I couldn't call my son Kick because someone in the school playground would definitely kick him. But I loved the sound of it. It had this sharpness, this energy. So James and I decided, if we ever had another child and it was a boy, we'd call him Kit, which had the same feel, just softer. Still strong and cool, but less likely to get him literally kicked.

I stayed in St Mary's for about a week. I was in bed, binge-watching *Breaking Bad* while stitching a flower pattern onto a handbag. That was me, for days – drug labs on the screen and delicate embroidery on my lap.

Then Samir came in and said, 'Right, I want you out of bed, and you need to make a decision. If you go back to Oxfordshire and you bleed again – that'll be the one. That's when the baby's coming. If you want to be delivered there, fine. But if you want me to deliver the baby and you want to be here in London, you've got to stay nearby.'

I must have been about thirty-three weeks by then, and I felt more relaxed. 'Okay, we've passed thirty-two weeks. The baby's lungs are probably developed enough. We're going to be all right.'

'I want you walking around,' Samir said. 'Go and see the sights, get some fresh air. You've been in bed too long. Get up and about.'

So James and I booked a hotel right next to the hospital and, while James went off to do voiceovers, I pottered. Each day, I'd get up, go for a wander around the area, nip into some shops, get a bit of food. Then I'd go back to the hotel and switch off. I'd play *Plants vs. Zombies* on my iPad, watch *30 Rock* and eat loads of Maltesers.

When I think about it now, I'd kill to have a whole week to wander about and stay in a hotel. At the time, though, I was bored out of my mind. Because we weren't at home, I couldn't nest. There was no chance of cleaning floors or anything useful like that in the hotel. All I had was the baby's rucksack and I'd been unpacking and repacking it obsessively – folding all the baby clothes, taking them out, refolding them, putting them back in. I spent some of the day wandering the streets of London doing a bit of shopping. I bought chocolate. I went to Patisserie Valerie and ate omelettes and great big ice-cream sundaes. But mostly I stayed in my room and played *Plants vs. Zombies* on my iPad while eating Maltesers.

The night before I gave birth, Ruth Jones came and kept me company while James was at work. She was just adorable. Honestly, the memories and laughs we've shared from *Gavin & Stacey* – she knows me so well, and I absolutely love her. She was brilliant. She told me about having just been interviewed on the same sofa as Jedward and what an experience that had been. After she left, James got back from doing his voiceovers, and I realised the baby had stopped moving.

'We need to go to the hospital,' James said.

'No, no, no,' I said.

Every time something big happens, I freeze – I completely refuse to move. Half of it is that I hate making a fuss. I don't want to turn up somewhere and have people flapping around me. And the other half is probably some animal instinct, saying, 'Stay away from me, I'll just deal with this alone.' So I stayed put.

James was worried sick. I couldn't sleep. I lay there eating Maltesers and playing *Plants vs. Zombies* all night. At about half past seven in the morning, I finally shut my eyes and crashed out. Then, around half past nine, I woke up and sat up in bed, feeling completely normal – because with placenta previa, you don't feel pain when you're bleeding – and when I pulled the bed sheets back, honest to God, it was like a bloodbath. There was blood everywhere. I'd been haemorrhaging in my sleep.

I jumped out of bed and shouted for James. He went into shock at the sight of the bed soaked with blood. The rucksack happened to be empty because I'd unpacked it the day before and now I was grabbing anything – babygrow, hat, nappies – and shoving them into the bag. No toiletries. No slippers. Just the bare minimum.

I phoned the hospital. 'I'm on my way and I'm bleeding.'

'Okay, we'll be waiting for you,' they said.

James was still rushing to get dressed, but I was already out the door. He kept yelling, 'Slow down! You're going to make the bleeding worse!' But I was sprinting.

I got to the lift and was pressing the button like mad. When it came, I heard someone cry, 'Hold the lift!' and a man ambled in slowly. When he saw me – a massive, manic, round pregnant woman with a towel stuffed between her legs and a rucksack on her back – he rushed in and hit the button.

He could see this was serious.

As soon as the doors opened, I was off. James was still calling after me, 'Slow down! Please slow down!' but I was running as fast as a big round ball can run, which actually, it turns out, is quite fast. I legged it down the road in Paddington, not saying a word – absolutely focused – straight to the Lindo Wing.

With James right behind me, I ran past the desk, straight into the lift, shot all the way up to where they were waiting for me. I stripped off, got the gown on and went straight into the operating theatre. Looking back now, I think that was actually the best thing. Everything was moving so fast, I didn't have time to look around at all the medical instruments laid out, or think, 'Oh God, they're about to cut me open.' There wasn't time to get scared.

They got me up onto the table and told me to hunch forward for the epidural. That bit was honestly the worst. The thought of a needle going into my spine was horrible. But I bent over and thought, *Just don't move.* It wasn't pleasant, but it was quick, and then they laid me back down. All of a sudden, my body went completely numb. It was the weirdest feeling. I felt like a cow. My limbs were so heavy, and I remember thinking, *They're going to have to lift me like a slab of meat.*

I asked, 'How will I know it's worked?'

'It's all about temperature,' they said. They sprayed something cold down my body. 'Does it feel cold?' I couldn't feel a thing and that meant it had worked.

Within five minutes, I could smell burning – a cauterising smell, like a hot soldering iron. That was the scalpel. And then, within about eight minutes, she was out. Eva Madelief Russell, born on 15 February 2013, at thirty-four weeks and five days.

There is a curtain between you and the surgeon so that you

can't see all the cutting and rummaging that goes on when you're having a C-section. When they dropped the curtain down and lifted her up for me to see, oh my God, she was absolutely perfect. Six pounds, four ounces – teeny-tiny. Like a little doll. Her ears were bruised because they had to pull her out quite forcefully, but she was just so, so beautiful.

The day before, I'd said to James, 'What if I don't love it as much as I love the dog? Genuinely, what if I just don't feel anything? What if I don't want to look after it?' and he'd said, 'Don't worry. If you don't want to, I'll do everything.'

But the second they placed her on my chest, I completely fell in love. It was instant.

They wheeled me into the recovery room and I couldn't stop looking at her. She was this perfect little thing. I love babies when they're tiny and like little hedgehogs, all snuffly and wriggly and curled up.

There was no need for her to have any special care. 'Let's get her on the boob straight away,' one of the midwives said.

I've always been completely flat-chested my whole life, right into my thirties, and there I was, propped up with a muslin across me, and they put her on the boob. I was so tired, completely out of it, and she wasn't interested in feeding. All she wanted to do was cwtch and drift off.

Then, all of a sudden, I was absolutely soaking. It felt like water was pouring out from under my arms. 'I'm sweating buckets,' I said.

The midwife smiled. 'No, it's your milk. Your milk's come in.'

I couldn't believe it. In the space of about ten minutes, my boobs had ballooned. I'm not joking; they looked like watermelons and were rock solid. I've never seen anything like it in my life. They'd just exploded. At the time I had no idea that I came from a line of women with superhero milk supplies, but I later learned that it ran in the family: my nan had always had loads of milk and my auntie Edna, Nan's sister, had such an oversupply that, when she had her boys, she'd hand express the excess and give it to premature babies.

Eva was sleepy and not really latching properly, but I was determined to breastfeed, so we started hand-pumping. I was exhausted. I was sitting upright in bed, nodding in and out of sleep, barely there.

The midwife said, 'Do you mind if we help express for you?'

I was so tired. 'Honestly, do what you like,' I said.

It's difficult to hand-express milk unless you've got the hang of it, and having such solid boobs made it twice as tricky. Luckily, James had goats when he was growing up, so he knew exactly what to do. His technique was amazing. So there I was, fast asleep in the middle of the bed, James on one side milking one boob and the midwife on the other side milking the other. Quite early on, you realise that dignity goes out the window.

We'd collect my milk in a syringe and try to feed Eva with that, gently squeezing little drops into her mouth. But she just wasn't feeding. I remember the midwife leaning in and saying, 'You can do it, Eva. Come on, you can do it.'

They were all so lovely, so encouraging.

When it was time to go home, one midwife wasn't happy about us going, because Eva was beginning to go orange. You could see it in her skin that she looked jaundiced. They said, 'Look, we can't let you go yet. We need to do some tests, check her jaundice levels. She'll probably have to go under the lamp.'

I was secretly relieved because I was absolutely shattered and more than happy to stay another night. Midwives and staff kept popping in to see us – they were so sweet and kind – but I was just wrecked.

On top of this, I was severely constipated. Nobody told me that after a Caesarean, with all the codeine and medication, you stop going to the loo. And as the days were going by, it got so bad that I was doubled over with pain. I genuinely wondered if you could die from not pooing.

Eventually, one of the midwives came in and said, 'We're going to give you a suppository.' She put it down and left the room to get something. 'I'll come in and help you in a minute.'

No, you won't, I thought. *I've been poked and prodded enough – I'm doing this one myself, thank you very much.*

James was in stitches because I was off that bed and into the bathroom like lightning. I probably set a record for fastest self-administered suppository.

We stayed the extra night. They even put a little sign outside our door saying, 'Please don't disturb.' I passed out completely and slept so deeply.

Eva went under the UV lamp for her jaundice and it worked. Her colour came back and she was doing much better, so we were finally allowed to go home.

Leaving the hospital, that first time you put your baby into the car seat – it's just mad. Surreal. And I could barely walk. I'd had abdominal surgery for the first time in my life, and everything felt fragile and strange.

'The first song that plays is going to be Eva's song,' we decided, turning the radio on. Straight away, 'Diamonds' by Rihanna came on. I sat there crying.

We drove home extra slowly, taking it easy over every lump and bump in the road. I was terrified she'd wake up, or that the jolts would somehow harm her. Before we left the hospital, I'd fed her loads and expressed a huge amount, about 80 ml. I didn't realise that the more you express, the more your milk comes in – I hadn't got my head around the whole rhythm of feeding yet. I was just winging it.

And then suddenly I was back home, with this tiny baby in my arms. I remember walking through the front door and seeing Daisy, our dog, who honestly must have thought I'd died, because I'd just disappeared. I passed Eva to James and Daisy jumped into my arms. Then we walked Eva around the house, taking her into each room and introducing her to it all, and I held Daisy as we went. It felt very special. 'This is your home now.'

And so began the whirlwind that comes with having a newborn. I got into bed and basically stayed there. I'd lost a lot of blood, and they ended up giving me iron tablets and a Bavarian iron supplement. I just couldn't get up. I had Eva in bed with me, feeding her constantly, cuddling her. I was so wiped out – completely exhausted and totally depleted. I was low on iron, sore from surgery and emotionally all over the place.

And then, two weeks after I'd given birth, my agent phoned.

'You need to get into London to audition for a period drama called *Breathless*,' she said. 'It's for ITV and it's a series about gynaecology in the NHS in the early 1960s. It's going to be the new *Mad Men*.'

And for the first time in my life, I thought, *No, I don't want to.*

12

Escape to the countryside

As an actor, you're conditioned to say yes. You say yes to every audition, every opportunity – because you have to. That's just the way it is.

This time, for the first time, I didn't want to go. I didn't want to be part of this brilliant new show. I just wanted to stay in bed. With my baby. But – because I'm an actress – I said, 'Okay, I'll go.' Even though I was still bleeding, still totally spaced out, still in recovery.

I wasn't expressing milk, then; I was feeding on demand. I'd bought Gina Ford's book – the one that tells you to feed at this time, wake the baby for half an hour, then put them back down – and I realised quickly it wasn't for me. I'd never really thought how much structure or routine I would like as a mum, but it turned out that I wasn't very regimented. Wherever we were, and whenever Eva cried, I'd just get my boob out and feed her. I was fine just going with the flow. But this led to some quite wonderfully embarrassing moments for my mum.

One day, we were walking by the river and Eva was having a huge crying fit. Looking back now, as a mum of four, I can see that she was overtired and just needed to be walked to sleep in the pram. But, as usual, with the slightest hint of a cry, I decided to sit on the floor, get my boob out and feed. Mum managed to drag me into a local cafe, which was heaving, with the only table and chairs right in the middle of everyone. We managed to squeeze through, sit down and then I unleashed the biggest bosoms I think anyone had ever seen.

The problem was, Eva was so tired and fussy that I just couldn't get her to latch on. Every time I tried, she'd wrench her head away, screaming, starting my milk going and leaving me to spray across the next table. Mum was mortified. 'Come on, Mum, we're going,' I announced, battling my way through the tables again.

When we first got home from the hospital, Eva was having trouble feeding. Tired and recovering from jaundice, she struggled to latch, leaving me with bleeding and cracked nipples. I'd imagined that breastfeeding would come naturally. Nobody ever tells you otherwise: that you have to learn how to do it, that your boobs need to readjust to their new job, and how forceful a new baby can be on them! Nothing quite describes the agony of having a screaming baby hanging loosely off the end of a bleeding nipple.

So we reached out to the most wonderful breastfeeding consultant and doula, Rachel, who turned up with a big knitted boob and taught me how to get Eva to latch properly. I'd read about all these positions – the rugby hold, this hold, that hold – and I was getting stressed about it all. In the end, I just thought, *Stuff this*. I picked up Eva, shoved her on the boob, didn't overthink it and she latched on immediately. I found that if I didn't think too hard about it and just got as much boob in her mouth as possible, she'd feed.

'Boob is more than milk. Boob is everything to a baby,' Rachel said. I took that on board.

Straight away I decided that the baby was sleeping with me. So we got rid of all the duvets and pillows. James, bless him, had to sleep on the very edge of the bed, with no pillow. I was in the middle with Eva. I'd stuffed towels and cushions down the sides so she couldn't roll out. No dummy, no bottles, just feeding on demand.

Mum was amazing. We were a real team. She was trying so hard to help, but she's a Virgo and I'm an Aries. She likes structure, routine, knowing when the next feed will be and I was wandering about with Eva strapped to me in a papoose. And every time she cried, the boob came out. Still, Mum was nothing but supportive.

Mum offered to look after Eva while I did the audition for *Breathless*. We went into town and I settled them in a hotel reception in Leicester Square. Eva was sleeping.

I said to Mum, 'I'm nipping off to the audition – just sit with her.'

Mum said, 'I don't have a dummy, I don't have a bottle. If she wakes up, what do I do?'

'Just hope she doesn't!'

Mum sat there, completely frozen, didn't move an inch, terrified Eva would start crying.

I went into the audition, two weeks after giving birth. What was I thinking? I sat down and started talking about my placenta previa, and all the blood I'd lost. I told them that I'd had a double placenta – how rare it was, and how I'd since learned that my amniotic sac had started to tear on my way to the hospital, and if I hadn't got there when I did, both me and Eva probably would have died.

That's all I talked about in the audition. I read the scene, talked about Eva and left. I didn't care one bit about the part.

Eva screamed the whole way home. She always hated being in the car seat. Mum would sit next to her, singing non-stop and shaking a plastic parrot rattle. This would go on for the two-hour journey home. Looking back, she was probably telling us to shut up!

I walked through the door at home, and immediately got a call from my agent. They'd offered me the part in *Breathless*. That's always how it goes. When you genuinely don't care – when you don't need the job – they always want you. But when you really want it and work your arse off for it, they never give it to you. Six episodes, ITV, a main part playing a nurse married to a doctor in a gynaecology department. Jack Davenport was starring. Filming started in four weeks.

And then my agent said, 'You've also been offered the part of Queen Elizabeth I in the fiftieth-anniversary special of *Doctor Who*.'

'Oh my God!'

I was stunned. I'd always wanted to be in *Doctor Who*. In fact, I had been offered a role in it years before but had to turn it down because I was filming *The Cazalets*. I'd never had another call for it until now.

All I could think was, *I don't want to do these jobs, but I'm going to have to say yes.*

I felt I had to. I was still in that mindset where the acting job came first, no matter what. Even though, in my heart, I had no desire to act, I accepted both jobs. I had another four weeks at home with Eva and, when she was six weeks old, I went back to work. It was awful. It felt like being ripped away from my family.

I said straight away, 'I'm bringing my baby to set, and I'll be feeding her on demand.'

'That's fine,' they said.

They were lovely about it, really kind and understanding. But putting it into practice was something else.

We went into rehearsals. Mum looked after Eva and took her for walks in her pram. She would pop in so that I could feed Eva and then head back out again. The only thing that kept me going was the thought that, at the end of the day, I'd get to be with her again.

On the first day, Jack Davenport looked at me and asked, 'How old is your baby?'

'Six weeks,' I said.

'Oh my God, you've just given birth. Why are you even here?'

I shook my head. 'I don't know why I'm here. I really don't.'

We filmed *Breathless* all around London and Mum went on helping out with Eva. We'd get to set in the morning and I'd try to feed Eva, and then Mum would have her in my trailer and take her out for walks.

Eva wouldn't sleep, and wouldn't lie down in the pram, so Mum had to prop her up. Then she would walk and walk and walk. One day, she managed to get Eva lying down in the pram, just about to drift off, when a motorbike roared past and woke her. I came back from set to find Mum standing next to the noisy generator, holding Eva and rocking her to sleep!

There were no bottles, no expressing – just me feeding her when she needed it. This meant that we'd be in the middle of filming and I'd hear the distant cry of a baby. It would set my boobs off straight away, and I think a big portion of the budget went on breast pads. Mum would arrive looking flustered, and have to go up to the second assistant director and say, 'Eva's crying. She needs feeding.' And then, regardless of what was going on, I fed her.

'My baby needs feeding. I'm feeding her now,' I'd say.

I'd walk off-set and find somewhere to sit down and feed. Everybody else would be standing around waiting. The third assistant director would come over, and very politely ask, 'Jo, how long do you think you'll be?'

'I've no idea.'

It was so hard to know, because she could be feeding for an hour or it could be fifteen minutes. It was usually about thirty.

When you think about it now, breaking for thirty minutes because someone's feeding their baby – it shouldn't be a big deal. But it is. They were so understanding, but time is money. You just don't have the time to spend half an hour feeding and have a lovely cwtch afterwards.

But I didn't care. I think I was halfway to thinking, *Fuck the acting job.* With acting you surrender so much of your life. Filming comes before everything. I've missed family weddings, celebrations, even funerals. I wasn't prepared to sacrifice this.

It can be very difficult for women to juggle first-time motherhood with work, especially in those first few months. Personally, I think you can't have it all. You just can't. You've just got to make a choice, and I'd made mine: *Sod the industry, I want to stay home.* However, I still had two jobs to complete.

I've never had opinions about what other women choose to do. Very early on, a midwife said to me, 'You need to eat first. You need to make sure you're okay. The baby is only happy if the mum is happy.'

That's a bit bloody brutal! I'd thought.

But you realise it's true. Your baby isn't going to be happy if you're not happy. So I've got no opinions about what other women choose to do – whether it's bottle feeding, breastfeeding, having a nanny, doing it yourself, staying home, going back to work – whatever makes you happy, whatever keeps you sane. You have to do what works for you, because it's hard enough as it is.

For me, I completely flipped direction. I'd spent the first ten years of my marriage working constantly. We had a holiday in Portugal, one in the Maldives and we went skiing – those were our only holidays together in ten years. The rest was just filming, filming, working, working. Then, overnight, I decided, *I don't want to do this any more.*

I got through it, but there was one scene I had to do in *Breathless* – a love scene with my on-screen husband, Shaun Dingwall. I was supposed to seduce him because the couple hadn't been sleeping together. Six weeks after giving birth, I had a very new mum body with gigantic boobs. They put me in a big billowing pink nightie that made me look like a strawberry blancmange. I had a matching pink dressing gown, also big and flowing, which only added to the size of me.

In the scene, I was meant to seduce him and slowly put his finger in my mouth. 'I can't. I can't do it,' I said. We were in fits of giggles. His wife was pregnant at the time. 'The most I can do is kiss you and be a bit sexy, but we've got to cut the finger-sucking thing,' I said. 'I've got massive tits, I'm breast-feeding, I look like a pink blancmange – I cannot pick your hand up sexily and start sucking your fingers. It's horrific.'

By then the whole cast was going around calling it 'the finger' and giggling about it. Thankfully, it was cut and I didn't have to do it in the end, but it was one of those moments where I thought, 'I'm just not in the mindset for this any more.'

I've always been incredibly professional. I've never been late for a job. I've never been difficult on-set. I've always been 100 per cent reliable. But there was one day I was bringing Eva to set and they wanted to send a car for me.

'Okay, as long as the car has ISOFIX so I can fit the baby seat properly.'

They said yes, but when the car turned up the next morning, it was pretty old, no ISOFIX – just a standard seatbelt to strap the car seat in. I was a brand-new mum and I was neurotic. So I said, 'Thanks very much, but I'm not getting in the car.'

I phoned the producers and said, 'I'll drive my own car with the baby.'

The thing was I had absolutely no petrol and it was really early – about five in the morning. We set off and I managed to get to a petrol station I knew, but it was closed. I drove to another – also closed. After finally filling the tank at a third petrol station, I turned up to the set about an hour and a half late. I was first up for that day.

Everyone was so understanding. The producer was really lovely and kind. Inside, they must've been thinking, *Bloody hell, this woman is ruining us.* But they couldn't have been nicer. And then I got on with the day and did my scenes. I didn't even think about the fact that I was late, which is so unlike me.

All through this, I was also filming *Doctor Who* in Cardiff. I was going back and forth – London to Cardiff, Cardiff back to London. I couldn't take Eva to her six-week check-up because I was being chased around a field in Cardiff by a Zygon. James had to take her. 'How's the mother? Where is she?' enquired our doctor. 'Oh she's doing fine,' replied James. 'She's dressed up as Elizabeth I running around a field at the moment.'

In the beginning, I was on the back of a horse, playing a young Queen Elizabeth I. I had a long red wig and was trussed into a tight corset over a big billowing dress. I could barely remember my lines. I hadn't even thought about the accent.

As the day went on, I could feel my boobs getting bigger and bigger in the corset. At lunchtime, I'd go into the trailer, open the corset and, oh my God, at the moment of opening the first hook and eye, my boobs would burst out and go 'poof' like inflating airbags. I'd breastfeed for half an hour, express for another twenty-five minutes, have about one mouthful of food and go straight back on-set. It was like that every day.

James would drive around for hours with Eva in the back of the car, up and down over the mountains, just trying to get her to sleep. When filming finished, we'd go back to the hotel, eat something, and I'd get into bed and cluster feed every twenty minutes until 4 a.m. Then I'd be picked up at 5 a.m. to go back to set to be dressed up as Queen Elizabeth I.

To say that I did not even know where I was at that point is an understatement. All I remember is sitting under a tent outside with John Hurt. He was like a lifeline – so wonderful, so understanding. 'Don't even worry about the accent,' he said. 'She wouldn't have spoken with RP. She probably had an accent more like yours, to be honest.'

I was so grateful to him. Thank you, John! Thank you.

All I wanted was to be in my trailer with Eva, but at least I got to sit under that tent with John, albeit dressed as Queen Elizabeth I, with gigantic breastfeeding boobs that she defi-nitely never had, wearing a wig. I don't think I looked much like a virgin queen.

It was thrilling to sit and listen to this actor I'd admired all my life, regaling me with incredible stories about his life, work and occasional drug taking with the Beatles. That's what got me through the job.

It was a wonderful job – of course it was – but it was also really difficult. I was supposed to be quite attractive as Queen Elizabeth I. It starts with me on the back of a horse with David Tennant, who was adorable as well, and had previously played my husband in *Nativity 2*. Then we're having a picnic, and I'm lying on my back, lifting my head to talk to David and my chin is basically touching my boobs – they were that huge. I can't even watch it. I've seen it once and I was horrified. My acting, the size of my boobs, the fact that I look like I've got no idea what I'm doing ... I just look like a massive milking machine. I shouldn't have been there. But I couldn't turn down *Doctor Who*. Not a second time!

We got through it somehow but I was crippled by anxiety and paranoia. I was so neurotic. Billie Piper was there, Jenna Coleman – they were really lovely – and Matt Smith, David Tennant, John Hurt ... and all I could think was: *Everyone's going to think I'm rubbish.*

But there was one brilliant bit at the beginning where David and I are chased by a Zygon – a big orange monster. I've always wanted to be chased by a monster on-screen, because I've always wondered, *Are you genuinely scared when you're filming a horror film and something is chasing you?*

Well, it turns out that you are! We saw the Zygon in the distance and it suddenly started sprinting towards us. David grabbed my hand and we ran as fast as we could. I was in this massive Elizabethan gown, my boobs bouncing, trying not to trip over, then I had to hide in this huge castle. It was surreal and genuinely terrifying.

I got the best photo ever of the Zygon holding Eva and looking like it was about to eat her. We also got photos of her in the Tardis, and one with a Dalek. I'd met my first Dalek at the read-through, but I still found them scary. The Daleks really scared me as a child. I had these slatted wardrobe doors in my room that you could just about peer through, and at night I was convinced the Daleks and Dracula were both hiding in there, watching me. I used to think the Daleks would appear and kill me, or Dracula would swing open the door and swoop. So to be in a read-through with a Dalek standing behind me was mad. Even madder was offering my baby up for a photo with it.

We got through *Doctor Who* and *Breathless* and then I thought, *That's it. I'm done.* I was completely finished.

It was a big decision. James and I were both self-employed and I didn't get any paid maternity leave. We were going to have to make some changes to the way we lived and money couldn't be spent the way it had before. Also, I had to realise that taking myself out of the acting world would have an effect on my career.

I plucked up the courage, rang my agent and said, 'I'm not working any more. I'm done with acting.'

And that was that. I ended up taking about six years off and it was absolutely wonderful. I spent all my time with Eva, and started having babies every two years. We were in the countryside; we had Daisy and then we got Lola, our springer spaniel. We had two ducks, Michael and Mabel, who would sit on our roof and then go down to the pond. We would go for walks. We had our cows. Honestly, it was blissful.

For a time, my agent would still phone and say, 'Do you fancy doing this? Do you fancy doing that?' and I'd say, 'No, no, no.'

'Okay,' she said eventually, 'I'm going to take you off my list. I'm just going to say to people, "She's not working at the moment."'

'I'm more than happy with that.'

I was with Eva constantly before the other kids came along. She learned to sit up and crawl, and I started thinking she might say her first word. One day I had a visit from Chris Gernon, who directed every episode of *Gavin & Stacey*, and who duetted with me on karaoke at every *Gavin & Stacey* wrap party. Many a time we would be drunkenly gossiping in the toilets, only to be interrupted over the speakers with, 'Page and Gernon, you're up! It's "Dancing Queen"!'

Chris hadn't really come to see me and James – she'd come to see Eva and bring her a toy.

While Eva was sitting on Chris's lap, I popped upstairs to get something. And in that moment that I was out of the room, Eva smiled at James, and said, 'Dada.'

Chris and James looked at each other in alarm. 'Oh my God. Don't tell Jo!'

They were going to lie to me and act as if I hadn't just missed Eva's first word.

I came back downstairs and straight away I could tell. 'What's happened?'

'Nothing,' they said.

'What is it? I can tell from your faces.'

'I'm so sorry,' Chris said. 'Eva looked at James and said "Dada".'

I had to laugh, but I couldn't believe it – her first bloody word and I wasn't even in the room.

After having Eva, I definitely wanted to have another baby. At the same time, James and I had the philosophy that whatever you are given, you are lucky. We were happy to take things as they came.

However, when Eva was about eighteen months old, I took myself down to the chemist and spent a small fortune on ovulation sticks to identify the most fertile time of the month. Very soon, I had a crampy feeling, and thought, *Oh my God, I'm pregnant.*

We were down at our caravan in Sussex, which we'd had for about five years. I'd brought some pregnancy tests with me but hadn't told James. I went into the toilet and the blue cross came up straight away again.

It was so exciting. Sitting at the window of our caravan,

I looked out and saw James coming back from a little walk he'd taken with Eva. He was holding her hand, and he had Daisy on her lead in the other hand.

As I watched them, I thought, *I know a secret. I know something that's going to change your lives for ever, and you don't even know it yet.*

I told them as soon as they got back and they were over the moon. Eva was very excited – she didn't really understand, but she was excited. And James was so, so happy. 'Oh God, I can't believe it.'

I had morning sickness straight away. It was exactly the same as with Eva – being sick all through the day, and when I wasn't being sick, constant nausea. But everything was going along smoothly. We found out very early on that it was going to be a boy, and I found it quite bizarre that I was growing a willy. We already had our first name – Kit – but couldn't think of a middle name. Then I thought, *Let's give him your name.* So we called him Kit James.

Around twenty-four weeks, my cravings for fatty food kicked in. I wanted Nando's, I wanted McDonald's. I would sit in bed, under the covers, with a tray on my lap, eating a huge Chinese takeaway, while watching *Love Island* on my computer. Fond memories.

I asked Samir to be my obstetrician again and my first question was, 'Can I have a vaginal delivery now, after having a Caesarean?'

He said it was completely up to me – he could book me in for a Caesarean, or I could try for a natural birth. I decided I'd wait and see, but I didn't go to any classes.

During my first pregnancy, I was treated like a queen. I was laid out on the sofa half the time, feeling sick, but honestly I was like the Queen of Sheba. I didn't have to lift a finger. Everyone did everything. It was heavenly.

Second birth – no one gave a shit. Everyone was just too tired because Eva never slept, even though she was in bed with us the whole time. She wouldn't even nap in the day. While I was pregnant with Kit, she would only put her head down if she was lying on top of me. And if I so much as moved – adjusted myself even slightly – she'd wake up and we were stuffed.

I was still breastfeeding Eva. She was fully weaned and eating food, but still feeding from me. My milk never dried up – I just kept going. We'd go upstairs, get into bed together, and she'd feed, then we'd both fall asleep.

I wanted to try for a natural birth, but we booked a Caesarean just in case. I knew what to expect from a Caesarean, even though I'd been so adamant about everything being natural in the beginning. It was scheduled for 2 April, a couple of weeks before Kit was due. The day before, on April Fool's Day, I had this plan to walk into the kitchen holding a pint of water behind my back, call James, start talking to him, and then tip the water down my legs and cry, 'My waters have gone!' just to freak him out.

What actually happened on April Fool's Day: I woke up in the morning, sat up and thought, 'Oh my God, I'm soaking. I need a wee.'

A couple of days earlier, I'd been walking through town with my mum and I'd had to stop and hold on to a shop window because I was cramping so much. *I don't know what's going on, but it'll be fine*, I thought. Looking back, I'd probably gone into labour.

Now I could feel a throbbing pain, and every time it pulsed, water poured out of me. I ran to the toilet and it just kept coming. I was so big and round I had no idea if my waters had gone or if it was just uncontrolled weeing!

James was downstairs with my parents. I had my phone on

me and called him. 'Can you just come upstairs? I think my waters are going.'

James looked at my mum. 'She says her waters have gone.'

'Yeah, right. It's April Fool's Day.'

When he came upstairs and saw my waters had actually gone, he panicked. 'We need to go now. We're in Oxfordshire – we've got to get to the Lindo Wing in London.'

Just then, I started getting full-on cramping and contractions. It was early morning. But then this weird part of me kicked in – the same one from last time – and I just dug my heels in. I said, 'No. I'm not going anywhere. I'm not turning up there looking like an idiot.'

'You're not going to look like an idiot,' James argued. 'You are quite clearly in labour.'

But I refused. 'We don't know that for sure.'

I went and sat in the living room, cross-legged on the floor, with a massive pad on, because my waters were still leaking. I cwtched Eva on my lap and sat and breastfed her for two hours.

James was in the kitchen panicking and saying to my mum, 'You've got to speak to her, Sue! She won't get in the car. She's in labour. Her waters have gone. She's just sitting in the living room feeding Eva.'

Eventually, they managed to talk me round and we left. I cried when I said goodbye to Eva because I felt so guilty, but she was absolutely fine. We got in the car and headed for London. As we reached the outskirts, James suddenly said, 'I'm absolutely starving. Please, can we pull in? I need to get a bacon sandwich.'

'Are you serious? I'm in labour and you want to stop for a bacon sandwich?'

He gave me a sheepish look. 'I'm starving!'

'Okay, fine – get me one as well,' I said.

Now, I knew that you're not supposed to eat anything in the lead-up to having a Caesarean. But I assumed that, as the baby was coming naturally now, ahead of the scheduled delivery, I would have to give birth vaginally, and it would take a lot of energy. I would need that bacon sandwich.

The bacon sandwich was delicious. We got to the hospital and Samir was there, gowned up and ready. He examined me, checked everything and said, 'Okay, we're good to go. Let's walk into theatre now.'

'We just need to confirm she hasn't eaten anything this morning,' said the midwife.

'Don't be ridiculous. Of course she hasn't,' Samir said, matter-of-factly. 'She knows she's in labour, she knows she's having a Caesarean – obviously she wouldn't have eaten anything.'

I felt so embarrassed. 'Oh no, I have,' I said. 'I'm really sorry – I've just had a bacon sandwich.'

He looked at me. 'What?'

'I was hungry, and I thought I needed the energy to push, because I thought I'd be doing it naturally now. '

Samir started laughing. 'Well, it's entirely up to you what you want to do. But even if you did want a Caesarean, I can't give it to you now – you've just had a bacon sandwich. I'm going to leave you for the day. You carry on, go through labour. I'll come back and check on you later, and we'll see how you're getting on.'

Off he went. 'I can't believe you had that sandwich!' James said in frustration.

'I wouldn't have had it if you hadn't stopped!' I said.

Five hours went by, mainly spent watching *The Real Housewives of Beverly Hills* on my phone.

Samir came back, examined me again and said, 'Your waters have gone, but you haven't progressed at all. Your cervix hasn't changed. And the baby's lying on the "wrong" side, with his back facing your back ... I mean, there's no "wrong" side, but it's not ideal. And now that your waters have gone, I can't manoeuvre him.'

Then he said, 'I'm telling you professionally – you can carry on as long as you like, it's your decision. But this labour is going to end in an assisted delivery. That could mean forceps, or being cut, or probably a Caesarean. So, I'm recommending a Caesarean because I already know what the ending is going to be.'

And I just thought, *I've been here all day. I've not progressed. I could go another twelve hours and end up with a forceps delivery, or worse – he could get distressed, and I'd still end up in theatre.*

Yes, I'd always wanted a natural delivery, but I wasn't so wedded to it that I'd put us through more stress just to tick that box.

'Stuff it,' I said. 'Just give me the Caesarean. Let's get him out smoothly.'

I once worked with an actor, after I'd had Eva, who commented, 'Too posh to push, were you?'

'No, I was haemorrhaging, you fucking twat,' I responded.

I came to terms with the fact that I'd never have a natural delivery, and I was okay with that.

I felt that Kit, like Eva, had picked his birthday – 1 April 2015. It was fast, but it felt good and everything went really well. They dropped the curtain, lifted him out, and he was big – eight pounds – and just utterly adorable. The first thing he did was wee all over Samir, which we all thought was hilarious.

Afterwards, I felt awful and really sick. I went into the recovery room and was vomiting for a good few hours. I got severely constipated again. That evening I couldn't stop crying, because I thought I was having a heart attack. I had this terrible pain in my shoulder, and I didn't understand what it was.

The midwives were just so lovely. They brought me peppermint tea and explained that I had wind. Of course, I hadn't done any research again. I'd just thrown myself into the pregnancy, same as before, and hadn't thought to prepare for things like wind or pain.

We came out of hospital quite quickly and Kit went straight on the boob, no problems at all. He was amazing.

In the beginning it was hard, having that realisation: *'I've got another one!'* That feeling of, *How does the love stretch?* (It just does – it sort of spreads out.)

For the longest time, we called Kit 'Baby Boy'. I don't know why. Eva used to say he was bald and ginger, which he was. He was so fair that he appeared to have no eyebrows, but after a couple of weeks he grew the most beautiful golden curls. Later on, he started growing thick, dark, curly hair and became the absolute spit of James. He's kind, caring and thoughtful. He's an Aries, like me, and I can see myself in him, but physically, he's the utter double of James.

I was up and about within a couple of days after that second Caesarean. I didn't have much choice because I had Eva to look after. I was walking around, feeling fine, getting on with it and driving when I shouldn't have been. Enjoying my disposable underwear because it was comfy.

Eva was over the moon that I suddenly had loads of milk again – newborn milk – and she wanted it. As she'd just got a new baby brother, I felt I couldn't say, 'You're not allowed the boob any more.' So I was breastfeeding two children, tandem feeding, which was hard.

Eva was two now and sucking really hard. One day she sucked so hard that, when she came off, she left what looked like a Minstrel chocolate on the end of my left nipple. It was this round, jelly-like circle, stuck right there. She'd made a massive blood blister.

I filled up the sink with warm water, put my boob in and tried to pull this blood blister off.

Afterwards, I said to her, 'I'm so sorry, darling, but Mummy can't breastfeed you any more. It's hurting me too much. It's just for the baby now.'

'Okay!' she said.

That was it – never said another word about it. No fuss at all.

Kit was just so sweet and, right from the get-go, you could see he was insanely intelligent. He was talking loads before he was eighteen months old. I wonder where he gets that from! And he loved taking things apart. Mum and Dad's breakfast bar stools – anything he could get his hands on – he'd just dismantle. He says now that when he sees something, he wants to look inside and see how it works. He's always doing something technical, always building something.

During Covid, he'd just started reception. We were school-ing from home on computers and Kit had been working on a circuit board. I'd set him up for morning assembly and while I was in the hall, setting up Eva, he proceeded to demonstrate to the class how if he touched two wires with his battery pack, he could make a spark and a flame.

I was just on the other side of the door. His teacher was desperately phoning me, but I didn't have a clue. Not until I read a message from one of the parents that afternoon.

'Oh my gosh, can you believe Kit and his flame this morn-ing? And you having a thatched roof!'

Needless to say, the battery pack was swiftly removed.

Eva once said that she loved him so much she wanted to take off his head and put an ice cream on his neck. Another time, she said she was going to put him in the bin. So it was really touch and go whether she was going to kill him or love him. She sort of dipped in and out of both. When he was about six months old, I caught her holding a big wooden xylophone above his head, ready to drop it. I managed to get there just in time and from then on I had to keep my eyes on them constantly. It was exhausting. Especially now that we had both of them in bed with us.

Mostly, she adored him. She loved shoving her finger in his mouth and was constantly poking him, prodding him and holding him. All while chanting, 'Kit's got a willy! Kit's got a willy!' Over and over.

There was one time she told Kit that it would be a long time before he got married, because he had a bad personality. She had an obsession with death. God knows why – probably from having such dramatic parents. She used to say, 'Will T-Rex die?' referring to her cuddly dinosaur. Or, 'I love my new shoes so much. Can I wear them when I die?'

It was just so gorgeous having the pair of them. I would spend hours with them, dressing up, making songs, playing games. James and I felt very lucky: we had all our animals, we had each other and we had our two children. Life was wonderful.

13

Shit happens

Trying to bridge the gap between the acting world and family life is really hard, because the world of showbiz just doesn't get it. In acting, everything is urgent: you've got to do it now, be there now, say yes now. You're used to people demanding everything of you immediately. But when you have a family, you can't just be available at the drop of a hat.

One of the reasons it's so difficult to carry on working is that you find yourself trying to merge these two completely different worlds, and they don't really fit. One's full of structure and demands, where acting comes above everything else, and the other's full of nappies and no sleep and just trying to get through the day. You're being pulled in two directions.

I wasn't going for auditions. You try being sent six A4 pages of dialogue to learn in a different accent for the next day when you're looking after two kids. But I did do the odd voiceover. There was one when James drove me to the studio. We parked up outside and I got Eva out of her car seat and fed her like mad, trying to get as much milk into her as

I could before I went in. Then I handed her back to James. 'Right, I'll be as quick as I can.' I was so out of it, trying to do a million things at once and stay focused.

I got out of the car and I was in such a state – flustered, rushing to get across the road – and a van driver started beeping the horn at me. *For God's sake*, I thought, *can a woman not go anywhere without a man signalling to her that he finds her attractive?* (Flash forward to the age of forty-eight and I wouldn't mind a few wolf whistles now. I know that's not the proper thing to say, but there you go.)

I ignored him, but he kept beeping and beeping, and eventually I turned around and snapped, 'What?!'

He started gesturing madly at me. I looked down to where he was pointing. My feeding bra was still open and I'd stepped into the road with my left boob hanging out of my top for all to see.

Oh my God! I popped it back in, smiled and gestured a massive thank-you to him. And then I crossed the road and carried on walking to the studio, a professional smile plastered on my face.

I ballooned while I was pregnant with Eva. I couldn't stop eating. I was even hungrier when I was breastfeeding her. I ate and ate and ate. By the time I had Kit I was absolutely starving. I was waking up in the night and having a pint of milk, a four-bar KitKat, another pint of milk, another KitKat. During the day, I'd have this gorgeous banoffee pie cake from the supermarket. I would eat half of it one day. Next day, I'd eat the other half and buy a new one the day after that, and on it went. It was a lot of rich food, but I think I needed it as I was feeding constantly.

I went on eating. When Kit was about ten weeks old, we went down to the caravan in Sussex. On the way, we stopped at McDonald's. I ordered twenty Chicken

McNuggets for me and James to share, but I ate most of them. Recently, I'd started suffering with slight indigestion but hadn't thought too much about it. The next morning, for breakfast, I had a can of Coke and a massive fry-up. We went to a surf cafe for lunch and I had a huge pineapple and cream smoothie and a pancake stuffed with Nutella. I don't know if it was the freedom of not having acting as my main focus, coupled with a clear sugar addiction, but whatever it was, I was going for it.

I had Kit in the pram and the dog with me, and I was sitting in the cafe's garden, surrounded by people, while James and Eva went inside to pay. Suddenly, the most excruciating pain I've ever felt hit me in my chest. It felt like someone had wedged their fingers up under my ribs and was ripping them off my body. I thought I was having a heart attack.

I stood up, trying to breathe. I'm not someone who would ever throw up in public. I mean, who is? But I projectile vomited in front of everyone. It was as if my body was purging. *I just need to survive this*, I thought. *I don't care what anyone thinks, I just need to survive.*

James came out of the cafe with Eva to the sight of his wife standing in her own vomit, Lola barking and Kit crying in the pram. 'Oh my God! What do I do?' he kept saying.

'Call an ambulance,' I replied, rushing inside to the toilets.

I knew straight away it was my gall bladder. I remembered my dad having the same symptoms when we were living in Treboeth. He'd collapsed walking Lady, our dog, outside St Alban's church near our house. He was sick in the street, collapsed on the ground, writhing in pain, with people walking past thinking he was drunk. He managed to drag himself home and get to hospital, where he was told it was his gall bladder. He'd been the same age I was now.

The pain was unbearable. It felt like an ice pick had gone

through me and was sticking out the other side. They call it the handbag of pain, because it covers the exact area where you'd wear a handbag over your shoulder.

The first responder turned up. They had to clear the restaurant. It was mortifying. I wasn't embarrassed then, but when we've been back since, the kids delight in shouting, 'Ooh look, Mummy, that's where you were sick!'

I sat on a chair and the first responder put sticky pads on my chest.

'It's my gall bladder. Same thing happened to my father, around this age.'

They put me in the ambulance and blue-lighted me to hospital. James followed, driving with the dog, the baby and Eva. He phoned my mum and she instantly set out to come and help.

I was throwing up in the back of the ambulance. I couldn't stop. The pain with your gall bladder is excruciating. I also had pancreatitis, and the cold, constant, gnawing pain just wouldn't go away.

They gave me morphine, but it didn't touch the pain. I felt like I was surrounded by cotton wool and floating, but deep inside my shoulder, the slicing pain was still absolutely killing me.

Mum arrived and took Eva and Lola back to the caravan. James stayed with me. They took me up to a ward and said a doctor would come to see me in the morning. 'Kit's staying with me,' I said. 'He's ten weeks old and breastfeeding.' Quite what I thought I'd be able to manage with him in that state beggars belief, but I wasn't giving up.

They went down to the maternity ward and brought up a cot for him. He stayed next to me, sleeping.

In the morning, the surgeon came with a group of students. I diagnosed myself before he could speak – gall bladder and pancreas. He decided to operate then and there. I agreed. The pain was too much.

Norma, my mother-in-law, who was a nurse, said, 'Don't let him operate yet, let the attack go down first.'

But I didn't listen. I was adamant. I said, 'No, I'm going to have it done.'

James looked after Kit. I had expressed milk for him. I went into surgery. When I came round, I found the surgeon hadn't gone through my belly button as planned, but just above it, leaving me with a strange little pin tuck at the top of my belly, which my stomach was now sitting on.

He gave me a bottle of liquid morphine and said I could go home. So I did. But the whole of that first week, I was still in so much pain. The pancreatitis and the cold, stabbing pain in my shoulder weren't easing. I kept downing the morphine. *You've just had an operation – you're meant to be in pain*, I told myself.

But it got worse. I was yellow. I didn't notice, James didn't notice. I was trying to look after a toddler and ten-week-old baby, but I was deteriorating. I couldn't do anything. I felt like I was dying. I felt weaker and sicker every day.

James phoned Samir and asked if he could recommend someone we could see.

'Go to Barry Paraskeva at the Lindo Wing – he's the best with gall bladder and pancreas problems.'

We booked in to see him, but I took a turn for the worse when James made me a cheese and pasta bake. Not the best thing to give someone recovering from gall bladder surgery, but I thought, 'God love him, he's tried,' and felt obliged to take a couple of mouthfuls. It was enough to push me over the edge, so we jumped in the car and drove straight there.

The journey from Oxfordshire to the Lindo Wing was excruciating. I was like a cat on fire on the back seat. I was doubled over with pain, screaming and unable to sit still.

We took Kit with us. When we got there, I ran out of the car with him.

I was sitting in the waiting area, bright yellow, hyperventilating and breastfeeding Kit, when Samir walked past. 'Are you all right?' he asked.

'No, I'm in agony,' I managed to get out.

With that, Barry called me in. I told him everything that had happened.

'Something's gone wrong,' he said. He suspected that I had a gallstone lodged in my system. 'I'm taking you in right now.'

But I needed to be sick, so I went to the toilet, shut the door and collapsed. They found me on the floor and carried me back. They needed to get painkillers and fluids into me, but it was proving difficult to find a vein. They couldn't get blood out of me. They tried everywhere, but nothing was coming out – or it would clot immediately, like little lines of iron filings. They made countless attempts on each arm. They brought in students, doctors, anyone who could help. Finally an older anaesthetist with white hair was brought up from the theatre. He took my right hand, moved it around, asked 'Are you . . . ?' and before I could answer, he stabbed the needle in just under my thumb, on the side of my wrist – hard and deep. I screamed, but it worked. He got the vein.

They moved me upstairs and gave me tramadol and codeine – one painkiller after another – but nothing helped. This started at seven-thirty in the evening and went on all night. I was constantly throwing up, going back and forth to the toilet, dragging my fluid drip behind me, in agony. In the end, I slept on the bathroom floor, it was just easier.

At about seven-thirty the next morning, I went to the loo and did the biggest poo I've ever done in my life and, just like that, the pain was gone.

'I've just done a massive poo and I feel absolutely fine,' I told Barry.

'You must have passed the gallstone,' he said.

He still wanted to do a follow-up procedure that involved putting a tube down my throat to check out my stomach, pancreas and other innards.

I agreed to it. Then we found out that the sedative I was having meant I wouldn't be able to breastfeed for twenty-four hours, so James had to buy formula and head up to the maternity ward to get some much needed help from the midwives.

Turns out Kit absolutely loved it, drained the bottle and proceeded to sleep for two hours.

In the meantime, I went to another hospital for my procedure.

I had to lie on a bed and have a black leather strap tied round my head to hold my mouth open. I looked like I was auditioning for *Fifty Shades of Grey*. They gave me something to make me woozy – not fully out, just nicely relaxed. While I was lying there, spaced out, I could see they were having trouble with the monitor. It only took them five or so minutes to sort it out, but by the time they had, the sedative had worn off.

I opened my eyes and the whole room came into focus. At that exact moment, a big tube was shoved down my throat. I felt the entire thing going down, like an alien, and shooting around from side to side, looking at my stomach and my pancreas. I could feel the force of it, searching around inside me. I started gurgling – trying to scream – and I heard a nurse say, 'Oh my God, she's eyeballing us – give her more, give her more.'

They topped it up, and I went under again.

Afterwards, they wheeled me out to the recovery room. I was lying there and the two doctors who'd performed the procedure came in, looking sheepish.

'So, something didn't go quite to plan during the procedure,' they said. 'We're not sure if you're aware.'

'Yes, I was wide awake. I felt the thing going down my neck and I could see there was something wrong with the monitor,' I said. 'But, to be honest, I couldn't care less now. What did you see? What's going on in there?'

'It's all clear. There's nothing left. When they flushed through your tubes, after the operation, the stones settled in your bile duct. What you went through last night was you passing the gallstone, and it came out with the massive poo this morning.'

'Oh my gosh, thank you!'

I came out of hospital that day, and never bought another banoffee pie cake again.

I've been fine ever since, touch wood. The thing is, you think your gall bladder doesn't do anything, but actually it does. It's there to collect all the bile and releases it when your digestion needs it. So when you've had it out, you're not supposed to eat anything with more than 5 per cent fat. Did I listen to that?

No, of course not.

But I was about to have a short, sharp shock.

During my gall bladder problems, I wasn't thinking about whether anyone recognised me because it was such an extreme emergency situation. But sometimes I did have to think about it – on top of the everyday pressures that every mum encounters. I was recovering from my gall bladder problems when I decided to take Eva and Kit out together, on my own, for the first time. We'd been watching *Mister Maker* on the telly, and Eva was obsessed, so when I saw that he was coming to a theatre in Oxford, I thought, *This is perfect!* and booked tickets.

I asked Mum to come with me, but she was busy, so I

decided to brave it alone. I gave myself three hours to get there, overestimated travel time and did it in thirty minutes. I found a space in an underground car park and got the massive Bugaboo Donkey pushchair out of the boot. I'd set it up and got the kids in side by side before I realised the car park didn't have a lift – just a big blue metal spiral staircase. I had to find someone to help me carry the pram up.

We got to the theatre two and a half hours early. I was nervous – it was my first time out properly on my own with the pair of them. We wandered around for the next couple of hours, getting egg sandwiches, crisps, chocolate and coffee.

I was hoping things would go more smoothly than they had at Christmas, when we'd taken Eva to see *Dick Whittington* in Reading. I was over the moon because I'd booked the tickets as soon as they went on sale, slap bang right in the middle of the front row. 'Wow, I'm on fire as a mum right now,' I thought happily.

But when the show started and King Rat came on, he had a green mohican and didn't stop shouting. He sat on a toilet, screamed, then the toilet shot into the air and Eva had a meltdown. Trying to manoeuvre a screaming, terrified child out of the middle of the front row without drawing attention to yourself is really quite a feat. She was traumatised. Other children had been taken outside too. He'd frightened them all. After that, Eva was scared of the theatre for ages. She kept asking, 'Is King Rat going to be there? Am I going to see King Rat?' I started panicking that we'd never set foot in the theatre again.

Now, we had finally got her back for *Mister Maker*, and she was excited. We walked into the foyer but, as people started coming in, she said, 'Mummy, I don't want to go in.'

There was something about going into the auditorium – the noise of the crowd, the music starting. It's magical. It gives you goosebumps. But she just completely freaked out. 'I'm not going in.'

There were lots of mums that we knew there. We tried to bribe her with chocolate. Someone said we could go to the top part and watch through the glass. But she wasn't having any of it. I tried for about twenty minutes. The music had started, the show was beginning, and she was saying, 'When I'm older, I'll go, Mummy. But not now, because King Rat's going to be in there.'

'Okay, if you're sure. We'll just go back to the car then,' I said.

They gave us *Mister Maker* colouring sets as we left. At the car park, I carried the pram down the stairs with someone's help, got Kit and Eva into their seats, gave them some Pom Bears and put *Dora the Explorer* on the iPad. Then, as I opened the boot and lifted the Bugaboo into the car, my stomach started griping.

It was proper griping pain. Bear in mind, I'd had chocolate, egg sandwiches, coffee, crisps, all sorts, on top of all the stress of getting there early, waiting around for two and a half hours and then having to leave. My stomach was really going. Then I got the sweats. *Oh Jesus, I'm going to shit myself*, I thought, *I've got to go now.*

I shut the boot and said, 'Mummy's just going to pop out for a minute.'

I locked the car and ran once around the perimeter of the car park looking for a toilet. I found someone and asked for directions. 'The nearest toilets are up the staircase, outside, across the road and into the bus station,' he said.

I couldn't do it. I couldn't leave the kids in the car while I ran across the road to the bus station. But I couldn't set the pram up again – it was too heavy and would take too long. And I couldn't carry a child under each arm, get up that staircase and get across the road without pooing in the street.

I realised I was going to have to go in the car.

When something awful like this happens, there's a strange sense of calm that takes over me once I've made a decision. *Right, let's just get on with it*, I thought. I had a Tesco carrier bag and I was parked facing a wall. There was a pay station alongside me, other cars parked behind and a few people about – not loads, but enough to make you nervous if you're about to shit in your own car. *At least I've got baby wipes and a bag*, I told myself.

I took off all my clothes from the waist down because I didn't want to get any poo on me. Then I climbed onto the passenger seat, facing backwards towards the rear window, so I could keep watch in case anyone was coming. The kids didn't have a clue. They were too engrossed in Dora, thank God, to notice their mother, naked from the waist down, squatting on a seat, with a Tesco carrier bag wrapped around her backside.

And then – I couldn't go. It was so unnatural. My body froze. The car behind me switched its lights on and I panicked. *Oh my God, what if I end up in* Heat *magazine? 'Stacey caught pooing in public!' I'll have to say I did it for my children, I had no choice.*

I buried my face in the headrest, relaxed and pooed.

Then I cleaned myself with baby wipes, wrapped everything in the carrier bag, put it on the floor and got dressed. And you know what? I was all right! I felt fine. I got into the driver's seat, ready to head home and that's when I thought, *I can't drive home with a bag of my own shit on the floor next to me. I just can't.*

This is the worst part of the story, and I feel utter shame about it.

'I'm so sorry, God, for what I'm about to do. Please forgive me,' I said, looking skywards.

I opened the car door, looked around, picked up the bag, placed it on the floor outside the car, shut the door, reversed out and drove away.

I drove home in shock. When I got through the door, I phoned Mum.

'Are you all right?' she asked.

'No. I'm not all right. I'm about to tell you something that's just happened to me, and when I start this story, you are never, ever going to imagine how it ends.'

As I told her, I was half hysterically crying, half hysterically laughing.

When James came home from work, I said, 'James, I drove all the way to Oxford today to shit in a car park. Then I turned round and came all the way home.'

And now I base everything in my life on that moment. If I've got a nerve-wracking audition, or a difficult meeting, I ask myself, *Is this as bad as sitting in a car and shitting in a carrier bag?*

And most of the time, it's not.

I always have a carrier bag in the car with me when I go out now. I've only needed it one other time as a makeshift toilet – and I'm leaping ahead now, but I'll tell the story anyway, as I think it only fitting to keep all poo stories together.

It was 2021 and I was in the early stages of pregnancy with Boe, so I had morning sickness. I was also feeling really nervous, because I was driving into London to meet Dermot O'Leary to do a read-through for a pet programme that I was co-presenting with him for ITV. It was an amazing opportunity: I love animals and think Dermot is fab. He's a brilliant presenter and I'd been watching him since his *T4* days. Now I was getting to work with him. So my tummy was feeling quite jittery all round.

I was just getting into London, passing a massive Dreams

showroom near a residential area, when my stomach started griping. *Oh my God, I'm going to poo,* I thought, in a panic. *I've got no control over my body right now because I'm pregnant, and I'm going to explode.* I looked around me. *I'm not going to make it. I'm going to have to pull over.*

I did a quick left and pulled into a cul-de-sac. It was about eight o'clock in the morning and I pulled onto the pavement. I was wearing a big, flowing, maternity dress and I jumped into the back of the car, lifted up my dress, bunched it around me, reached for the carrier bag and exploded.

I cleaned myself and wrapped it up, let my dress fall back down, ran out of the car, put the carrier bag in the middle of a nearby skip, got back into the car, looked around, thought, *Bloody hell, nobody's even seen me!* And set off again.

Before I went into the rehearsal room at the read-through, I went into the toilet to wash my hands and check I was okay. Once I was sure I looked absolutely fine, I put a face on, walked into the room and sat down next to Dermot, thinking, *Oh my God, I'm sitting next to Dermot O'Leary and I've just shit in a car.*

This is the reality of being a mum and an actress, pregnant and trying to keep it all together. Trying to make the kids' lives fun, entertaining and full of love. Trying to get through the day and keep everyone fed and alive and also survive myself. Trying to work in a business where you've pretty much got to be perfect most of the time. But sometimes, every now and then, you can't be. Sometimes, you just have to shit in a skip.

14

Just remember I'm pregnant . . .

I felt so lucky to have two children that I started to worry when I got pregnant a third time.

'You can't be that lucky,' I said to Samir, when I went to see him. 'Something's going to go wrong because it's the third.'

'No, it's absolutely fine. Just get on with it,' he said.

The morning sickness was worse than ever. I first noticed it when the smell of the fields being cut next door turned my stomach. Then it was the brown leather sofa I'd ordered from John Lewis. I hadn't thought about how much the leather would smell, but when it arrived, it was like someone had slit the throat of a buffalo in the middle of the kitchen. The morning after it was delivered, I woke up, opened the bedroom door and the smell of skin, blood and iron hit me like a wall. We had to phone John Lewis and get them to take it back.

The third pregnancy was hard. I already had two kids

hanging off me and Eva was just starting school. I was the mum at the gates with a child attached to her. On Eva's first day, her teacher noticed that I was getting a bit worried and upset.

'She'll have a lovely day, nothing to worry about,' she said reassuringly.

'I'm not worried about Eva having an all right day,' I said. 'I'm worried because I have a baby-carrying harness on, and Kit's in it, and I'm pregnant, and I know that when I collect Eva later, she'll have had gym and her shoes will be off, and I'll need to squat down to put them back on. And when I push myself back up, I'm probably going to wet myself. That's what I'm worried about.'

She looked a bit shocked. 'I wasn't expecting you to say that!' Then she laughed.

I was the mum who'd turn up early to school pick-up, park in the car park and fall asleep in the car. One day I was sitting there, feeling so tired, and I saw another mum getting out of her car. She was wearing tight grey trousers – and they weren't even leather, they were suede – and really high heels, and she had blow-dried, beautiful blonde hair. As I watched her walking into the school, I thought, *I don't know how she even exists! That is just so not what my life is like.*

My third Caesarean was booked in for 13 December, so I got everything for Christmas sorted by October. I just had to, with two kids and being pregnant. And when I was in central London towards the end of my pregnancy with Noah, I decided on a whim to get my ears pierced again, because my piercings had sealed up. You're not supposed to get piercings when you're pregnant and your immunity is low, but I thought, *Stuff it*, and went for it.

I was wandering down Carnaby Street and saw Liberty, the department store. *They'll be good*, I thought. I walked in and there was a new section and it looked amazing.

'Can I get my ears pierced, please?' I asked.

The woman looked at me and said, 'Oh gosh, you're really heavily pregnant – we can't do it.'

'I'm right at the end, I'll be absolutely fine,' I assured her.

She went to ask someone and, while she was gone, someone else brought over a tray of earrings for me to choose from. I picked a pair and waited ages while everyone was checking that I'd be safe to have my ears pierced. After about twenty-five to thirty minutes of sorting it all out, they finally said, 'Yes, we're willing to do it.'

I went to pay. 'Have you chosen your earrings?' they asked.

I showed them the ones I'd chosen and the total came to £2,000. Oh my God. I had no idea it would be so expensive! I thought it would be like going into your local Samuels and saying, 'Can you pop a gold stud in?' Apparently not.

I stood there with my credit card in my hand and said, 'Ooh now, let me just have another little look at these, I just want to make sure I'm getting the pair that I really like.'

Scanning the tray as fast as I could I picked the cheapest pair I could find, and they were still £500 each. Absolutely ridiculous. But I was committed now. *What the hell am I going to say to James?* I thought. But I couldn't back out now. I'd been there ages, they'd fussed over me, so I had to go through with it.

Now, at forty-eight, I would have said, 'Oh gosh, I had no idea – sorry!' and walked out. But at thirty-nine, pregnant and flustered, I chose not to. I handed over my card and laid down £1,000 to get my ears re-pierced with little hoops. It was my first time being pierced with a proper needle as well, which was terrifying, but I got it done, and they looked good.

When I got home and saw James, I said, 'Right, before anything else, you need to remember that I'm pregnant, and I'm not of sound mind, and I've done something.'

'Oh God, what have you done?' he asked.

'Well, I was in Liberty and I wanted the holes in my ears re-pierced. So, I chose some earrings, and got them done. Then I realised that each ear cost £500. Basically, I've spent £1,000 to get my ears re-pierced.'

He was stunned. 'I can't believe you've done this.'

'Well, I can't go back now,' I said. 'So what I'm going to do is I am never going to buy another pair of earrings again for the rest of my life. I'm thirty-nine. So if I wear them every day now until I turn ninety, then the cost will spread out and it'll be just like they cost me a fiver or something – they'll basically be a bargain.'

He didn't agree. But that's how I spent £1,000 getting my ears pierced. Oh my God.

As I write this, I would just like to point out that I am wearing those earrings right now.

Noah didn't come early. There was no emergency this time. It was a calm lead-up. We travelled into London the night before, stayed in a hotel and I got up at four-thirty in the morning. No signs. No twitching. No labour. Nothing. Just movement, but no drama.

At the hospital I was first in for surgery. Everyone was re-laxed. Music playing. People laughing. It was all really weird. For the first time ever, I had a chance to look around the theatre properly and I didn't like it. I could see all the scalpels and surgical tools laid out in rows. I'm not squeamish, but it was very off-putting lying there about to be cut open with all that around you.

'Okay, James, we're about to go,' Samir said.

James was sitting next to me, by my head. He's never been good with medical stuff – he can't even be in the same room as me when I have blood taken – but for some reason, he leaned back and looked behind the curtain, just at the moment the scalpel was going in. So he saw everything – the scalpel slowly sinking into me, me being cut open, steam rising off me. He smelled burning flesh.

He went completely green and I thought he'd spilled water on himself because his face was soaking wet. 'Are you okay?' I asked.

'No,' he said. 'I just saw the knife going in. I think I'm going to faint.'

He was helped off the stool by the midwives who had to lean him up against the wall, with his head between his knees. I was laughing. He was no help to me at all. I just kept looking down at him and saying, 'Oh my God, are you on the floor? Are you actually on the floor?'

He eventually pulled himself together and sat back down, still pale. And then Noah came out in a meditating pose, legs crossed, hands up. So calm. Noah is gentle, kind and thoughtful, so it totally fitted him to be in that position.

He was completely bald for ages and we wondered if he'd ever get hair. But now he's got the same blond hair as me, past his shoulders because he wants to be like Erling Haaland, the Manchester City footballer.

'What the hell do we call him?' we wondered.

We were thinking of names like Harry, Henry and Otto. I've always wanted to call one of the kids Bodhi. But James was against it. 'I am not having a child being named after Patrick Swayze's character in *Point Break*!' he used to say.

We started leaning towards Noah, which we also liked, and then the night before I gave birth we realised we hadn't come up with a middle name. 'Wilder' must have been in my head somewhere and, completely out of the blue, I said, 'What about the middle name Wilder? What do you think about that?'

'Okay . . .' James said.

'So we're still undecided on Noah – but we're going to have Wilder Russell,' we agreed.

After I gave birth to him, I just started calling him Noah, because I was so bloody tired.

'So is that what we're going with?' James said.

'I've started using it now, and it sounds nice. Let's just keep it?'

And so that's how he became Noah Wilder.

I only stayed in hospital one night. But that was enough time for Kit and Eva to toddle into the hospital to meet their baby brother. Kit was dressed in his little check shirt and cords, and holding a little balloon, and Eva was excited to have her two boys to play with. They were adorable.

Noah weighed eight pounds and fed straight away. No problem at all. He was so active that he didn't want to breastfeed beyond a year; he was constantly pulling away to see what was going on behind him. I called him my little monkey because he was always climbing, jumping, and getting bruised shins from leaping around. If my kids were James Bonds, Noah would be Sean Connery – solid, sporty, a rugby type – and Kit would be Roger Moore – slimmer, charming, charismatic. Women have always loved Kit.

When I came home after having Noah, I was straight back into it. First day home I was crawling around on the floor with one of the kids, while the other one was on my back. I had three of them now – I had no choice. I remember when there were just two, and I had to change both nappies at the same time, thinking, how do you cope with this? But with three, you just get on with it. You've only got two hands and suddenly they're outnumbered.

Communication between me and James was reduced to barking orders. 'You take that one. I've got this one. Watch the dog!' 'Is everyone wearing shoes?' Leaving the house was like a military operation because of the amount of stuff we had to take with us.

My agent rang. She was losing patience after years of coming to me with enquiries from casting agents and having to go away and tell them I still wasn't interested in working. 'Look, you're going to have to decide what you want to do, because there's no point in me looking after you if you're turning everything down and refusing to go for auditions.'

'All right, then, send me up for everything,' I said, but I was thinking, *I'll turn up to the auditions and just be shit. That way, I'll have shown willing but I won't get the job.*

That was my strategy for the next few years while I focused on the kids.

The house became ever more chaotic. Eva's first word was 'Dada'; Noah's first word was 'bum'. The other two taught him it in the back of the car, just repeating it over and over.

Eva had steamed swede and turnip as her first food. Kit's first food was sweet potato and broccoli. And Noah's was a lick of a lollipop in the car. It's funny how you stop bothering about the little things.

I've never worried about being the perfect mum. I just decided from the get-go, *The boob is going to solve everything. If she's hungry, if she's tired, if she's upset, if she's hurt herself, if she's bored, shove her on the boob, and she'll be absolutely fine.*

More often than not, she was – and the boys were too.

They've got gorgeous manners; they know how to behave and you can have lovely conversations with them. But, although I've not let them go feral, I think it's really important that they're wild and expressive. I don't panic about stuff. I let them jump in the mud and roll around; every day, we're painting our faces, acting out different stuff; there is always music and singing and it's noisy and it's loud. And it's just the way I like it.

With the first one, it's 'We've got to do this, this and this; we've got to get her through the day and make sure she's okay.'

Then, by the time you get to the fourth, you're like, 'Oh God, your food's dropped on the floor. Don't worry. It's fine. Pick it up and eat it, before the dog gets it.'

I'm very relaxed now. I've never been worried about fitting in. I'm not the perfect mum at the school gates and I'm happy with that.

Eva and Kit used to call Noah the Bald Terror. He dragged himself around before he could walk and then would jump from one bit of furniture to another. He never walked anywhere – he was always throwing himself around and covered in bruises.

That was when I got massively into my sugar addiction. I would drop Eva off at school, drop Kit off in nursery, and Noah, who was dinky then, would have fallen asleep in the car seat. I'd pull into a petrol station, get myself a caramel latte, a magazine and a Curly Wurly, and I'd sit in the car and polish them off while reading the magazine.

That then became two Curly Wurlys every day, and then it was, *Well, if you're going to have two you may as well have three.*

So I'd eat three in a row and, after the third one, I'd think, *Well, I just want to keep chewing.* So I started buying five. Soon five Curly Wurlys wasn't enough. So I got eight. Well, if you're going have eight you may as well round it off at ten. And then I finally topped it off at eleven. By the end I was eating eleven Curly Wurlys and having a caramel latte every day. I would drop Eva and Kit off in school, Noah would fall asleep and I'd get my coffee, my magazine and my Curly Wurlys. Often, by the time I got to the seventh, I didn't want any more, but I wanted to keep chewing. I should have just eaten carrots.

Eleven Curly Wurlys a day. I did it for ages, until I thought, *This is ridiculous. You've got three children now. You're going to get diabetes or something.*

I began to cut down on the Curly Wurlys.

James had always wanted four children. I didn't mind how many we had, but after the first couple, I thought, 'Yeah, we're definitely going to have four.'

I would have liked to have had them all in my thirties, but Noah was born when I was thirty-nine, and James said, 'That is it. We're done. We cannot have a fourth. It will break us – emotionally, financially, mentally, physically.'

'Are you serious? You're one of four and they're all boys – how can you be so soft?' I said. 'What the hell difference is one more going to make? It's mad as it is. It's like a zoo. And it's really good fun. Let's just get on with it.'

But he was adamant. 'No. We're not having another one.'

I wanted to leave it open. Before my third Caesarean, Samir had asked me: 'When I'm operating on you, would you like me to tie your tubes – if you don't want any more?'

'Definitely not,' I said. 'Don't tie my tubes. But we aren't having any more.'

For the next two years I was hugely broody and desperate for another baby. But James stayed adamant, so I thought, *Okay, we're not going to have another one, we'll just get another dog*, and got on with things.

I'd been doing voiceovers, dipping my toe into work, doing little bits and bobs when, in 2018, completely and utterly out of the blue, I got a text from Ruth Jones.

'I need to speak to you.'

It sounded worrying. My first thought was, *Oh no, what if there are nude photos of me on the internet? Are the papers about to do something awful?*

I stupidly said this in an interview once, when they asked

how I first found out we were doing the 2018 special. I said, 'I thought Ruth was going to tell me there were nude photos of me out there, or something.'

Then it was all over the place: 'Joanna Page feared nude photo leak!'

Luckily, I have never had a nude photo taken. Well . . .

I've never had a 'sexual' nude photo taken. But when I was twenty-nine, and really into yoga, I met the most wonderful woman from London. She was a photographer who specialised in portraits of pregnant women. She would photograph them and their huge blossoming bumps in the woods, or leaning against trees, or in the garden, basically, however they wanted to have their bump captured. I asked her if she would take my photograph because I was twenty-nine, and I wanted to capture my youth and beauty before I turned the ripe old age of thirty. Oh, what I would give to be thirty now.

She was wonderful. She told me to come to her house in Camberwell, wearing a loose flowing dress, and she'd be delighted to. So off I went.

I was a bit nervous in my long, flowing dress, as I had no idea what to expect. Yes, I'd done sex scenes, but I was being someone else then. This was me; I wasn't playing a character. Putting my fears aside I got off the bus and walked down the road. It was a normal street, lots of terraced London houses, a lovely climbing rose, and then I arrived. It was a little orange door, hidden up a path, quite under the radar and nondescript. Who knew that behind this door all manner of nudity was going down. I hurried up the path and knocked on the door. It opened and I was greeted by the earthiest, most at-home-in-herself woman I've ever met. She had long, flowing white-blonde hair and an aura that I was drawn to. The smell of patchouli and sandalwood hit me and I thought, *This is right up my street.* I went in. She had a huge warehouse apartment and the floors were all concrete. Oh my God, it was so cool. There was all manner of art on the walls, tap-estries, macramé. She had plush red rugs scattered about and a huge leather sofa, and right in the middle of the room was a thick metal winding staircase. It felt so bohemian. There was a little raised platform area to the side with a bed of red roses laid out. She told me to stand up there, and handed me some banana bread.

We talked for a while as she set her camera and lights up, then she suddenly told me to take my knickers off. I felt so calm and centred in her presence that it felt fine. I imagined all the pregnant women who'd gone before me with their huge heavy round bellies and thought, *My God, aren't women wonderful!* She talked to me for a little while longer, then she told me to take off my dress and lie in the roses.

Flash forward to October, and James was sitting in our living room, celebrating his birthday. He'd had some cake and now he was opening his presents. I handed him the photo in a large and heavy wooden frame. It was all wrapped up. He excitedly ripped the paper off and nearly had a heart attack.

'Oh my God, who took this photo?' was the first thing that came out of his mouth. I don't know if it was the sight before him in the frame that had shocked him, or the fact that his wife had actually gone and done something like this, but he was speechless. After explaining what I'd done, he thought it was quite wonderful, albeit insane.

It's good to keep him on his toes.

The frame now stands upstairs in our attic, covered in bubble wrap so that no one sees it who shouldn't. As much as I loved it, it became quite clear that I couldn't hang it in the house – it drew too much attention!

I think one day, when I get to my nineties, I'll hang it above the fireplace.

When I phoned Ruth back, she said, 'How would you feel about doing a *Gavin & Stacey* special?'

I just went hysterical on the phone. I couldn't believe how exciting it was.

I went off to Cardiff for six weeks to film the special. It was one of the first times I'd been away from home since having the children. Noah was two. I stayed there the whole time, popping back and forth at weekends, so it was quite a long stretch. James had to take over. Mum and Dad came to live with him, and for those six weeks they all looked after the kids.

It was very strange leaving the kids and James after such a long time being 'Mum'. I was excited to be back with the gang again, but I was different now – I had kids. I didn't look the same as I had at twenty-nine. I might have even joked about it: 'I wonder what the papers are going to say about Stacey not looking the same any more?

One day, Mat Horne texted me and said, 'Don't look at the newspaper today.'

Obviously, I went straight away and got the paper.

They had published a close-up photo of my stomach taken by a photographer with a long lens. I must have been lifting up my top to have the microphone put on, and my stomach was considerably bigger than it had been when I was twenty-nine and filming *Gavin & Stacey*.

The article said something like: 'We've got a clue about the *Gavin & Stacey* storyline. Stacey must be pregnant – look at Joanna Page's belly. She's obviously wearing a prosthetic bump.'

But it wasn't. It was my own belly.

I found it incredibly funny. Mat was really concerned that I'd be upset, but I thought it was hilarious.

The week after that, I was on the front of another newspaper in a pink dress that Stacey wore – with a gigantic cleavage – and the article was saying how amazing my figure was, because my boobs were huge. So there you go. That's what it's like.

I did some more pieces of acting work and, in 2019, I started doing my first ever presenting jobs. I hadn't considered this as a possible new direction until then. Well, not since I had presented *The Paul O'Grady Show* in 2007, with Daisy, our Jack Russell, which was a terrifying experience. I raced through the show, read the autocue too fast and didn't enjoy a single minute of it.

Now I was given the chance to co-present *Shop Well for Less* with Mel Sykes at the BBC. The premise of the show was going to people's houses, chatting to them and suggesting how they could save themselves a load of money. We started filming: me and Mel Sykes got on well. She was lovely and so down to earth.

Soon after we started filming, Covid happened and we had to stop. A few days earlier, the *Gavin & Stacey* special was up for a big award at a ceremony at the Mandarin Oriental Hotel in London, and Alison Steadman, Melanie Walters and Ruth Jones all phoned me and said, 'You've got to come!'

But James had become obsessed with the virus that was coming out of China. He was showing me loads of videos and getting worried. He stopped sleeping and was constantly drenched in sweat, thinking, *I need to protect my babies from whatever it is that's coming.*

So I decided not to go to the Mandarin Oriental in the middle of London and be among loads of people at an awards do, and stayed away. At least one person I know of got Covid.

On the one hand, lockdown was hard for me and James, because we were self-employed, meaning all our work stopped. As we didn't qualify for furlough handouts, we re-alised we were going to have to start living off our savings.

We built ourselves a wooden voiceover studio, got a load of equipment, set it all up, covered it in duvets and mattresses and went for it.

On the other hand, lockdown turned out to be the most wonderful family time. I only lasted for a couple of weeks trying to home-school the three children. After that, I thought, *This is absolutely ridiculous. Eva is so distressed – and so would I be if I was being forced to sit in front of a bloody computer from eight-thirty in the morning until three o'clock in the afternoon.*

You can't just stare at a computer constantly when you're a child.

I told the teachers. 'We're not doing online lessons. We're reading, we're doing art, we're baking, we're playing in the garden, we're looking for insects. That's what we're doing.'

It was lovely after that. We had our own veg patch, we were eating like we were in *The Good Life* and drinking lots of wine. We were quite sad when it all ended and we had to get on with real life again. It had been hard with three young children, but we'd been a team and we'd got through it.

After Covid I shot the cover of *Fabulous* magazine – and when I was interviewed for the accompanying article, the journalist, a woman, asked how lockdown had been.

'Oh my gosh, it's been exhausting!' I said.

I talked honestly about what it had been like during Covid – how lovely it was all being together, but how difficult it had also been.

Later that year, I was doing some more press around Christmas. It got to the end of the day and I had a glass of sherry before my final interview, to celebrate. It was just a quick thing, nothing major. The interview was over Zoom with a young guy – about twenty-two. 'I read your *Fabulous* interview, all about your sex life with James,' he said.

I laughed. 'I haven't been talking about my sex life with James. I might've been talking about my relationship.'

He asked how things had been during Covid and I loosened up and laughed and said something like, 'Yeah, it was like we were going to get divorced every single day.' Which was similar to something I'd heard Alex Jones say as a joke. Obviously, it wasn't meant seriously. We were just looking after three kids and exhausted and bickering.

And that was that. Until Christmas Day. We'd put the kids to bed and we were both exhausted. We made a plate of meats and gherkins, poured a glass of sherry and sat down. We turned on Sky News to watch the press preview and the front pages started flipping past. Then I saw something flash up that looked odd, a bit familiar – a top banner on a paper. I rewound it, paused it, and there it was on the front page: a huge close-up of my face with the headline: 'Joanna: My Divorce Hell.'

James and I just looked at each other. 'What is that?'

It was awful. I couldn't believe it: the front of the newspaper, a big picture of me, smiley face, blonde bob and I had no idea where it had come from.

My agent phoned up the next day. The newspaper had said they were going to print another story – that James and I were selling Lavender Cottage because we were separating. That we'd split up during Covid and couldn't live with each other any more. They said if I didn't give them a statement, they'd run it.

I was furious. 'You can print what you want,' I said, 'I'm not being bullied by anyone.'

Someone from my agency was on the phone to them all day and, after hours of argument, they dropped it. But it didn't go away. Every other paper picked it up and now there were big double spreads and photos of me looking serious, with the headline: 'My Divorce Hell.' All based on that one quote: 'It was like we were going to get divorced every day during Covid.'

That's all I ever knew about it. I didn't read the rest. But James did – he even read the comments. The one that stuck out most for him was when someone wrote, 'Look at her husband! He's wearing those brown shoes again. He wears them in every photo.'

I, of course, thought this was hilarious!

As soon as Covid was over, me and Mel went back to filming *Shop Well For Less*. So, if you watch it, in the first couple of scenes I'm quite slim and wearing the clothes that I'd chosen for it – and then I walk through a door, going into someone's house, and suddenly I'm about a stone and a half heavier from all of the wine, pies and potatoes I'd consumed during lockdown.

Still, I was presenting and enjoying it.

It wasn't something I'd trained to do. But I could quite clearly talk, and chat to anybody, and get on with them. And I could think of loads of questions to ask, because I'm interested in people.

And I thought, *You know what? I actually love doing this.*

15

What are the chances?

Noah was about to start school. For the first time since 2013, I was going to have some free time. *I can do yoga,* I thought. *I can go and have a coffee. I can just wander around and take the dogs for a walk. It's going to be amazing.*

Then I started to feel broody again. I wasn't using ovulation sticks but I'd had three babies, so I could sense when I was ovulating. One morning, after I'd dropped the kids off at school, I drove up to the house and saw James standing in the garden, bare-chested, in low-slung tracksuit bottoms. He looked really manly and sexy, like a dirty, rough gardener. I'm not saying that all gardeners are dirty and rough, but if you were going to see one that was, this is what he'd look like.

I got out of the car and I said, 'Quick – get upstairs. Let's have sex.'

'What's the matter with you?' He was used to me being absolutely knackered all the time.

I laughed. 'Nothing. You just look really sexy. Just get upstairs.'

He still looked dubious. 'Are you ovulating?'

'I don't know,' I said. 'I'm not doing any ovulation sticks, if that's what you're asking. I'm not trying to get pregnant.' Then I said, 'Quick – before I change my mind.'

So we went upstairs. And before we had sex, he said, 'You're ovulating, aren't you?'

'I genuinely don't know,' I said. 'But I'm forty-four. What are the chances that I'm going to get pregnant? They're not very high, are they?'

So we did it. And that was the only time we had sex in the month – because we were so tired and had three kids.

Two weeks went by and I got my period on the Monday. I was disappointed, although I wasn't intent on getting pregnant. Then I stopped bleeding and, all the way through until Saturday, my stomach was cramping weirdly. There was something wrong and I started worrying that it was serious.

I had started presenting my own radio show on BBC Radio Wales every Sunday. So every Saturday, I was going down to Cardiff, to BBC Wales, to record the show the next day.

I was in my hotel room on the Saturday night. My stomach was cramping and I thought, *I know what this feeling is. I feel bloated. I feel full. I feel like . . . there's something in me.*

Luckily, I had a mask lying around somewhere – because if you're in *Gavin & Stacey*, and you've got a really recognisable voice like mine, and you're in Cardiff, everybody knows you.

The last thing I need right now is somebody recognising me while I'm buying pregnancy testing kits, I thought.

I went to a chemist and bought about ten kits. Back at the hotel room, I weed on a stick and it just went boom and came up with a really strong blue cross.

I couldn't believe how fast it came up. I was in complete and utter shock. I'd had sex once in the last month, I was forty-four, I already had three children – and we'd said we weren't going to have any more.

I did loads more tests. And then I phoned James. 'Hi, it's me. Are you with the children?'

He laughed. 'Well, of course I'm with the children.'

'Okay – can you just leave the room and go somewhere where you're not with them? I have to tell you something.' I sounded so serious – it was very out of character.

'What's the matter?' He thought I was going to tell him I was seriously ill, he told me later.

'I'm pregnant.'

There was a pause. 'How are you pregnant?'

'We did it once, remember?'

The penny dropped. 'You were ovulating!' he burst out. 'I can't believe this. What are we going to do? We're not going to be able to afford it. This is impossible.'

'Well . . . we're just going to have to find a way to make it work,' I said.

I could almost hear the cogs of his mind turning as he took in the news and processed it. Suddenly, he was welcoming it. 'This is the fourth – it's exactly the same as me! I was a surprise. This is amazing. This is the most wonderful news. We're going to do it, okay? We're going to do it.'

With all the other pregnancies, he had been very conservative in the beginning – even though everything was mostly fine. But with this one – with Boe – he threw caution to the wind and said, 'It's going to be fab.'

I had to go into work at the radio, knowing I was pregnant and dying to tell everybody. I think I told my producer straight away, because I can't keep a secret. I mean, when Ruth told me we were doing a *Gavin & Stacey* special, I told my mother and James straight away – because I couldn't keep it to myself. Thank God they *can* keep secrets.

I remember sitting the kids down on the bed to give them the news about the new baby. 'Mummy's got something to tell you.'

At first, they thought I was going to say I had Covid. Then Eva said she thought I was going to tell her that I was a snake – she'd had a dream recently where I had turned into one. When I told them they were going to have a baby sister, Eva screamed with excitement, Kit started crying with shock and happiness and Noah sat there giggling.

All through the pregnancy, we were going to call her Margot. That was the plan. But right at the end, I thought, 'Stuff this – I've always wanted to call a baby Bodhi.' I couldn't call her by a boy's name but I could shorten it to Bo. *I'll spell it B-O-E, so she won't always have to say, 'It's B-O,' when people ask*, I decided.

And that's how she became Boe. It was only right near the end that I decided on her middle name, Willow. I didn't even know where I got the idea – it just came to me.

Every weekend, I was doing a live morning radio show from BBC Wales with the worst morning sickness ever. I had a bin underneath the table in case I needed to be sick and my desk was crammed with Coke, water and loads of different bits and bobs: ginger biscuits, chocolate bars, Percy Pigs, crisps – anything I could nibble on.

I'd be taking deep breaths because the smell of everything made me queasy, and my body would be aching. It was so hard to get through it.

I carried on filming *Shop Well for Less* when I was pregnant – and that was fine. The crew were all really lovely and I was so relaxed. There was a very female atmosphere there.

Then I was offered the job of *The Pet Show* for ITV, with me and Dermot O'Leary presenting together. I accepted it, but then I found out I was pregnant and started worrying that

I was going to be fired. Not that ITV would ever probably –
legally – be able to fire me. But I thought, *I can't tell them!*

So I kept it to myself. I didn't tell anybody.

Now I was having to go into all of the VTs – short films –
for *The Pet Show* and film with animals. One VT involved
flying up to Glasgow from Stansted to film a field full of
sheep. I did my research and made sure it would be safe for me
to go. Fortunately, none of the sheep were pregnant, as there
are risks to expectant women associated with close contact
with sheep during lambing – they were all old, adopted sheep
that a woman had rescued.

At Stansted Airport, I was about fifteen weeks pregnant
and suffering from terrible morning sickness. I was being
sick, carrying a carrier bag around, sweating – it was really
bad. As I was going through security, when my hand luggage
was going through the scanner, I realised I'd forgotten all
the rules. Because of Covid, I hadn't flown in ages, and I'd
packed all of my shampoos and toiletries in my hand luggage.

The security guy stopped me, opened the suitcase and said,
'You can't take all of this through.'

I was so emotional, I just started crying. I said, 'Oh dear,
I'm an actress, I'm presenting, and I've got all of my make-
up and shampoo with me – I'm going to look awful without
them.'

He tried to reassure me: 'Don't worry, you can just go
through and buy it all again.'

But I was in bits. 'It's such a waste of money, and I really
don't want to . . .'

Right in the middle of this, Ollie, our producer, came
through security and saw me. 'Jo – are you all right?' he
asked.

By now I had the sweats. I hadn't eaten and I felt faint and
dizzy, like I was going to throw up. It was absolutely horrific.

Ollie looked worried. 'Are you okay?'

I cracked. 'I haven't got my shampoo, and – oh my God – I'm fifteen weeks pregnant.'

He froze.

I felt even sicker. 'You're going to fire me, aren't you?'

'No! Of course not,' he said. 'Let's just get you through security.'

He helped me through and I went off to repurchase all my shampoo and toiletries. He was laughing by that point. 'Look, don't worry about it. We'll just let them know. It changes the insurance and everything but it's absolutely fine. Of course you can be pregnant.'

So that was it – it was out in the open. Everyone knew from then on. I carried on filming while pregnant, gradually getting bigger as the shoot went on, and it was completely fine.

I did another memorable VT before I started filming in the studio with Dermot. It was in East London, in quite a rough area. When we got there, my stomach was really feeling gripey. We were there to find a cat detective – an investigator who was going to uncover the disappearance of a cat.

We got to where the cat had disappeared, but it was a dead end in a rundown area. Suddenly I needed to go to the toilet.

So I said to the driver, 'I'm going to have to—'

'No, you can't just go off running here.'

'I've got to!'

I jumped out of the car and ran into the nearest shop. There were loads of men around this pool table and it felt a bit dodgy. They were watching something. I didn't even want to think about what was going on in there, but it made me uneasy.

'You shouldn't be in here,' one of the fellas said.

'I really need to go to the toilet,' I said. 'I'm pregnant. Please – will you help me?'

So he said, 'Yes – come with me.'

He took me across the road into a food shop where there was another load of men sitting around a TV. It looked quite dodgy in there, too. 'Here's the toilet,' he said.

It was right next to the men and I had to get past them to get to the door. And when I opened the door, I saw that the toilet was quite a distance away – and there was no lock on the door, and no way I could hold it shut.

But I was so desperate, I genuinely didn't care. By then I'd have pooed in the middle of the room in front of them. I went in, only to find that there was no toilet paper, so I had to go back to him and say, 'Excuse me, there's no toilet paper in there. Have you got any?'

He reached for a kitchen roll out and gave me one sheet.

'This couldn't get any worse!' I said in embarrassment. 'Could you just please give me the roll?'

He gave me the rest. I went into the toilet and thought, *You know what? If they open the door and they all sit there watching me, I couldn't even give a shit any more. I've just had enough.*

I went to the loo, came out and then we carried on filming.

My cravings during my pregnancy with Boe were peculiar. With Eva, I was really craving Percy Pigs. And with the boys, it was fatty stuff like Chinese takeaways, McDonald's and Nando's. With Boe, I think I developed pica, which is an excessive desire to smell certain odours, and eat certain things that are not normally intended to be consumed, because all of a sudden I just loved the smell of rubber. Oh my God, I couldn't get enough of it.

I would go to John Lewis when I was in town and walk up to the fourth floor – which is where all the kids' stuff is – and I would stand amongst the rubber wellies sniffing them. And then I would pick up the wellies, put my nose in them and just stand there sniffing.

When I was at home, I chewed constantly on tooth-brushes – and then I wanted to start chewing rubber. And, one day, right before school, the kids were on their way out and I picked up a stone from the driveway.

'Mummy – what are you doing?' they asked.

'I have to chew this stone.'

I put it in my mouth and started sucking and chewing on it. They thought I'd lost my mind.

I went to the post office and bought a bag of a hundred elas-tic bands. I'd carry them around with me and, every morning, I'd put one in my mouth and chew it all day. I loved it. I still do – even now, if I start chewing one, it feels amazing.

Boe was due around Christmas Day – another Christmas baby. I was booked in for a Caesarean on 17 December. By then, I had stopped going to some of my appointments. I'd say, 'Don't worry, Samir, I'm not coming in for a scan – I know what I'm doing.'

I wasn't the least bit worried. It was my fourth baby – I knew the drill.

But Mum was worried. 'It's your last baby and later babies always come earlier,' she said. 'You're not booked in until the seventeenth, but I think she'll come before that.'

I tried to reassure her. 'I'm absolutely fine. There's nothing to worry about.'

But on 1 December, she said, 'I just want to be in the house. I'm coming up with Dad.'

'You are just huge,' Mum said, when she saw me.

That night, James and I were in the middle of watching *Succession*. We were in the living room at Lavender Cottage; everyone else was in bed. Mum and Dad were in the annexe.

I was eating Parma ham and cheese and stuffing my face. It was the birthday party episode. I was really enjoying it, when it suddenly felt as if someone had punched me in the stomach. It was like a proper blow – Boe must have kicked me really hard, because it completely winded me. I doubled over with a sharp cramp.

I waited it out, breathing through the pain, and then it passed. 'Blinkin' heck, that really hurt!' I said.

It must have been about quarter to midnight. I settled back into the sofa and carried on eating my ham. A few minutes later, out of nowhere, my waters went. I went straight to the loo, sat down, and thought, *This isn't wee – this is definitely my waters.*

Back in the living room, I walked in circles, repeating to James, 'My waters are going. I can feel them.'

I started panicking and getting ready to go, but then I stopped. 'No, I don't want to. What if I'm not actually in labour?'

'You are. We've done this before,' James calmly replied.

Still, I kept saying, 'No, I don't want to go.'

I walked around in circles, waters still going, not wanting to believe it was happening.

'Right, I'm getting into bed,' James said eventually. 'Come and wake me when you're ready to go to the hospital.'

'Okay,' I said. He went upstairs. I stayed downstairs, pacing.

I started getting contractions – proper, full-on contractions, unlike anything I'd experienced before. With Kit, they were mild – but these went from zero to one hundred. I don't think I'd ever truly felt a real contraction until then.

I started timing them: eight minutes apart, right from the start. They continued for forty-five minutes until I went upstairs and got into bed. Then they started to become more frequent – every five minutes. I let it go for about an hour, maybe a bit more, and then they dropped again to three-minute intervals. By that point, I was properly bracing for each one. They were intense.

James was asleep, so I got out of bed and phoned the Lindo Wing.

A calm voice answered. 'Hello, love. You all right?'

I gave her my name, explained I was a patient, and said, 'My contractions are three minutes apart and have been for about forty-five minutes. I'm getting worried now.'

'Is it your first?'

'No, it's my fourth,' I said.

I heard a sharp intake of breath. 'Just get in here now! Your baby is coming.'

I told her we lived in Oxfordshire – a two-hour drive away.

'Just start driving. Stay on the phone if you need to. If anything happens, call straight away. Just get here.'

I went straight to James. 'We need to leave. Now.'

By then I couldn't even walk. The contractions were coming too fast.

James ran downstairs to the annexe and knocked on the door. Mum answered.

'The baby's coming!' he said.

She looked at him with her eyes wide. 'Shit, shit!' she replied.

I couldn't get into the car at first. The contractions were coming so close together that I couldn't move. We set off while the kids slept upstairs. We were just about to get on the motorway when James – who used to drive into London every day before Covid – suddenly veered off towards Marlow. He was in such a state that he took the wrong turning.

By this point, the contractions were constant and I couldn't sit properly. I was holding myself up off the seat, groaning like a cow. The pain was unbearable.

James turned around and floored it down the motorway. I was in the front seat, holding onto the dashboard. 'For God's sake, hurry up!' It was all happening so fast.

When we pulled up outside the hospital, I couldn't even cross the road. I had to stop every time a contraction hit. Eventually, we made it in. I got upstairs and onto the bed. James went to park the car.

While he was gone, they started putting stockings on me, getting everything ready. I got off the bed and went to the toilet – and then I wouldn't get off it.

The midwife stood next to me saying, 'You need to get off the toilet – what you're feeling is the baby. The baby's coming.'

I refused. 'I'm not getting off. I just need to poo.'

'This baby's going to be born in the toilet!' she said.

Eventually, she got me up and out of there. I tried to squat in the corner, still groaning, 'I need to poo. I need to poo.' Then came the worst contraction – a searing pain that climbed like it was going up a mountain. It got to the top, I waited for the relief, but instead it just got worse. It kept climbing. I had a bowl in front of me and I was being sick into it.

James walked in, fresh from parking the car. He looked at me, shocked. 'I can't believe how much worse this has got in such a short space of time!'

'I'm going to poo!' I said

The midwife smiled. 'It's the baby's head. You can feel the baby's head.'

Everyone started getting ready for the theatre. They wanted me to walk there, but I couldn't. I was in so much pain, it was unbelievable. When I finally managed to lie on the bed and have an epidural, all of that pain just went away and the relief was out of this world.

But I'm glad I actually experienced contractions. And just knowing she was on her way – that she'd decided it was time – was wonderful.

My births were nothing like I'd planned or expected. I always thought I would be this woman who did hypnobirthing and yoga and who had vaginal deliveries with no epidural and no pain relief. That was the person I thought I was. But you know what? You find out that life doesn't go to plan. As long as your baby comes out healthy, that's all that matters.

They dropped the curtain, and there she was. All seven pounds and three ounces of her. Not as big as the boys, but absolutely perfect. Someone took photos of her with just her little head peeping out of my stomach.

The whole procedure was smooth. Once we got back to the room, I felt absolutely fine. I wanted food immediately; I was starving. Boe latched onto the boob straight away and started feeding, no problem. I'd come prepared for the dreaded post-partum wind with peppermint tea and two huge cartons of prune juice. 'Just have one glass,' I was told. I drank both cartons.

I was on the toilet all night but I had no wind at all.

I stayed in until the next day. This time I video-called the children and showed them their new sister. In person, she was beautiful – a tiny, dainty doll. But somehow, on camera, she looked exactly like Ross Kemp. Seeing her on the video call, my mum thought she was huge. When this tiny creature came home, she said, 'I wasn't expecting that!'

Everything felt very easy, and she was just perfect. We went home, and the kids were over the moon to see her. They took turns to sit and hold her, and read books to her. And then we all sat around together and watched *Doctor Who*, and it was really sweet and loving and relaxed.

That's the way it has been now with four – because they all help to look after Boe, and life is lovely and busy, just how I always wanted it to be.

Since having Boe, I haven't worked much. I've done loads

of voiceovers, but very little filming. *No – this is my life*, I've decided. *This is what I love doing. I'm with the children. I want to be with them all the time. And I just want to enjoy it.* Especially as I know I'm not going to have any more.

During the Caesarean, I asked Samir to cut my tubes, and he did. Which was lucky, because only a couple of months after having her, I got really, really broody again.

'Well, thank God you had your tubes tied,' James said. 'We can't have five children.'

Boe's upbringing has been different from the others, because we've done no classes. I've not done 'toddler time' or any of those sorts of things. She's got three siblings and they don't stop talking to her. They carry her around everywhere and they're always reading to her, so her classes are happening in her own house, with her siblings and the dogs. Recently, we got four guinea pigs. The kids had been asking for guinea pigs for ages. They even did a mood board and I thought, *Yes, it's time we had some smaller animals, as well.*

So now we've got four male guinea pigs – all very butch, with a lot of testosterone flying around. They were given the snip recently, which has calmed things down a bit, so we might introduce a few females as well. It's been a brilliant experience for the children – they've all been helping with feeding, cleaning them out and taking care of them. Kit made a salad bowl for them today, which looked like it had just walked out of Pizza Hut. All he needed was some Thousand Island dressing and some croutons to finish it off. Boe absolutely adores hers. They've been such a lovely addition to our family, and it's been wonderful to watch all the children getting involved.

Boe's arrival meant we needed more space. It was quite hard work keeping up the thatch on Lavender Cottage, because there was a green woodpecker that used to fly over and pull it all out in one corner. Obviously we would never kill a bird, but eventually James said, 'We need to find a way to stop the woodpecker destroying our roof.'

So he went to a garden centre and bought a gigantic model of an owl, which he put in the garden to scare off the wood-pecker. In the weeks and months that followed, every time I walked past it I thought there was an Alsatian loose in the garden. Once, feeling a presence behind me, I turned around thinking it was a wolf.

So now we had each bought something that the other found a blight on the garden – and just like the enormous 'gnome pig', the gigantic owl will no doubt move with us from house to house to house.

When Boe was less than a year old, we found the per-fect place with an extra bedroom a bit further into the countryside.

James said, 'Hang on, let's give it some time.'

But, being impulsive as ever, I insisted, 'Come on, let's be in by Christmas – before her first birthday. It'll be fun!'

Honestly, I can't believe how much he lets me get away with sometimes. He's just a very kind and patient man. It was ridiculous, trying to move when the baby hadn't even turned one yet – packing up our life and starting over. But we did it. We moved into the house we're in now, and we've been here ever since.

Then 2024 came around. I was putting Kit in the bath and feeling awful – I had tonsillitis – and, as I was running the water, I stepped out of the bathroom for a moment. When I came back in, I noticed a message from James Corden on my phone. *Oh my God*, I thought. *This actually means . . .*

That's how it always happens with us – completely out of the blue. James and Ruth never tell us anything in advance. So when something *does* happen, it's a total surprise.

After the last Christmas special – the one where Nessa goes down on one knee and proposes to Smithy – I had no idea what the answer was going to be. I remember sitting in my car, reading the script on my phone, and scrolling to the end thinking, *Wait . . . what? Oh my God! They can't finish it like this!* We were all left hanging, just like everyone else.

So when I got that message in 2024, I phoned James straight away. 'Ah,' he said when he answered. 'Have you heard of a wonderful, lovely actress called Ruth Jones and her marvellous body of work?'

'Yes . . . ?'

'Well, I was wondering – would you like to be a part of more of that wonderful work?'

'Oh my God – yes! I can't believe it!'

'We're doing a special. Are you up for it?'

Of course I was. I was so excited I could hardly contain myself. But then came the hard part – we weren't allowed to tell anyone. Obviously, I told James and my mum, but apart from that, we had to keep everything quiet.

After that, it was all about waiting. Everyone had said yes, but then we had to get into all the contracts, schedules and logistics. Who's free when, who wants what, who's doing what. That whole side of it takes ages.

Filming kept getting pushed back. Then James had his play, and rumours started swirling that we were doing a special. We all had to deny it, because the truth was, we didn't even have a script yet. We genuinely didn't know what was happening at that point.

That carried on right up until I was finishing on my wildlife programme (*Joanna Page's Wild Life*) – the first job I'd done since having Boe. I'd finished filming for the day and was at a service station, waiting to get a burger, when I glanced down at my phone – and there it was. An email had come through with the subject line: Toffee Apple. That was the code name for the script. The *Gavin & Stacey* special had landed.

16

How's it going to end?

As I looked around at all the people in the service station, I thought, *I've got a secret on my phone that nobody here knows about.*

I knew most of them would be as eager as I was to know what happened in the script, especially at the end.

I got my burger and went and sat in the car. Then I hesitated. *I don't want to start reading it,* I thought. *It would mean I'll see how it all ends!*

And a part of me didn't want it to end. I didn't want to find out. I wanted to carry on with this sense of anticipation because I knew as soon as I opened that email and began reading, it would be the beginning of the end.

I opened it. The first scene was Stacey saying, 'Gav, it's a wedding!'

I sent Ruth a voice note. 'There's a wedding! Who's it going to be?'

I read a bit more. I got to the bit in John Lewis, then Sonia turns around in the chair. I sent another voice note to Ruth. 'Oh my God, he's marrying Sonia. I can't believe it.'

All the way through the script, I went on voice-noting her. 'Gwen's got a boyfriend, hasn't she? Gwen's got a boyfriend!' And then: 'My God – he's coming down the stairs!' The next voice note was completely manic: 'It's Dave Coaches! Gwen's boyfriend is Dave Coaches!'

I managed to read half of it in one service station, then had to drive to another service station to avoid getting a ticket. I voice-noted Ruth all through the second half. I was laughing and I was crying. Ruth heard it all in real time as I was actually experiencing it. She was playing my voice notes to James.

I got towards the end and it said that the last few scenes would all be filmed together, and would be improvised. There weren't any lines. It was just: 'Bryn sings karaoke'; 'Gavin and Stacey are dancing together'; 'Gavin's dancing with his children.'

Tears welled in my eyes as I read on. The theme tune plays underneath it all, and then it stops for a bit. Stacey looks at Gav and says, 'Smithy and Nessa, who'd have thought?' And Gavin replies, 'I know, only took 'em seventeen years.'

Then we run and join our family in a photo, which is then frozen in time, and our theme tune starts again with the words, 'Tell me tomorrow, I'll wait by the window for you.'

After reading those lines, I sat in the car and cried, thinking of all these people I've known since I was twenty-nine, and all the filming we've done together and everything we've been through, and how they've become my family. Then it says, 'Tomorrow I'll wait by the window for you ...' And then the music finishes.

I drove home. I spent the evening reading different bits out to James, which I really wasn't supposed to do. I swore him to secrecy and lied to everyone and said that I hadn't let anyone read it. Then I let Mum read it, because she's good at keeping secrets – obviously better than me! Mum cried and just thought it was fabulous. She didn't breathe a word to anybody.

We were due to start filming at the end of September 2024. I was still feeding Boe, but knew I had time to get my head back into Stacey mode.

After finishing my wildlife show, I came home, we went on holiday and when I got back we went straight into doing the last ever *Gavin & Stacey*.

I was very nervous before the read-through, which took place in Soho House in White City. Outside, I saw Sophie Hebron, who was our second assistant director, and Steve Roberts, our first assistant director. They'd come back especially to do their old jobs and to say goodbye like the rest of us. Sophie took me in.

It was really warm and I was so nervous that I practically had a panic attack. Sophie took me to the toilet so I could take my vest off because I was boiling. God knows why I was wearing a vest at the end of August. She gave me a glass of water.

It was packed in the rehearsal room. There were so many people wanting to watch, including Ben Winston, our executive producer, who was on the laptop being Zoomed in from America. It was just lovely to see all these familiar faces from throughout the years. Many of us now have children and time's moved on, but putting us all back in the same room together, we went straight back into being family.

We sat down. I was next to Mat and opposite Ruth and James. Chris Gernon was opposite and Rob Brydon was to my right. Chris gave a little talk. It all felt so huge and momentous. I got a bit teary – nothing unusual there! Then Ruth said a few words, and I think she got a bit teary too.

James took over and started speaking. He's always so good with words and great at the talking. He wrapped it up and said, 'Right, come on then, let's go for it.'

It was terrifying. There was a lot of pressure. I had the first line, and I was thinking, *What if I can't do this any more? I mean, my God, I've now had four children. I'm still breastfeeding. What if motherhood is draining me of all of my sort of talent and power? What if I can't do it? What if I can't speak?*

Then I opened my mouth and Stacey came out.

When we got to the bit where Baby Neil plays the guitar and sings the Beatles song 'Blackbird', Oscar, who plays Baby Neil, got out his guitar and started singing. It was really, really beautiful. As he was singing, we all just started crying. There wasn't a dry eye in the room.

By the end of the read-through, I'd laughed, I'd cried – I felt like I'd been wrung out. It was a really moving, amazing experience. We just knew it was special.

And so began the start of a couple of months of staggered crying for me.

We went straight into rehearsals in a church in the middle of London. We'd come in every day, arriving separately. At first, they were taking us in through the back door because they didn't want anybody to spot us. It was lovely being with the gang again, rehearsing and reading together. Saying good morning to Larry when he turned up by bike in his snazzy cycling shorts and helmet. Watching Uncle Bryn come to life, discovering Gwen's boyfriend and trying not to giggle too much during the scene. Trying to muster up some sexiness and mild aggression for Stacey's role play!

We had our costume fittings in the building, and it was important to me that Stacey's clothes reflected what she had worn in the very first series. I'm pretty sentimental, and I think I was starting to say goodbye to her.

But it worked because I felt like I was back to the good old days of Stacey in the very first series. Sexy, very Welsh and a bit rough. But I did have to put fake tan on every single day, just to give me a bit of a glow. When you've had four kids you need every bit of help you can get!

We rehearsed for two weeks, then we were off down to Cardiff for filming, where I spent six weeks.

At first I was worried about it. I was still sleeping in bed with Boe and couldn't bear to be apart from her. She was still breastfeeding, just for comfort, and I was worried about how she'd cope in my absence.

Well, it turns out, just fine. Boe was ruling the roost, ordering everyone around and enjoying finally having a bed to herself.

So I gave myself permission to enjoy lying in my massive hotel bed, getting lots of sleep and drinking a couple of gin and tonics every night. I thought, *She's going to be feeding less while I'm away, and then she'll stop quite naturally.*

I'd film all week, then at the weekend I'd go home. As soon as I got through the door, she'd jump on my lap and say, 'I want boob. I want boob!' And so the breastfeeding managed to continue.

I went home every weekend, apart from one, when I thought, *No, I'm going to treat myself.* I sat in my hotel room, ordered steak and chips and a load of side dishes, two big glasses of red wine and watched the telly.

It was amazing. Oh my God, it was amazing.

I tried to make it look to the hotel staff like there had been two people staying there that night, because I felt so embarrassed about how much food I'd ordered.

Filming this *Gavin & Stacey* was weirdly joyous, and that was because we all knew it was goodbye. We knew it was going to be the last time that we did this together, and so we thought, *Right, let's go for it and have a laugh.*

Saying that, I was crying from the second day of filming. My first scenes were Nessa and Stacey down the slots in Barry Island, riding in the back of Nessa's rickshaw. We filmed all day. It was a riot. I was excited to be back on-set, huge crowds had come to watch and cheer and I was filming with Ruth, which I loved. I laughed all day long.

Then they said, 'That's a wrap on Nessa and Stacey in the slots.' I burst out crying, and I think I cried every day at some point from that moment until the end of the shoot.

Ruth was crying, Chris Gernon our director was crying and I was a state. And I continued like that until I found out they were serving chicken breast for lunch and I'd missed putting my order in. That soon shook me out of the tears.

It was, *That's the last time I'm filming in Stacey's house*, and I'd cry; *That's the last time I'll be in Pam and Mick's house*, and I'd cry. I was like that with every scene.

But there was so much laughter, too. Particularly when I tackled Stacey's suggestion of role play to Gav, to spice up their sex life. We had to test out numerous pairs of old man glasses. Stacey had found a pair in a charity shop and wanted to wear them and call herself 'Stephanie' in order to be a dominant landlady with Gav. Everything ended up looking too trendy and too good, because that's the style these days. I must've tried on about twenty pairs until we found the right ones for the job.

There's a scene where Stacey comes into the bedroom and starts role-playing with Gav, puts on the glasses and forcefully bends him over while he's looking through the suitcase.

I was outside the bedroom before one of the takes. James Corden had said to Chris Gernon, 'Pass her this message.' And Chris came up and said, 'Next time, bend Mat over the bed and slap him on the arse, but don't tell him that you're going to do it.'

I giggled. 'Okay.'

We started doing the take. I spun him round, bent him down and slapped him across the backside, really hard. It made a massive noise and he shot up with a shocked expression on his face. But we carried on going and managed to get through to the end of the scene, even though we were on the edge of laughing.

On the second take, I hit him even harder. Oh my God! The crack of his backside! It was like a gun had gone off! I panicked, thinking, *Oh my God, I think I've physically hurt him.* We tried to carry on but I could barely look in his eyes. We almost got to the end of the take, before we both just collapsed into fits of giggles. I think that's the one that was used in the show.

So we were having an absolute hoot. The only problem was we couldn't share any of it with Laura Aikman, who played the controversial Sonia. Her part in the finale had to be a complete surprise because James and Ruth wanted the audience to be shocked when they found out that Smithy was marrying Sonia, not Nessa, as they would naturally assume. After all, Nessa had proposed at the end of the previous special, five years earlier. So we hadn't even been allowed to meet and rehearse with Laura in London.

The first time we got to see her was when we filmed the wedding between Sonia and Smithy. She had arrived on-set early in the morning, hidden and disguised. She'd been told that she would have to sleep overnight in the hotel that we were filming in until the whole sequence was finished. Only problem was, there were no staff working there because it was closed, so she'd have to stay, alone, in a big, scary hotel and hope for the best. Luckily Sophie Hebron and a couple of the other girls agreed to stay too.

It was exciting filming the wedding because we had a lot

of extras in there, and they didn't have a clue what was going to happen. The looks on their faces when they walked into the wedding room and saw the banner with the words 'Sonia and Smithy' was priceless! Nobody could quite believe it.

Before it started, Ruth stood at the front of the room. 'What you are about to see is going to ruin your Christmas Day. We trust that you're not going to say anything. Please come along on the ride with us and keep it a secret, because you now are part of our journey.'

There was an audible gasp in the room.

We began filming.

We'd got to the point when Stacey stands up and says, 'I don't think it's right for either of you . . .' Then Anna Maxwell Martin, who plays the wedding celebrant, asks everyone to stand who thinks Smithy shouldn't marry Sonia. There were two extras on Sonia's side of the room, who were clearly supposed to be her relatives or friends. Completely out of the blue, the two extras stood up and agreed that he shouldn't be marrying her. We were all so shocked but kept on going to the end of the scene, when Chris called 'Cut!' and we all collapsed in fits of giggles.

Afterwards they apologised. 'We're so sorry – we just got carried away, because we really didn't want him to marry her!'

Some of the time we were in fits of giggles but most of that day was spent crying.

I remember when Mat went up to say, 'Mate, just don't do it. I think this is wrong' – oh my God, you could see the tears just falling from his face and landing on the floor.

At one point, Chris said to him, 'Mat, can you please stop crying? I don't think Gavin would cry this much.'

'I'm sorry, Chris,' he said. 'It's just so emotional. I've got no control over it.'

I was worse. There were a few times, before takes, when

I'd have to go into the bathroom and pull myself together. *This is really embarrassing*, I told myself. *You're out of control on-set and you can't stop crying.* It was difficult. At one point, I was in the toilet and Anna Maxwell Martin had to come in and shake me out of it, by making me laugh.

When Smithy said, 'I did fall in love . . . seventeen years ago in Leicester Square . . .' we all looked at each other, and I thought back to that time – all those years ago – when I was twenty-nine, starting out on just another job.

The emotion of it all just overrode everything.

It wasn't all tears, though.

When we got to Pam and Mick's house, we all properly started partying. Even when there's no alcohol on-set, and you're just pretending to be drunk, because you're physically acting it, your brain somehow becomes convinced that you are!

It was written into the script that we would end up doing something mad and wild when we were getting drunk. Chris Gernon decided not to tell us what to do and just let us improvise and get on with it. We were all dancing and singing to Abba, when Mat suddenly launched himself onto the sofa. One by one, we all followed, until I was the very last and threw myself on top of the pile, shooting over everyone and falling onto the floor. My dress rose above my bum and my top dragged down under my boobs. I felt like an accordion.

'Mum!' I screamed to Mel, and she raced over and did her best to cover everything up, but she didn't know which end to start with!

We laughed all day throughout the argument with Dawn and Pete. It was only intended to be a couple of lines originally, but when Adrian Scarborough walked in in his costume and Julia Davis launched herself at him, it was too good to not put in. Watching them go at each other was such a highlight, and I had to bury my face in Mat's shoulder, pretending to be upset, because I couldn't stop laughing.

Also we had to film James doing his own stunt and throwing himself down the stairs. We had a stuntman on-set, but James thought it would be far more authentic and shocking if you could see it was actually him. They put a huge amount of sponge under the carpet so it felt like walking on air. We all knew he could only have one go at it, so we rehearsed the lead-up a couple of times, and then he went for it. He properly threw himself down the stairs and we were all in shock! But it worked, and it was great!

Outside at Unit Base, where all our trailers were, we'd had a problem with photographers hiding in the bushes. One day, our lovely second assistant director, Sophie, found a man in the bushes and went for him. She started posing and being very sarcastic, and asked him if he fancied taking her photo that day. Turns out it was just a normal man trimming his hedge, who didn't have a clue what was going on and was quite thrown at the sight of this woman parading herself in front of him!

The evening before our last day of filming, we all met up at the hotel for a glass of wine and sat around in a circle, reminiscing for the behind-the-scenes documentary. Normally, I wouldn't stop talking, but the thought of saying goodbye the next day was all too much for me and I spent the evening mostly mute.

Throughout the eighteen years of my *Gavin & Stacey* experience, whenever I'd said, 'We're not doing any more,' at the back of my mind I'd always thought, *But they're probably going to.*

But now I knew it was over.

I would never see and work with this glorious group of people in this set of circumstances, in these costumes and as these characters ever again.

So I sat there, barely saying a word. When it finished, I left straight away, thinking, *I can't talk to anybody. I'm going to cry.*

I didn't wait for the lift. I went up the back staircase, got to my room and cried. I was dreading the following day. *I don't know how I'm going to get through it. It's too emotional.*

The next day – the last day – I got up in the morning and thought, *Right – pull yourself together. You've cried so much, there can't be any tears left.*

I'm not good at goodbyes. I'm incredibly sentimental. I'd rather do a French exit and not say goodbye to anybody. But I thought, *I've cried so much that surely I've got it out of my system.*

I got in the car and was driven to set, keeping it all together. I was all right. Then I got out of the car, walked to my trailer and saw Steve Roberts, our first assistant director. I looked at his face, he looked at me and I started crying. 'Steve, I can't look at you,' I said, and rushed off to my trailer.

Then Sophie Hebron, our second assistant director, came in and I said, 'Sophie, I can't look at you. I can't talk.' We'd had Sophie and Steve throughout nearly all of it. They didn't do the previous special because they're not first or second assistant directors any more – they've gone on to do other jobs in the business. But for this last finale, they'd come back to do their original job and to say their goodbyes.

Sophie sat in my room and Julia Davis came in too, and I sat between them crying. 'What am I going to do? I mean, I can't stop crying – how am I going to act?'

I went into make-up. I was in such a state that they gave me a cup of coffee. I sat down and spilled it all over my jeans – which, to be fair, was quite good because it snapped me out of it. I had to go straight into costume, take off all my clothes and say, 'Please, can you wash and dry my jeans?'

I went back into make-up, looked at Ruth and started crying again. Mat came in and gave us goodbye presents. I looked at mine and started crying again. I basically couldn't talk to anybody. Thank God for Sharmilla, my wonderful make-up artist, who kept me going with tales of her Halloween escapades!

Before we went onto set, I had to be sewn into Stacey's last costume, the lovely yellow dress. The shoulders kept falling down, so they sewed everything onto my control pant suit underneath, which meant every time I needed the loo, I had to quickly rip myself out of the costume.

I got to set and we were filming in the same pub that we'd done Baby Neil's christening in, and the New Year's Eve party from the last special. We started improvising and it was honestly like a real-life wedding reception – we just partied and had fun.

They put the music on and Ruth started the karaoke as Nessa. It was all quite raucous and very funny and not in the least bit perfect, because we knew that the theme tune would eventually be playing over all of it, so the audience wouldn't hear what we were saying. Nevertheless, Rob Brydon took his singing very seriously. We heard these noises from behind a curtain, and found Rob, with headphones on, doing a full vocal warm-up. Well, we just ripped him to shreds.

The tears started when Alison and Larry got up to sing 'Leaving on a Jet Plane'. As I write, it still brings a lump to my throat. It's such a great song and they were so sweet together, such a history between them. It wasn't perfect – they were messing up the words – but it was lovely and beautiful and so poignant, and we all started crying.

We were sitting on the chairs and Rob Brydon turned to look at us all. I didn't know if he was acting or being serious, because when he turned around, his face was contorted like a baby's face when it's crying. He was just full-on sobbing. 'I'm sorry, I'm sorry,' he said. Then they shouted 'Cut!' and he just kept sitting there, sobbing, and saying, 'I'm so sorry, this is just so sad. It's just so sad.'

The boys got up and did karaoke, and Nessa and Stacey joined in with them to dance, then we all got up as a family and started dancing. We did the conga, which we'd done all those years ago in the 2018 special. Everyone joined in, all the crew, and we went outside the pub, through the garden, onto the pavement, waved and said hello to all the fans on the road, then conga'd back into the pub.

I was worried because the script said, 'Gavin stands up and does a speech. Stacey stands up and does a speech. Then Nessa and Smithy say such and such . . .'

What am I going to do? I thought. *Just stand up and improvise as Stacey*, I told myself. *She wouldn't write a speech. She'd just stand up and say something. Just say what you feel in the moment.*

So we were all sitting around and Mat stood up for his speech. He'd gone and got the little beer mat from the props department – the one Stacey had given him in the 2018 special, saying, 'Meet me down at the beach.' He had obviously written a speech and knew exactly what he was going to say. He got out the little beer mat – I was really surprised and touched by that – and then got out the 'Right, this is a toast' fake piece of toast prop that Smithy was supposed to use for his best man speech in episode six of the first series when he completely goes to pieces at the wedding. It was a brilliant speech by Mat.

Then I stood up and lifted my glass. I looked at Ruth and James and said, 'I just want to do a toast to all of the people that I love.'

I spoke from the heart. I told them – all my friends – just exactly how I felt about them. 'I love you all so much. Thank you for making every single day so wonderful. I know we're together now, and you're getting married, but I just want to say – I love you with all my heart.'

I was glad I hadn't written anything because I didn't have to. I just said something from my heart naturally and started crying – which is just what Stacey would have done.

And then it came to the very end: mine and Mat's last ever lines and the moment where we run into the family group and take the little freeze-frame photo of all of us. We'd known it was coming all day but suddenly it was like, 'Bloody hell – this is it. This is the last bit.'

Just before we began, Ruth and James stopped everything – all of us and all of the crew – and gathered us together to say how thankful they were for everything that everyone had done, and just how amazing an experience this whole thing had been.

I was crying of course. Mat, sitting in front of me, had kept it together all day. He had stayed strong and hadn't been emotional. But as they were talking he put his head in his hands and started crying. You could see the tears coming off his face and landing on the ground.

When they finished speaking, Mat and I started marking out what our last two lines were going to be. We kept going to rehearse and I just couldn't get my one line out because I was crying.

I had to pull myself together. I went to the toilet and told myself, *Sort yourself out, this is ridiculous.*

When I went back in I don't know what I'd managed to do to myself, but suddenly I had this serenity, this calm. While everybody was getting ready for the photo, I stood quietly with Mat by the camera. I looked around the pub and thought, *Just take it all in. Just remember this moment. Remember how wonderful it's all been.*

They shouted action. We did our last lines. We did it once, then went back and did it again. And Mat and I did our last two lines to each other.

We got into the group and took the photo, and they shouted cut. Then Ruth and James came and hugged us. The four of us stood and cried and hugged.

'We love you so much,' they said. 'Thank you for everything you've done.'

'Now we're going to do the last bit,' Chris Gernon said. 'We're going to turn the camera round so it's facing all of you guys for the photo, and we're going to film that bit.'

Normally, when you're filming things with music you don't get to hear it, unless you have an in-ear monitor. But this time Chris had made sure the music was set up so that we could hear it. She wanted us to take the photo and, while we were standing there, she was going to play the *Gavin & Stacey* theme-tune song, 'Run', but she didn't tell us she was going to play it. She was going to surprise us.

So Mat and I ran round and jumped in for the photo while the camera was still running. Then they cued up the music, pressed play and suddenly our theme tune came on.

And what was really funny was, because we're all professional actors, we kept it together and didn't move. She hadn't shouted cut so we knew we had to stay in our roles while the music was playing. We all stayed there frozen ... until she finally shouted, 'Cut! Cut! You can stop. Cut.'

Immediately, Mat and I turned to each other and hugged. And then we sobbed and sobbed and sobbed.

I remember Ruth pulling me out of that and I started hugging her. And then I was just going round and round, sobbing and hugging everybody.

Then we all went outside to say goodbye to the wonderful crowds of people who'd turned up and supported us every single day. The fans had been so adorable and kind and really dedicated – we wanted to thank them for being so lovely.

We all got in our van and drove off. It was a really big van with little LED lights on the top and our driver had taken out the coffee machine that was usually in there and put in a beer pump. He poured me a pint straight away and I drank it on the way to the hotel.

We got to the hotel, I quickly changed and we went straight to the wrap party.

The next morning, I had the worst hangover I've ever had in my life.

It was dreadful. I was supposed to check out of the hotel by twelve o'clock. At one o'clock, Melanie Walters, who played Gwen, was in my room trying to help me pack because I was in no fit state to do anything. I lay on the bed as my TV mum packed my suitcase, trying to jam everything in.

I'd gathered so much stuff after being in the hotel for six weeks that I couldn't fit it all in my suitcases. Mel tried her best, but in the end she took the rest of my stuff back home to Swansea in her car, bless her, then she went round to Mum and Dad's house and dropped it all off there.

I was supposed to be going home on the train, but I was in such a state that, in the end, I just thought, *Stuff it*, and spent £380 on a car to drive me home. I felt so sorry for myself. For starters, I couldn't drag the two suitcases onto the train, not in my state, and, secondly, I would have thrown up on said train. So I had no choice but to get a car.

'Oh my God, you look absolutely awful,' James said when I got in, and then all the kids jumped on me with excitement and love. At long last, Mummy was home!

17

Being me

There's a part of me that dreams of being a farmer. We've got two dogs and four guinea pigs but I'd love to have real pigs, a couple of sheep and maybe a goat. I want to be in the countryside and to grow my own food. And, most of all, I want to spend more time with James and the kids.

I'd also like to become a trained yoga instructor. And a sex therapist, with a little hut in the garden where people can come for counselling. Also a breastfeeding advisor and helper. I've breastfed four children. I've had cracked nipples, bleeding nipples, blood blisters, mastitis . . . I've been through the whole shebang and I'd love to be able to help new mums – talk to them about it and be there for them.

But for the time being – and I imagine I'm not the only one – some of my dreams are going to stay on hold while I do other stuff.

We said goodbye to *Gavin & Stacey* in the best possible way. Over twenty million people sat down together on Christmas Day 2024 to watch the final episode. My family included.

Mum and Dad had come to stay. All of the kids, including Boe, were cwtched up on the sofa. From the minute *Gavin & Stacey: The Finale* started to when it ended, everybody was silent and behaved themselves – even the dogs. Not one single word was said. You could hear silent crying from Mum as she sniffled all the way through it. And, by the end of it, we were all crying.

My dad was crying, James was crying, I was crying. The kids were crying a bit, but also sort of laughing at the fact that all the adults were crying. This is what we were doing on Christmas Day – together. And the thought that millions of other UK families were doing exactly the same as my family in that moment – well, I mean, it's just wow. It is an honour. It's amazing.

Hats off to Chris Gernon, who directed every single episode of *Gavin & Stacey*, for her incredible work. To make an audience first fall in love with characters in 2006, all the way through until 2024, and to still have people invested in them, and their story, is not an easy thing to do, but Chris managed it.

And then, in May 2025, we all went to the BAFTAs. We met at a hotel in town. Rob Wilfort arrived first. Then Mat, and it was gorgeous to see him. James Corden got there looking very dapper. Then Ruth arrived with Chris Gernon – they'd been getting ready together. Alison and Larry were sitting in the car waiting for us, because Alison had broken her leg in Dubai. The next to arrive was Rob Brydon with Claire, his gorgeous wife. And then Mel arrived.

Now, when Mel plays Gwen, she's very mumsy. It's always a neat little blouse, little short, cropped cardigans. Gwen was a bit sexier this time because she's got a boyfriend, but still very neat and very nice. But when you see Mel in real life, she's got such a cracking body. She's a qualified yoga and Pilates instructor – so slim, so toned – and she turned up in this gorgeous emerald-green, long dress with a corset. She looked like she'd been dipped in ink and the effect was stunning. It's very funny seeing her like that, because I'm used to her being my mum and making me omelettes – and suddenly this sex bomb turns up with this dress dripping off her.

Ruth had insisted that we all stay together for the red carpet. That was lovely. It's always scary turning up for the photographers. Everyone's screaming your name, and all I can normally think about is holding my stomach in and not squinting. But this time we didn't feel we were having to do our own thing. We turned up as the wonderful family that we are, in a big gang. It felt so safe, because you've got your bestest mates, your family, around you. And they really are like family.

So we were there as this big gang of people on the red carpet. We turned up and did all our interviews together. We did all our photos. We were outside having so much fun that we missed the entire champagne reception and couldn't get a drink. As we walked into the theatre I glanced at the waiters holding everyone's empty glasses and was very tempted to knock back all the dregs and leftovers, but Rob Wilfort pulled me to my senses!

We took our seats, a bottle of water between us. By the time we'd got through the three-hour ceremony, I hadn't eaten for about four or five hours. I thought about Mum, who always advised me to take a pack of jelly beans with me everywhere, in my handbag, just in case. This was the one time I hadn't taken her advice and I was absolutely starving.

But it was a joy. What was amazing was that Ruth won Best Female Performance in a Comedy. The couple from *Colin from Accounts* were presenting. When you or your show is nominated for something, before it happens, a cameraman comes, kneels at your feet and puts a camera on your face. So you need to remember that and keep your happy face plastered on for when your name isn't called and you have to give a very gracious, 'Yes, yes, they deserve it, they should have won,' and have a smiley little look around, a bit of a laugh, a clap of your hands, when inside you're thinking, *Just make my face look natural and good, because I haven't won. And the camera is filming me.*

The camera was on Ruth, and there were cameras on the rest of us. When they announced she had won, a bolt of adrenaline shot through us all. James Corden started crying. It was just beautiful. It was such a raw, vulnerable moment. We all stood up. We all screamed. I mean, it was a real guttural 'Yes!' because it was so, so deserved.

Ruth has played the character of Nessa since 2006 and, aside from being a wonderful comedic actress, to have created a character that's so iconic that you can just look at a drawing of her, just the outline, and know it's Nessa – that's an achievement.

In that moment, I thought again of how, as an actor, at drama school, you just want to get a job. When I left RADA, I wasn't thinking about doing something that loads of people would watch, that people would like, that people would ever talk about. A job that is reviewed on *Newsnight*. A job where people start knowing your character's name. A job where people start knowing your *real* name! A job where people recognise you in the street and go, 'It's Stacey. What's occurring, Stace?'

I'm just so grateful.

For the last couple of years, people have been saying, 'You need to do a podcast.'

'Just sitting there talking?' I'd say. 'I can't imagine how difficult that would be.'

'Are you kidding me? You don't stop talking. Doing a podcast would be perfect for you,' everyone said.

Fifteen years ago, I had the same thoughts about voice-overs. I couldn't imagine what it would be like to work without delving down into the depths of my emotion. Then I started doing voiceovers and found them quite easy, because I like sight-reading. You don't have to remember any lines, you don't have to do any research, you just turn up and do it there and then, and then go. It's good fun.

I was already branching out and doing more presenting. In 2023, I started appearing as a guest panellist on ITV's *Loose Women*. I didn't do a lot of it last year because I was filming other programmes, but I really enjoyed sitting on that panel with such strong, opinionated women. These were people I'd seen in TV shows and presenting for years and it was amazing to find myself sitting next to them. Now it feels like I'm inside a lovely, warm cocoon every time I go on the show. It's especially good the more you get to know them. They're wonderful women who offer a lot of good advice.

And it's always exhilarating when you're on a panel with Janet Street-Porter. You've no idea what she's going to do, or what she's going to say to you. It's normally something quite sarcastic and cutting, but that's what I've always loved about her – from watching her on the telly when I was younger to experiencing it first-hand sitting next to her. She's straight-talking.

One day, Natalie Cassidy was interviewed on *Loose Women*. Afterwards we started chatting and got on like a house on fire. She said she was doing a pod and asked if I'd like to do it with her. It was just chatting and reviewing things on TV for the BBC.

My natural reaction these days – because I'm so tired and life is so incredibly busy with all the kids – is to say no. But on that occasion I thought, *Stuff it, I need to start saying yes to everything and just do that for a bit.*

'Yeah, okay, let's give it a go and see what happens,' I said.

So Nat and I started doing our pod, *Off the Telly.* It was brilliant fun. We chatted about TV shows, what we liked and didn't like, but the thing I loved most was the pair of us meeting up. 'What have you been up to this week? What's your opinion on such and such?'

Those were the best bits for me.

What's brilliant with a podcast is that you can decide what you're going to talk about – and off you go. I've come to re-alise that I'm quite good at it, because, believe it or not, I'm a bit of a talker.

The first person we interviewed on our pod was Sir David Jason. I couldn't believe I was sitting there interviewing Del Boy. If, like me, you grew up watching *Only Fools and Horses*, it becomes part of your family life. You watch the Christmas spe-cials, you've got your favourite episode, you know most of the lines. And here was little old me, interviewing Sir David Jason.

It was an utter joy. He was an utter joy. He was funny, he was cheeky, he was just lovely to chat to. He told us brilliant stories. For our first ever interview together on our pod, we couldn't have asked for more.

So I've decided that the root of what is next for me is being myself. The whole entertainment world is so different from when I first came out of RADA. You can do whatever you want and be whoever you choose. Everything's on social media, everybody's posting. You don't have to depend on any press department doing your interview or any agent putting you forward for this or that. You've got yourself, and you've got your own independence, strength and confidence.

I can wake up one morning and think, *Yes, I've got my own platform. I can act, I can present, I can pod.*

That is the way that I see myself now – it's exciting.

Last year was so busy and hectic, with all the excitement, stress and secrecy of *Gavin & Stacey*, and then presenting *Joanna Page's Wild Life*, that right now, I don't fancy leaving the kids and going away to a film set for weeks on end. But maybe when they're all older and in college, I'll think, *You know what? I fancy doing a play now.*

This is the last year I'll have with Boe before she starts nursery and school. Eva's nearly a teenager, and my boys are creeping up on me, about to make me the shortest member of the family, aside from the animals and Boe. Although I'd probably put Boe in the animal category at the moment as well.

It's all going so fast, but I reckon I've done well to keep my career going while looking after four magnificent kids.

I used to love being onstage. That's where it all starts – the youth theatres and drama school, the magic of waiting in the wings, the feel of the audience, the warmth of the lights.

When I see a play now, it makes me feel nostalgic for the theatre, nostalgic for that world.

One day, I'll belong to a theatre company again.

But, for now, I don't want to play someone else. I want to be me.

Acknowledgements

When I realised I was going to write a book I got over excited, thought I was Carrie Bradshaw from *Sex and the City* and went straight out to buy a handbag I could carry my notepad and pens in. Then I realised I was going to have to actually write the thing and shit myself. So, I have a lot of thank yous to the people who supported me and kept me going when I wanted to run away shouting 'I can't do this!'

First and foremost, I am hugely grateful to my wonderful agent Rebecca Johnson-Honey for convincing me to write this book in the first place. Supportive, funny, loyal, loving and always there for me when I messaged panic stricken at 3 a.m. You truly are my rock. A special thank you to my literary agent, Ben Dunn, you're just brilliant. Always encouraging, optimistic, totally honest, calming, you made me believe I could do this, gave me the confidence I needed but also gave me a kick up the arse when required. Quite simply, you were there for me and I appreciate it hugely. Rebecca Cripps, thank you! This book simply wouldn't exist without you. Gentle, kind, calm and funny. What a lovely person you are and a true delight to work with, thank you from the bottom of my heart. My fab team at Encanta, Grant Michaels, Lizzie Ronayne and Abbie Tucker. You continually support me, are so understanding about the chaos of life and work with four children, I couldn't ask to be surrounded by better people and couldn't do any of it without you. Kelly Ellis, my publisher, you completely got me, didn't make me change, accepted me as I was and let me run with it, thank you for your passion, enthusiasm and just being a really cool woman I wanted to work with, and also being very understanding with my deadlines! My editor Ifrah Ismail and project editor Zoe Carroll, for being great when receiving seventy-eight emails of a morning from me. Ellen Turner, you make press a joy. Lucie Sharpe, Hannah Wood, Linda Silverman, Marie Hrynczak, Louise Harvey, Charlotte Chapman, Louise Hayman, for all your research, design and work on this book. Thank you Little, Brown for taking me into your world. Lottie Brooksbank, you kept me sane and glowing. Tess Wright, you made me feel and look good. Big thank you to Jez and Rachel Felwick for looking after my kids when I thought I couldn't do this any more and had a meltdown, and Aunty Pam Phillips for being a cheerleader and helping clothe my children for the last twelve years.

Ruth Jones and James Corden, I thank you both from the bottom of my heart. You changed my career and my life. I waited years for a part to fall in love with, to have a character whose world and voice I completely knew and loved, and then along came Stacey. Brilliantly written by the pair of you, a joy to act, a wonderful family to become a part of. I'm so grateful for everything you've given me and I love you both very much.

My family, I honestly couldn't have done any of this

without you! James, my amazing husband, I love you. You've kept the house running and the kids fed and watered while I sat in car parks until 5 a.m. writing this. Always by my side, the best teammate, strong, supportive, loving, keeping my spirits up and keeping me fed. Engulfing me in your big arms, providing French Martinis and shoulder massages on demand. My four children Eva, Kit, Noah and Boe, you are everything. Thank you for inspiring me every day and bringing lightness, love, joy and laughter into my life. Making me realise nothing really matters and there's no point in panicking, fuck it, just have fun. Mum and Dad, thank you for your endless love and unwavering support. Always there, giving me the belief I can achieve anything I put my mind to. I'm so grateful for everything you did for me, I love you both with all my heart. Nan, I carry your strength and determination in everything I do, thank you for giving me that. Daisy, you made me the mother I am today. And lastly, Lola, Bess, Rusty, Scamp, Lady, Bonny, Sooty, Smarty, Tiddles, Tarzan, Avocado, Messi, Scruffer Dante and Charlotte. You make life what it should be. Love you all.

RAISING READERS
Books Build Bright Futures

Dear Reader,

We'd love your attention for one more page to tell you about the crisis in children's reading, and what we can all do.

Studies have shown that reading for fun is the **single biggest predictor of a child's future life chances** – more than family circumstance, parents' educational background or income. It improves academic results, mental health, wealth, communication skills, ambition and happiness.[1]

The number of children reading for fun is in rapid decline. Young people have a lot of competition for their time. In 2024, 1 in 10 children and young people in the UK aged 5 to 18 did not own a single book at home.[2]

Hachette works extensively with schools, libraries and literacy charities, but here are some ways we can all raise more readers:

- Reading to children for just 10 minutes a day makes a difference
- Don't give up if children aren't regular readers – there will be books for them!
- Visit bookshops and libraries to get recommendations
- Encourage them to listen to audiobooks
- Support school libraries
- Give books as gifts

There's a lot more information about how to encourage children to read on our website: **www.RaisingReaders.co.uk**

Thank you for reading.

[1] OECD, '21st-Century Readers: Developing Literacy Skills in a Digital World', 2021, https://www.oecd.org/en/publications/21st-century-readers_a83d84cb-en.html

[2] National Literacy Trust, 'Book Ownership in 2024', November 2024, https://literacytrust.org.uk/research-services/research-reports/book-ownership-in-2024